BERGSON AND HISTORY

SUNY series in Contemporary French Thought
—————
David Pettigrew and François Raffoul, editors

BERGSON AND HISTORY
Transforming the Modern Regime of Historicity

LEON TER SCHURE

Published by State University of New York Press, Albany

© 2019 State University of New York

All rights reserved

No part of this book may be used or reproduced in any manner whatsoever without written permission. No part of this book may be stored in a retrieval system or transmitted in any form or by any means including electronic, electrostatic, magnetic tape, mechanical, photocopying, recording, or otherwise without the prior permission in writing of the publisher.

For information, contact State University of New York Press, Albany, NY
www.sunypress.edu

Library of Congress Cataloging-in-Publication Data

Names: Schure, Leon ter, 1980– author.
Title: Bergson and history : transforming the modern regime of historicity / Leon ter Schure.
Description: Albany : State University of New York Press, [2019] | Series: SUNY series in contemporary French thought | Includes bibliographical references and index.
Identifiers: LCCN 2018052656 | ISBN 9781438476230 (hardcover) | ISBN 9781438476247 (pbk.) | ISBN 9781438476254 (ebook)
Subjects: LCSH: Bergson, Henri, 1859–1941. | Historicism. | History—Philosophy.
Classification: LCC B2430.B43 S382 2019 | DDC 194—dc23
LC record available at https://lccn.loc.gov/2018052656

10 9 8 7 6 5 4 3 2 1

Contents

List of Illustrations	vii
Acknowledgments	ix
Abbreviations	xi
Introduction: History, Presentism, Bergsonism	xiii
1. The Case of the London Cenotaph	1
2. Historiography, Modernity, and the Acceleration of Time	23
3. Bergson and the Crisis of the Modern Regime of Historicity	59
4. A World Made Out of Time	75
5. The Survival of the Past	117
6. Historical Creation	147
7. The Dream of Progress	175
Conclusion: Assessing Presentism	211
Bibliography	223
Index	237

Illustrations

Figure 1.1 Photograph of the London Cenotaph, 1920. 26

Figure 3.1 People listening at the window to a course by M. Bergson, 1914. 84

Figure 5.1 Bergson's memory-cone. 149

Figure 7.1 Front page of *Le Matin*, August 4, 1914. 205

Acknowledgments

I wish to acknowledge those who contributed in various ways to the realization of this book. This work evolved from my doctoral thesis and I want to thank the University of Groningen for allowing me the opportunity to conduct the research on which it is based. While working at the Faculty of Philosophy, I benefited a lot from the feedback that I received from my colleagues. My special thanks go out to René Boomkens and Eddo Evink, who took the time to discuss earlier drafts of this manuscript and who gave many useful suggestions for improvement. This also goes for Eelco Runia, who pointed me to the history of the London Cenotaph. I am appreciative to Marc Cooper and James Harbeck for their help in improving the English of this text. I would like to thank the editors and staff of SUNY Press for the pleasant way in which they have guided me through the publication process, especially Jenn Bennett-Genthner, Andrew Kenyon, Chelsea Miller, and Kate Seburyamo. I also owe gratitude to the two anonymous readers for their insightful reports. I acknowledge the Mary Evans Picture Library and the Bibliothèque nationale de France for giving me permission to use a number of images in this book. Many people have contributed to this book by giving me new insights and inspiration, or by reading and commenting on previous versions of this text. In particular, I want to thank Thijs Lijster, Daniëlle Aalten, Auke Kranenborg, Joost van Driessche, Bjinse Sikma, Frank Ankersmit, and Sandra Ramírez. I am deeply grateful for the encouragement and support of my friends and of my family, Inge and Jeroen, Jurre and Lize, and Pauline. I thank my girlfriend, Hiske, for her invaluable love and support. I dedicate this book to my mother and father.

Abbreviations

Whenever possible, references to the works of Bergson are given to the authorized English translations, which were approved by Bergson, who was fluent in English. Abbreviations are used in the notes to refer to Bergson's writings. The French originals are included in Bergson's *Oeuvres* (1959), to which I refer below:

CE   *Creative Evolution* (*L'Évolution créatrice*, 1907). Translated by Arthur Mitchell. 1911. Reprint, Mineola, NY: Dover Publications, 1988. In *Oeuvres*, 487–809.

CM   *The Creative Mind: An Introduction to Metaphysics* (*La Pensée et le mouvant*, 1934). Translated by Mabelle L. Andison. 1946. Reprint, Mineola, NY: Dover Publications, 2007. In *Oeuvres*, 1249–1482.

ML   *Mélanges*. Edited by André Robinet. Paris: Presses Universitaires de France, 1972.

ME   *Mind-Energy: Lectures and Essays* (*L'Énergie spirituelle*, 1919). Translated by H. Wildon Carr. London: Henry Holt and Company, 1920. In *Oeuvres*, 811–977.

MM   *Matter and Memory* (*Matière et mémoire*, 1896). Translated by Nancy Margaret Paul and W. Scott Palmer. 1912. Reprint, Mineola, NY: Dover Publications, 2004. In *Oeuvres*, 159–379.

OE   *Oeuvres*. Edited by André Robinet. Paris: Presses Universitaires de France, 1959.

TFW   *Time and Free Will: An Essay on the Immediate Data of Consciousness* (*Essai sur les données immédiates de la conscience*, 1889). Translated by F.L. Pogson. 1913. Reprint, Mineola, NY: Dover Publications, 2001. In *Oeuvres*, 1–157.

TS   *The Two Sources of Morality and Religion* (*Les Deux sources de la morale et de la religion*, 1932). Translated by R. Ashley Audra and Cloudesley Brereton. 1935. Reprint, Notre Dame, IN: University of Notre Dame Press, 2006. In *Oeuvres*, 979–1247.

INTRODUCTION

History, Presentism, Bergsonism

We have been thrown into a time in which everything is provisional. New technologies alter our lives daily. The traditions of the past cannot be retrieved. At the same time we have little idea of what the future will bring. We are forced to live as if we were free.[1]

—John Gray, *Straw Dogs: Thoughts on Humans and Other Animals*

A "return to Bergson" does not only mean a renewed admiration for a great philosopher but a renewal or an extension of his project today, in relation to the transformations of life and society, in parallel with the transformations of science.[2]

—Gilles Deleuze, *Bergsonism*

Time is what hinders everything from being given at once. It retards, or rather it is retardation. It must therefore, be elaboration. Would it not then be a vehicle of creation and of choice? Would not the existence of time prove that there is indetermination in things? Would not time be that indetermination itself?[3]

—Henri Bergson, *The Creative Mind: An Introduction to Metaphysics*

---

1. John Gray, *Straw Dogs: Thoughts on Humans and Other Animals* (London: Granta Books, 2002), 110.

2. Gilles Deleuze, *Bergsonism*, trans. Hugh Tomlinson and Barbara Habberjam (New York: Zone Books, 1991), 125.

3. Henri Bergson, *The Creative Mind: An Introduction to Metaphysics* (*La Pensée et le mouvant*, 1934), translated by Mabelle L. Andison (1946; repr., Mineola, NY: Dover Publications, 2007) (hereafter CM), 75.

In 1989 Francis Fukuyama famously proclaimed the "end of history." The fall of the Berlin Wall and the failure of communism had, according to Fukuyama, ended a centuries-long, political-ideological evolution of mankind. Liberal democracy had prevailed over rival ideologies such as monarchy, fascism, and communism, and would soon establish a uniform political reality based on equality and freedom. To Fukuyama, the end of history was also a sad time. The world would now be free from irrationalities and there would be nothing left to fight for: "the worldwide ideological struggle that calls forth daring, courage, imagination, and idealism, will be replaced by economic calculation, the endless solving of technical problems, environmental concerns, and the satisfaction of consumer demands."[4]

Fukuyama's predictions have since been widely criticized and rejected. Now, more than twenty-five years after its proclamation, the end of history is often considered as a utopian symbol for the "happy '90s," when liberal democracy seemed like the "finally found formula of the best possible society."[5] The only thing left to do was improve liberal-democratic capitalism and make it even more just and tolerant than it already was. The ideological striving that had determined the course of the twentieth century appeared to belong to the past once and for all.

We could therefore maintain that Fukuyama was not all that wrong and that history did indeed come to an end after 1989. Yet this has not been the end of history as such, but of a very specific idea about the nature of history. What has come to an end is the notion that we as human beings are part of history as an all-encompassing process that we are collectively shaping. This idea came into existence at the end of the eighteenth century with the invention of the "modern" future.[6] History, in this view, was the road upon which we collectively travel toward a utopian future, while the past represented the distance already covered, measuring how far we have removed ourselves from the traditional, premodern world that we have left behind.

Nowadays, we no longer consider ourselves historical beings. Of course, we still live in times of constant change. Technological innovations transform on an almost daily basis the ways we communicate, transport ourselves, and produce. "Just about everything" seems to accelerate, as James Gleick puts it, while paradoxically we seem to have less and less free time and collectively

---

4. Francis Fukuyama, "The End of History?" *The National Interest* (Summer 1989): 1–18.
5. Slavoj Žižek, *First as Tragedy, Then as Farce* (London and New York: Verso, 2008), 88.
6. Chris Lorenz, "Blurred Lines. Memory, History and the Experience of Time," *International Journal for History, Culture and Modernity* 2 (2014): 43.

suffer from "hurry-sickness."⁷ However, despite the continuous acceleration of time, it seems that history has come to a standstill. It is as if we have lost the ability to "make history." The changes among which we live are overwhelming and appear without direction. In spite of our hectic daily lives, it seems that in contemporary society "nothing essentially changes anymore and nothing new occurs."⁸

Commentators have therefore noted that twenty-first-century societies are no longer oriented toward the future, but increasingly to the present moment. Douglas Rushkoff even speaks of "present shock" to describe our current condition. He argues that while futurist Alvin Toffler spoke in 1970 of "future shock" to describe what happens to people when they are "overwhelmed by an acceleration of change,"⁹ the future that we were waiting for during the twentieth century has now arrived:

> Everything is live, real time, and always-on. It's not a mere speeding up, however much our lifestyles and technologies have accelerated the rate at which we attempt to do things. It's more of a diminishment of anything that isn't happening right now—the onslaught of everything that supposedly is.¹⁰

With the waning of the modern future and the progressive notion of time that went with it, we now find ourselves trapped in an infinite present that has drawn the past and the future into itself.

The French historian François Hartog has related contemporary presentism to what he calls a "crisis of the modern regime of historicity." Within the modern regime of historicity, symbolically operative between 1789 and 1989, the past and the present were illuminated by a "view from the future." But since the fall of the Berlin Wall the future has lost its appeal. The future is no longer a source of enlightenment but, if anything, has turned into a threat, a location of uncertainty, the disastrous continuation of the present. Hartog's diagnosis is confirmed by social surveys in the Netherlands that

---

7. James Gleick, *Faster: The Acceleration of Just About Everything* (New York: Pantheon Books, 1999), 16.

8. Hartmut Rosa, *Social Acceleration: A New Theory of Modernity*, trans. Jonathan Trejo-Mathys (New York: Columbia University Press, 2013), 15.

9. Alvin Toffler, *Future Shock* (New York: Bantam Books, 1971). Future shock describes, according to Toffler, "the shattering stress and disorientation that we induce in individuals by subjecting them to too much change in too short a time" (2).

10. Douglas Rushkoff, *Present Shock: When Everything Happens Now* (New York: Penguin Group, 2013), 1.

show time and again that people are convinced that future generations will be worse off than their parents.[11] Such expectations reflect the feeling that we are, as Slavoj Žižek puts it, "living in the end times," that "the global capitalist system is approaching an apocalyptic zeropoint."[12] Paradoxically, this apocalypse is not only conceived as a disaster but also welcomed as a relief. The destruction of the world almost seems like the only way out, as sociologist Hartmut Rosa states, "a kind of exciting antipode to the creeping apocalypse of an everyday existence that . . . appears rigid in virtue of its contingent openness and ubiquitous simultaneity."[13]

Because the future has been drawn into the present, the same has happened with the past. The past no longer refers to "what lies behind us," but instead refuses to "go away."[14] Symptomatic is the proliferation of heritage in the last decades, which shows how "confidence in progress has given way to a desire to preserve and save."[15] Under the flag of the UNESCO charter, it seems that anything can be declared heritage—not only monuments or cultural and historical sites, but also landscapes, animals and plants, know-how, languages, folk traditions, and even the gene pool.[16] In the Netherlands, "consumer fireworks" have recently been declared immaterial cultural heritage.[17] Without direction from the future, it has become impossible to determine what merely belongs to the past and what pertains to history.

The emergence of an eternal present has affected the social and cultural significance of history as a discipline. History is no longer considered crucial for our individual and collective self-understanding. Presentism implies "a fundamental change in the experience of time,"[18] as a consequence of

---

11. "Volgende generaties slechter af" [Coming Generations Worse Off], Dutch Broadcast Foundation (NOS), accessed January 2, 2016, http://nos.nl/artikel/236012-volgende-generaties-slechter-af.html.

12. Slavoj Žižek, *Living in the End Times* (London and New York: Verso, 2010), x.

13. Rosa, *Social Acceleration*, 274–275.

14. Lorenz, "Blurred Lines," 43.

15. François Hartog, *Regimes of Historicity: Presentism and Experiences of Time*, trans. Saskia Brown (New York: Columbia University Press, 2015), 185.

16. Ibid., 182–183.

17. "Consumentenvuurwerk is cultureel erfgoed [Consumer Fireworks are Cultural Heritage]," De Telegraaf, accessed October 20, 2016, http://www.telegraaf.nl/binnenland/24812086/__Vuurwerk_is_cultureel_erfgoed__.html. Thijs Lijster relates this to a present-day "torpor of time." See Thijs Lijster, *De grote vlucht inwaarts: Essays over cultuur in een onoverzichtelijke wereld* [The Great Flight Inward: Essays on Culture in a Chaotic World] (Amsterdam: De Bezige Bij, 2016), 105–130.

18. Lorenz, "Blurred Lines," 46.

which the "motor of history(-writing) has stalled," as Hartog puts it.[19] This motor consisted in a conception of time as linear and progressive, a time that "passes irreversibly and annuls the entire past in its wake."[20] History as a discipline is based on the idea that the past is distant and absent from the present.[21] This has given historians the task of carefully reconstructing the past in every detail, before it would be forever consumed by time.

Simultaneously, historians themselves have also increasingly refrained from providing orientations for the future. During the nineteenth century, history not only professionalized and developed into a scientific discipline, it also became an important source of culture. Historians had an important political and cultural role. History books were being written for a broad and educated public and became of central importance to the formation of national and social identities.[22] Yet because of the cataclysms of the twentieth century, historians became wary of speculation and entrenched themselves behind the high walls of Academia. Nowadays, history as a discipline, as Georg Iggers puts it, "is caught in an iron cage of increasing professionalization and specialization with all the limits they set on the imaginative exploration of knowledge."[23]

Recently, a number of attempts have been made to recuperate the existential task of history. In *The History Manifesto* (2014), Jo Guldi and David Armitage argue that history needs to restore its relationship to the public future. The authors register a "crisis of short term thinking" that has pervaded our whole society and culture, leading as a consequence to a retreat of history from the public realm. In a crisis of short-termism, Guldi and Armitage state, "our world needs somewhere to turn to for information about the relationship between past and future." In their eyes, "history—the discipline and its subject-matter—can be just the arbiter we need at this critical time."[24] *The History Manifesto* wants to restore the *longue durée* by bringing history beyond the biological timescales of individual human lives.

---

19. Hartog, *Regimes of Historicity*, book cover.

20. Bruno Latour, *We Have Never Been Modern*, trans. Catherine Porter (Cambridge MA: Harvard University Press, 1993), 47.

21. Lorenz, "Blurred Lines," 43.

22. Georg G. Iggers, *Historiography in the Twentieth Century: From Scientific Objectivity to the Postmodern Challenge* (Middletown, CT: Wesleyan University Press, 1997), 25–30.

23. Georg G. Iggers, "Historiography in the Twentieth Century," *History and Theory* 44 (October 2015): 471.

24. Jo Guldi and David Armitage, *The History Manifesto* (Cambridge: Cambridge University Press, 2014), 7. See also the website of Cambridge University Press, accessed May 14, 2016, http://historymanifesto.cambridge.org.

Another historiographical approach that seeks to restore the public function of history is "big history," which wants to unite "natural history and human history in a single, grand, and intelligible narrative."[25] Big history does not start with the first human activity, but with the Big Bang some thirteen billion years ago. Instigator David Christian sees big history as a contemporary version of the ancient, but now rarely practiced, tradition of "universal history" that transcends existing disciplinary boundaries: "It will treat human history as one member of a large family of historical disciplines that includes biology, the earth sciences, astronomy, and cosmology."[26] Big history wants to generate a sense of "global citizenship" by constructing "histories of humanity" that are "as powerful and inspiring as the great national histories of the nineteenth and twentieth century."[27] Within the universal maps of the past, Christian argues, "it will be easy to see that all human beings share a common and quite distinctive history."[28]

The History Manifesto and big history are admirable attempts to recuperate the relevance of history in a presentistic society and culture. However, it is my contention that a merely wider historiographical perspective will not be enough to accomplish this task. We will need to start by "rethinking history," meaning by critically assessing our ontological presuppositions regarding the nature of history. The way we understand history has been ontologically shaped by the modern regime of historicity. It is therefore no more than logical to suggest that historical thought has entered a state of crisis, given that the arrow of modern time is dissolving in an unending now.

In this book, I want to seize the contemporary crisis of the modern regime of historicity as an opportunity to critically reflect on the ontological foundations of the modern understanding of history. I want to examine whether we can overcome this crisis by adopting a perspective on history, and ourselves as historical beings, that is grounded in an alternative, nonmodern ontology of time. In so doing, I will turn to the philosophy of duration of the French philosopher Henri Bergson.[29] A Bergsonian approach, so I will argue, breaks with two important prescriptions of what Bruno Latour calls the "modern Constitution," which have also shaped the modern view of history:

---

25. David Christian, *Maps of Time: An Introduction to Big History* (Berkeley, CA: University of California Press, 2005), xv.
26. David Christian, "The Return of Big History," *History and Theory* 49 (December 2010): 7.
27. Ibid., 26.
28. Ibid., 7.
29. For an assessment of the nonmodern character of Bergsonism, see Suzanne Guerlac, "Bergson, the Void, and the Politics of Life," in *Bergson, Politics, and Religion*, ed. Alexandre Lefebvre and Melanie White (Durham, NC: Duke University Press, 2012), 40–60.

firstly, the separation of the world into two purified ontological zones, that of Nature and Culture; and, secondly, a linear, progressive notion of time that supports this separation. Bergson's philosophy of life implies an approach to history that is based on a creative mode of time in which Nature and Culture are indissolubly connected. I hope to show that Bergsonism allows us to reconceptualize the categories of past, present and future, and that we may thereby regain an understanding of ourselves as "historical beings."

∼

Henri Bergson (1859–1941) lived and worked in a world that in many ways resembled the beginning of the twenty-first century. He wrote the majority of his works during the Belle Époque, the quarter-century that preceded the outbreak of World War I.[30] This was a period marked by a "feeling of living in an accelerating world, of speeding into the unknown."[31] As it is today, everyday life was transformed by a series of important technological innovations that reconfigured temporal and spatial experience, such as the telephone, the bicycle, photography, the cinema, the automobile, and the airplane.[32] Artists, politicians, scientists, and intellectuals sought ways to deal with these changes. In the artistic realm, this resulted in a second wave of modernist innovation.

It was against the background of this "culture of time and space" that Bergson's philosophy of time gained an enormous popularity and influence. Bergson became a vital point of reference for the most important artistic and political movements of the day, such as cubism, symbolism, anarchism, and modernism.[33] Contemporaries considered Bergson the greatest philosopher of his era. The philosophical revolution of Bergsonism was compared with those of Socrates and Kant.[34] John Dewey stated that "no philosophical problem will ever exhibit just the same face and aspect that it presented before Professor Bergson." And William James, calling *Creative Evolution* in

---

30. Charles Sowerwine, *France since 1870: Culture, Politics and Society* (New York: Palgrave, 2001), 94.

31. Philipp Blom, *The Vertigo Years: Europe, 1900–1914* (New York: Basic Books, 2008), 2.

32. Stephen Kern, *The Culture of Time and Space, 1880–1918* (Cambridge, MA: Harvard University Press, 1983), 1.

33. Alexandre Lefebvre, introduction to *Henri Bergson* by Vladimir Jankélévitch, trans. Nils F. Schott (Durham, NC: Duke University Press, 2015), xiii.

34. By Edouard Le Roy in 1913. See Richard A. Cohen, "Philo, Spinoza, Bergson: The Rise of an Ecological Age," in *The New Bergson*, ed. John Mullarkey (Manchester: Manchester University Press, 1999), 18.

1907 "a true miracle in the history of philosophy," posed the question of whether Bergson's work marked "the beginning of a new era."[35] Bergsonism was rejected equally passionately. Bertrand Russell considered it a dangerous form of anti-intellectualism and later wrote that it "harmonized easily with the movement which culminated in Vichy."[36] The left-wing French writer Julien Benda even claimed that he "would have happily killed Bergson if this was the only way to destroy his influence."[37]

All the more remarkable, therefore, is the pace at which Bergson fell into oblivion after World War I. The dissipation of Bergson's influence has been attributed to different causes. Some writers note that the themes that dominated the philosophical agenda changed and metaphysics fell out of fashion. Other interpreters point out that the Bergsonian worldview was so ubiquitous that its originality lost distinctiveness as its ideas were incorporated by movements whose longevity was more secure, such as phenomenology, existentialism, and structuralism.[38]

The famous confrontation between Bergson and Einstein that took place on April 6, 1922, in Paris—and that Bergson, in the eyes of the public, lost—also contributed to the demise of Bergsonism. This encounter has recently been described by Jimena Canales as a "debate that changed our understanding of time," because it consolidated "a world largely split into science and the rest."[39] During the meeting, Einstein remarked that "there is no philosopher's time; there is only a psychological time different from the time of the physicist." Einstein hereby denied the cosmological meaning that Bergson had attributed to his conception of time and space. What Bergson was after, according to Einstein, was nothing more than the subjective time of psychology, which had nothing to do with the "real world" with which science was concerned. Bergson came to be seen as a philosopher who had been unable to keep up with the innovations in physics. He was situated on the losing side of a dichotomy that opposed objective reality to subjective illusion.[40]

---

35. Ibid.

36. Bertrand Russell, *A History of Western Philosophy, and Its Connection with Political and Social Circumstances from the Earliest Times to the Present Day* (New York: Simon and Schuster, 1945), 791.

37. Robert C. Grogin, *The Bergsonian Controversy in France 1900–1914* (Calgary: University of Calgary Press, 1988), ix.

38. John Mullarkey, "Introduction: La Philosophie nouvelle, or Change in Philosophy," in *The New Bergson*, ed. John Mullarkey (Manchester: Manchester University Press, 1999), 1.

39. Jimena Canales, *The Physicist and the Philosopher: Einstein, Bergson, and the Debate that Changed our Understanding of Time* (Princeton, NJ: Princeton University Press, 2015), 7.

40. Bruno Latour, "Some Experiments in Art and Politics," *E-flux Journal* 23 (March 2011): 5.

Yet since the 1990s interest in Bergson's philosophy has increased, especially as a result of the popularity of Gilles Deleuze, who was profoundly influenced by Bergson; as John Mullarkey put it in 1999, "many now believe that the neglect of [Bergson's] work is both unfair to him and irresponsible to philosophy."[41] In this book we will see that Bergsonism has also gained a renewed topicality in light of the contemporary crisis of the modern regime of historicity.

What was the make-up of the philosophical revolution unleashed by Bergson which provoked such strong and manifold reactions at the beginning of the twentieth century? Bergson himself remarks in one of his essays that the work of a philosopher can often be traced back to one very simple intuition, yet precisely because of its simplicity, this intuition is very hard to put into words, which is why the philosopher "went on talking all his life."[42] With this statement Bergson certainly also referred to himself. If we wish to trace back through Bergson's entire oeuvre to a primary intuition, then this would be the intuition that time endures. We can experience duration, for example, when we want to mix a glass of water and sugar. This process can be captured in mathematical terms by a scientific formula, but this hides from view the fact that we have to wait until the sugar has dissolved. According to Bergson, "this little fact is big with meaning."[43]

This example shows us that it is extremely difficult, if not impossible, to put duration into words or formulae. St. Augustine already realized this in the fourth century, when in book XI of his *Confessions* he posed the question "What then is time?": "If no one asks me, I know: if I wish to explain it to one that asketh, I know not."[44] Already in his first book, *Time and Free Will* (1889), Bergson remarks that we deal with the elusiveness of time by understanding duration in spatial terms. Think only of the spatial metaphors that we make use of when we speak about time: we say that something happened "long" ago, that our future is "in front of us" or that time "moves slowly." The time of the clock is also based on a spatial conception of time—it imagines time as a homogeneous and empty medium, in which temporal "units" are arranged side by side.

Of course, the measurement of time conveniently structures public life. Yet by quantifying time in this way, Bergson argues, we eliminate the

---

41. Mullarkey, "Introduction: La Philosophie nouvelle," 1.
42. CM, 88–89.
43. CM, 9.
44. Augustine, *The Confessions of St. Augustine*, trans. E.B. Pusey (1921; repr., Auckland: The Floating Press, 2008), 332.

qualitative aspect of time, which is its duration. This is problematic because it is duration that turns time into a positive and creative force that brings about change. Bergson describes duration as the "continuous creation of unforeseen novelty."[45] In Bergson's later works, he emphasizes that duration is much more than merely the psychological experience of time. Our own duration can disclose other durations.[46] In *Creative Evolution* (1907) Bergson states that duration is immanent to the universe. It is the universe itself that endures. Duration becomes the way in which Bergson conceives of the evolution of life as a non-mechanistic and non-finalistic creative process, "the continual elaboration of the absolute new."[47]

Although temporal change is also of crucial importance for history as a discipline, historians and philosophers of history have largely neglected Bergsonism.[48] One of the reasons for this is undoubtedly that historians feel that a philosophical reflection on the nature of time is not of any concern to them. The timeline in history is unquestioningly accepted as a "neutral" way to organize historical time and to "measure" the distance between past and present. Historians tend to neglect how the assumption of an empty and homogeneous time structures their understanding of history.[49] As Michel de Certeau puts it, "the objectification of the past has made of time the unreflected category of a discipline that never ceases to use it as an instrument of classification."[50]

Another reason why the implications of Bergson's philosophy of duration for the study of history have rarely been interrogated is that Bergson himself seems never to have had a particular interest in history. Besides some scattered references throughout his oeuvre, history only makes a sudden and unexpected appearance in the final remarks to Bergson's last book, *The Two Sources of Morality and Religion* (1932). As Maurice Merleau-Ponty noted, "It is hard to understand why Bergson did not think about history from within

---

45. CM, 73.

46. Keith Ansell-Pearson, *Philosophy and the Adventure of the Virtual: Bergson and the Time of Life* (London: Routledge, 2002), 10.

47. Henri Bergson, *Creative Evolution* (*L'Évolution créatrice*, 1907), transl. Arthur Mitchell (1911; repr., Mineola, NY: Dover Publications, 1998) (hereafter CE), 11.

48. There are of course exceptions, such as the universal historian Arnold Toynbee, who applied a Bergsonian ontology to history. See Christian Kerslake, "Becoming against History: Deleuze, Toynbee and Vitalist Historiography," *Parrhesia* 4 (2008): 17–48.

49. See for instance Donald Wilcox, *The Measure of Times Past: Pre-Newtonian Chronologies and the Rhetoric of Relative Time* (Chicago: University of Chicago Press, 1987).

50. Michel de Certeau, "History: Science and Fiction," in *Heterologies: Discourse on the Other*, trans. Brian Massumi (Manchester: Manchester University Press, 1986), 216.

as he had thought about life from within."[51] Furthermore, interpreters have often set Bergson's philosophy of life in opposition to historical thought. They emphasize that Bergson's philosophy of life has to be conceived as an attempt to go "beyond the human state" and that human history is therefore not a primary concern for him.

In this book I will argue, nevertheless, that Bergson's philosophy of life is not antithetical to history, but, on the contrary, has to be understood as historical through and through. One of the intentions of this work is indeed to establish Bergson as an important philosopher of history. The relevance of Bergsonism to history becomes clear once we understand that Bergson refers so little and inconsistently to history because his philosophy of life implies a fundamental revision of the conventional modern meaning of the term. Instead of isolating human history from the history of the natural world—or, in other words, evolution—Bergsonism implies an understanding of historical time within the broader framework of the time of life. Bergson's conception of time unites the domains of Nature and Culture.

Bruno Latour has introduced the metaphor of a "modern Constitution" to show how the modern world has been divided into two ontologically distinct zones: on the one hand that of human beings (Culture), and on the other that of nonhumans (Nature). The modern Constitution warrants the transcendence of Nature, which is not made by human beings but only discovered by them.[52] Simultaneously, it guarantees the immanence of society (Culture), where human beings freely determine their own destiny.[53] For the modern Constitution to function, the scientific representation of things cannot be confused with the political representation of human beings. Otherwise we would neither obtain objective knowledge of the laws of nature nor achieve the political emancipation of humanity.[54]

---

51. Maurice Merleau-Ponty, "Bergson in the Making," in *Signs*, trans. Richard C. McCleary (Evanston, IL: Northwestern University Press, 1964), 187.

52. Joost van Driessche, "Muishond: Techno-wetenschappelijke, literaire en ethische bewegingen van taal" [MouseDog. Techno-Scientific, Literary and Ethical Movements of Language] (PhD diss., University of Groningen, 2016), 127.

53. Latour, *We Have Never Been Modern*, 30. According to Latour there is a paradox at the very core of the modern Constitution to which the moderns are blind. The separation of Nature and Culture simultaneously causes a proliferation of hybrids of nature and culture. The division of the world into two purified domains of Nature and Culture hence is a modern myth.

54. Hans Harbers, "Van mensen en dingen: Bespreking van: Bruno Latour, wij zijn nooit modern geweest" [Of Humans and Things: A Review of: Bruno Latour, We Have Never Been Modern], *Krisis* 58 (1995): 7–8.

The modern Constitution separates and purifies the domains of Nature and Culture through a modern conception of time. Time passes, according to the modern Constitution, in a very particular way, as if it abolishes the past behind it. Because of the elimination of the past, the moderns experience time as an "irreversible arrow, as capitalization, as progress."[55] The arrow of time sustains the modern Constitution by turning the asymmetry between Nature and Culture into an asymmetry between past and future: "The past was the confusion of things and men; the future is what will no longer confuse them."[56] History, as the "science of men in time" (Bloch), sanctions this asymmetry by constantly confirming the break between a premodern past and a modern present.

Bergson, however, does not regard Nature as the "polarized opposite" of Culture, but as its "underlying condition." Interestingly, this does not imply a reductionist sociobiology. Bergson does not merely understand social phenomena in terms of biological categories. Instead of a static domain "out there" that functions according to fixed laws, Bergson views Nature as imbued with a creative mode of time. Bergson associates life with an immanent creative tendency, which explains its evolution. According to this conception of life, as Elizabeth Grosz puts it, nature "does not contain culture but induces it to vary itself, to evolve, to develop and transform in ways that are not predictable in advance."[57]

Bergson's nonmodern ontology hereby allows us to explore an alternative understanding of history, one that goes "beyond the human state" and that gives us a unique sense of history's creative potential. I will argue that this perspective has significant topicality in the context of the contemporary crisis of the modern regime of historicity. While presentism has turned past and future into nonentities, parts of an omnipresent present, a Bergsonian ontology of time and history allows us to imagine the past instead as a living resource for the invention of the future.

∾

In the coming chapters, the contemporary crisis of the modern regime of historicity forms the background for an exploration of the historical relevance of Bergson's philosophy of duration. This is a wide-ranging topic for which I

---

55. Latour, *We Have Never Been Modern*, 69.

56. Ibid., 71.

57. Elizabeth Grosz, *Time Travels: Feminism, Nature, Power* (Durham and London: Duke University Press, 2005), 44.

have drawn upon a variety of sources. This is also reflected in the structure of the work. Although each chapter can be read and understood perfectly well on its own terms, in their sequence the different chapters may be imagined as stops on a journey. This journey strings together contemporary debates in the philosophy of history, Bergsonism and its contemporary interpretations, social and historical studies of modernity, and the philosophy of culture. We will also travel back and forth in time: from the twenty-first century to the period around 1900, and back again, toward the future. When we have arrived at our destination, I hope that we shall have obtained a glimpse of how an alternative perspective on time and history can help us to rethink the place of history in our presentistic society and culture.

We take off in chapter 1, entitled "The Case of the London Cenotaph," with the evaluation of a current debate in the philosophy of history. While the philosophy of history for decades mainly focused on questions of historical epistemology, recently theorists like Eelco Runia ("presence") and Berber Bevernage ("transitional justice") have instigated an "ontological turn" with the objective to "rescue the past from its current status as a nonentity."[58] In this chapter I will explore the idea of a "present past" by means of a case study, that of the history of the London Cenotaph. This is the most important war memorial in the UK, commemorating the British casualties of the First World War. I claim that the Cenotaph succeeded in turning the past into a "disquieting presence," and explore how the memorial interrupted the official narrative of the war.

In chapter 2, "Historiography, Modernity, and the Acceleration of Time," we will take a step back and see how the ontological turn in the philosophy of history is related to a broader crisis of time in contemporary society and culture. By discussing the work of such diverse authors as Martin Heidegger, Reinhart Koselleck, François Hartog, and Hartmut Rosa, I will show how modern historical consciousness has been shaped by a modern regime of historicity. Contemporary presentism can be understood as the crisis of this modern regime. In order to overcome this crisis, I will explore an alternative, nonmodern conception of time and history that is implied by Bergsonism.

We turn in chapter 3 ("Bergson and the Crisis of the Modern Regime of Historicity") to a previous crisis of the modern regime, one to which the history of the Cenotaph also testified: the period around 1900. In many ways, these "vertigo years" resemble the "neue Unübersichtlichkeit" ("new

---

58. Michael Bentley, "Past and 'Presence': Revisiting Historical Ontology," *History and Theory* 45 (October 2006): 349.

indistinctiveness") at the beginning of the twenty-first century.[59] These years were also marked by an acceleration of social life that dramatically revealed itself in the wake of World War I when international politics and diplomacy were overwhelmed by the sheer swiftness of events. We will see how Bergson's philosophy of duration can be seen as part of a broader cultural response to a reconfiguration of time and space between 1880 and 1920.

This forms the cue for an introduction to Bergson's philosophy of duration in chapter 4, "A World Made Out of Time." I will argue here that Bergson's metaphysics is paradoxically both non-systematic and empiricist. Bergson maintains that the systematic unity of the world may never be presupposed. Philosophy should always depart from concrete experience, which he designates as intuition. Intuition reveals, behind our perception of a stable world of "beings" that are placed in geometrical space, a reality of becoming, of duration. We will see that Bergson's oeuvre displays a consistent effort to explore the intuition of duration. It will become clear how Bergson develops duration from a psychological and subjective notion in his first book, *Time and Free Will*, into a philosophy of life and an ontology in *Creative Evolution*.

Chapter 5, "The Survival of the Past," is the next stop on our journey. It is dedicated to what I consider as the first of two contributions of Bergsonism to the ontology of history, namely, that Bergson can help us to reconceptualize the historical past. While historians tend to regard the past as an "absence" placed at a "distance" from the present, Bergson's theory of memory introduces us to a past that survives as a vehicle for creative change. Bergsonism shows us that the historical past is not fixed—an "object" that can be studied on its own terms—but that the past is constantly being reshaped in the present. I suggest that a genealogical approach may potentially offer us a historiographical tool allowing us to account for "the new" in history.

This brings us to chapter 6, entitled "Historical Creation," a second contribution of Bergsonism to historical thought: Bergson offers us a unique perspective on the creative nature of historical change. I compare Bergson's philosophy to the ontological presuppositions regarding the nature of history in nineteenth-century German historicism. This reveals some remarkable similarities between Bergsonism and the historicist worldview. Yet while the historicists oppose human history to the natural world, Bergson argues that the vital underlies the social. This provides the foundation for a conception

---

59. See Blom, *The Vertigo Years*, and Jürgen Habermas, "De nieuwe onoverzichtelijkheid: de crisis van de welvaartsstaat en de uitputting van utopische krachten" [The New Indistinctiveness: the Crisis of the Welfare State and the Exhaustion of Utopian Forces], in *De nieuwe onoverzichtelijkheid en andere opstellen*, trans. Geert Munnichs and René von Schomberg (Meppel: Boom, 1989).

of history that goes "beyond the human state," which is to say that human history, according to Bergson, unfolds within the ontological framework of the evolution of life. By comparing Bergsonism to Hegel's holistic philosophy of history, I will show that a Bergsonian approach allows us to conceive of history as an open whole.

In chapter 7, "The Dream of Progress," we come to the end of Bergson's life. In 1932, Bergson published one last book, *The Two Sources of Morality and Religion*, in which he tried to understand the historical situation of the Interbellum through his philosophy of life. Bergson specifically addressed the problem of war and how to evade it. Hereto he makes a famous distinction, later popularized by Karl Popper, between the open and closed society, which allows him to rethink the modern idea of historical progress. I will expose the theory of history that underlies Bergson's treatment here of the problem of war. Although this theory of history is a product of the Interbellum, we will see that its contemporary significance lies in its revelation of a historical dimension within Bergson's philosophy of life. This confirms my hypothesis that Bergsonism can be conceived as a nonmodern form of historicism.

An exploration of the currency of Bergson's philosophy would justify a critical approach that focuses on the shortcomings and contradictions that can be found in Bergsonism. Yet in this work I have chosen an approach that has more affinity with what Elizabeth Grosz calls an "affirmative method," one that wants to "assent to" rather than dissent from, and seek out "positivities, crucial concepts, insights on what is of value in the texts and positions being investigated."[60] A fundamental problem of the current presentistic regime of historicity is, so I claim, a lack of perspective, as past and future have been drawn into the present. I hope to bring out in the following what Bergsonism can still—or, maybe more accurately put, again—offer us, which at times may be more than Bergson himself envisioned.

---

60. Grosz, *Time Travels*, 2.

CHAPTER 1

THE CASE OF THE LONDON CENOTAPH

> A generation that had gone to school in horse-drawn streetcars now stood in the open air, amid a landscape in which nothing was the same except the clouds and, at its center, in a force field of destructive torrents and explosions, the tiny, fragile human body.[1]
>
> —Walter Benjamin, "Experience and Poverty,"
> in *Selected Writings*, vol. 2

> Every conception of history is invariably accompanied by a certain experience of time which is implicit in it, conditions it, and thereby has to be elucidated. Similarly, every culture is first and foremost a particular experience of time, and no new culture is possible without an alteration in this experience.[2]
>
> —Giorgio Agamben, *Infancy and History:
> On the Destruction of Experience*

In the middle of Whitehall, in the center of London around the corner from 10 Downing Street, stands a high, white, massive sculpture. While this edifice at first sight resembles an abstract work of art, it is in fact the Cenotaph, the

---

1. Walter Benjamin, "Experience and Poverty," in *Selected Writings*, vol. 2, *1927–1934*, ed. Howard Eiland, Michael W. Jennings and Gary Smith, trans. Rodney Livingstone and others (Cambridge, MA: Harvard University Press, 1999), 732.

2. Giorgio Agamben, *Infancy and History: On the Destruction of Experience*, trans. Liz Heron (London: Verso, 2007), 99.

most important war memorial in Great Britain, constructed to commemorate the British dead of the First World War. What immediately catches the eye is that the monument differs radically from traditional memorials. The design by Sir Edwin Lutyens carries no religious or patriotic representations. Instead, the Cenotaph has an apparently simple form imagining an empty tomb on a high pedestal. Its only decorations are some sculpted wreaths and the short text "The Glorious Dead."

By now the Cenotaph is fully integrated into the townscape of London, which makes the enormous impact of the monument soon after the First World War barely imaginable. Yet when the Cenotaph was revealed as a temporary sculpture made out of wood and plaster for the Peace Day Parade in July 1919, it unleashed an unprecedented public response that eventually led to the construction of a permanent version made out of stone. During the Interbellum the Cenotaph had an almost sacred aura and it was customary for people to raise their hats when passing by.[3]

Although the remarkable history of the Cenotaph has been extensively mapped in a number of publications, one of its most interesting features has gone virtually unnoticed. Contrary to its nineteenth-century predecessors that were based upon metaphorical representation, the Cenotaph principally commemorates by way of metonymy. By means of Eelco Runia's notion of "presence," this chapter shows that its metonymical form allowed the monument to constitute a "present past" in postwar London, which makes the Cenotaph highly significant to philosophers of history. The Cenotaph problematizes the status of the past as a nonentity within the present-day philosophy of history, a discipline predominantly influenced by the postmodern linguistic turn instigated by philosophers such as Hayden White in the 1970s and Frank Ankersmit in the 1980s.

Comparing the work of historians to monuments may seem problematic at first sight. I should stress, however, that metaphor and metonymy are being conceived in this chapter not as merely linguistic or literary phenomena, but as cognitive figures, conceptual in nature, that allow us to make sense of the world.[4] Hence, a historical representation can be seen as a metaphorical "thing made out of language" (Ankersmit) that does not fundamentally differ from other metaphorical "things" such as, indeed, monuments.

---

3. Allan Greenberg, "Lutyens's Cenotaph," *The Journal of the Society of Architectural Historians* 48 (March 1989): 12.

4. George Lakoff and Mark Johnson point to the cognitive importance of metaphor: "our ordinary conceptual system, in terms of which we both think and act, is fundamentally metaphorical in nature." George Lakoff and Mark Johnson, *Metaphors We Live By* (Chicago: University of Chicago Press, 1980), 3.

Section one will analyze the current status of the past as an absence in White's narrativism and Ankersmit's representationalism. Sections two and three investigate the theoretical importance of the Cenotaph as a "present past" on the basis of a detailed description of its realization. In the fourth and last section I will return to the philosophy of history and point out why it is so important to take the present past into account. I will argue that the philosophy of history should comprise more than merely an analysis of the epistemology and methodology of the historical sciences; it should also thematize the way past and present are related by addressing the problem of time in history.

1. HISTORICISM, POSTMODERNISM, AND THE ABSENT PAST

The philosophy of history is traditionally divided into two branches. Speculative or substantive philosophy of history, on the one hand, purports to uncover the essence of large-scale historical processes and is generally associated with eighteenth- and nineteenth-century philosophers like Vico, Herder, Hegel, or Marx. Critical philosophy of history, on the other hand, focuses on the epistemology of the historical sciences and the status of historical knowledge. It came into being as a reaction to the grand narratives of the speculative theoreticians, which it put aside as fruitless enterprises.[5] Since the 1970s, thinking about history has been almost exclusively dominated by a critical philosophy of history through narrativism and representationalism, which focus on the way historical meaning is constructed in textual representations of the past.

Historians tend to the belief that the past contains a meaning that can be uncovered by showing "what has actually happened." In the 1970s Hayden White refuted the realist pretensions of historians by showing that narratives about the past are fundamentally mediated by the historian who writes them. In his groundbreaking *Metahistory* (1973), White shows how the famous nineteenth-century historians Ranke, Michelet, Burckhardt, and Tocqueville prefigured the historical field they studied.[6] Although the historicists pretended to "wipe themselves out," they actually projected their ideological dispositions onto the historical past in a way that was not fundamentally different from that of the speculative philosophers of history. In other words,

---

5. David Carr, *Time, Narrative, and History* (Indiana: Indiana University Press, 1986), 1.
6. Hayden White, *Metahistory: The Historical Imagination in Nineteenth-Century Europe* (Baltimore: Johns Hopkins University Press, 1973).

according to White, meaning is not *a priori* part of historical reality but is established through narrative emplotment, and history has therefore more similarities to literature than to the sciences.

Following White, Frank Ankersmit has pointed to the importance of metaphor for establishing historical meaning on the level of the historical text as a whole: the historical representation.[7] While historical data are captured in single-sentence statements, it is through the historical representation that they obtain a historical meaning. Ankersmit sees the historical representation as an aesthetic substitute for an absent past similar to the way paintings, statues, or monuments substitute what they represent. Historical representations are not descriptions that can be true or false, but metaphors. Like metaphor, historical representation *is about* what it represents. It is an invitation to see a past reality *in terms of* X, like Johan Huizinga's invitation to see the late Middle Ages in terms of the autumn and Jacob Burckhardt's proposal to conceive of fifteenth-century Italy as a renaissance.[8] These kinds of metaphors are inherent to the narrative structure of the history text and allow historians to make sense of the historical data they encounter.

Despite these epistemological revisions, I think that there is also a fundamental continuity between historicism and the postmodern theories of White and Ankersmit. Although narrativism has made us aware that the grand narratives of historical progress are metaphorical constructions, it does not depart from the metaphysics of modern time that underlies the historicist worldview. Modern temporality conceives of time as a linear succession of now-points placed side by side in homogeneous space.[9] In historiography,

---

7. Ankersmit actually prefers "historical representation" over "historical narrative" because the latter suggests that history is merely a form of literature, while the term representation expresses the point that justice has to be done to what is represented, i.e., the historical past. As Ankersmit writes, "there is no representation without a represented." Frank Ankersmit, *Sublime Historical Experience* (Stanford: Stanford University Press, 2005), xiv.

8. See Johan Huizinga's *The Waning of the Middle Ages: A Study of the Life, Thought, and Art in France and the Netherlands in the Fourteenth and Fifteenth Centuries*, trans. F. Hopman (London: Arnold, 1924), and Jakob Burckhardt, *The Civilization of the Renaissance in Italy* (1860), trans. S.G.C. Middlemore (London: Penguin Books, 2004). These examples are mentioned in Frank Ankersmit, *Historical Representation* (Stanford: Stanford University Press, 2001).

9. The roots of modern temporality are explored in chapter 2. See also Reinhart Koselleck, *Futures Past: on the Semantics of Historical Time*, trans. Keith Tribe (New York: Columbia University Press, 2004); Peter Fritzsche, *Stranded in the Present: Modern Time and the Melancholy of History* (Cambridge, MA: Harvard University Press, 2004); and François Hartog's *Regimes of Historicity: Presentism and Experiences of Time*. Interestingly, all of these authors trace the origins of the modern notion of time back to the French Revolution.

this has its equivalent in the timeline that diachronically orders historical facts. The modern regime of time is marked by what Bruno Latour calls the arrow of time, which expresses that we progress through time "toward" the future and that the past is annihilated "behind us."[10] The past is thus fundamentally an absence. While the historicists assumed that historical reality was gone but still accessible, the narrativists have denied this possibility. As Michael Bentley notes, "The past-in-itself became an absence, a nothingness, a page on which to write, a place for dreams and images."[11]

The ontological status of the past in the philosophy of history of the last decades can be summarized by a quote from representation-theorist Alun Munslow: "the narrative logic of history is the only means we have to engage with the now absent past."[12] The past, in other words, is "broken off" from the present and has to be constructed as an object of knowledge before we can say anything meaningful about it. There are, however, dangers attached to reducing the past to the subject of "aesthetic whim."[13] As Walter Benjamin has argued, temporal regimes are not neutral ordering principles but can serve as instruments in the hands of those who have an interest in proclaiming that the past is over and done with.

Ewa Domanska, for instance, has pointed out that the ambivalent status of the disappeared person (dead or alive) resists "the dichotomous classification of present versus absent" that underlies modern historiography.[14] The disappeared person or body offers a paradigm for the past because it shows how the past is simultaneously continuous and discontinuous with the present—it both is and is not. As an example, Domanska mentions the case of the Madres de Plaza de Mayo, mothers whose children disappeared during the military dictatorship in Argentina. According to Domanska, the Madres

---

10. Latour, *We Have Never Been Modern*. Latour considers the tendency towards the preservation of the past (heritagization, monumentalization, musealization) a direct consequence of the modern, linear temporal regime. It serves as a counterweight to the notion of an "absent" past that is implied by linear time. This argument is similar to Nietzsche's critique of the antiquarianism of historicism in his second Untimely Meditation.

11. Bentley, "Past and 'Presence,'" 349.

12. Alun Munslow, "Editorial" *Rethinking History* (2010): 161.

13. Bentley, "Past and 'Presence,'" 349.

14. Ewa Domanska, "The Material Presence of the Past," *History and Theory* 45 (October 2006): 341. A similar point is made by Berber Bevernage, who describes the status of the Argentinian *desaparecidos* as "in between life and death." He reads the Madres' discourse as "a radical resistance to the irreversible time of history" and considers the *desaparecido* as part of a sophisticated "politics of time." Berber Bevernage, *History, Memory, and State-Sponsored Violence: Time and Justice* (New York: Routledge, 2012), 23–24.

used the ambivalent status of the *desaparecidos* in their quest for justice because they understood "that the junta's crimes would not be forgiven and forgotten as long as the relatives for whom [they] were looking retained the status of desaparecidos, situated in the 'between' that separates life and death."[15] A group of Madres even objected to the exhumation and identification of victims, because they feared that the closure that would result from this would avert the prosecution of the guilty. A similar phenomenon occurred with the disappearance in 2014 of forty-three students in Iguala, Ayotzinapa, in the Mexican state of Guerrero, which continues to spark national outrage. These examples bring the political dimension of temporal regimes to the fore. The "non-present past" implied by modern historiography subjects the past to the danger of domination and manipulation by fitting it into established discourses. Domanska, instead, prefers to think of the past as "non-absent":

> the non-absent past is the ambivalent and liminal space of 'the uncanny'; it is a past that haunts like a phantom and therefore cannot be so easily controlled or subject to a finite interpretation. It is occupied by 'ghostly artifacts' or places that undermine our sense of the familiar and threaten our sense of safety.[16]

In the following I would like to explore the conceptual space of the uncanny past that Domanska sketches, by means of a case study: the history of the London Cenotaph. The Cenotaph is unusual because by depicting an empty tomb on a high pedestal it avoids traditional metaphorical meanings by metonymically "presenting" the war dead of the British Empire in the center of London. But before discussing the theoretical significance of the Cenotaph, it is first necessary to examine in detail its realization.

2. LUTYENS AND THE CENOTAPH

The trench warfare in places such as Ypres, the Somme, and Verdun made the First World War a historical cataclysm of unprecedented scale. When the war had come to an end, Britain had suffered more than 700,000 fatalities, soon to be referred to as the "lost generation." Already during the war, practices of commemoration had begun with the erecting of shrines for the dead, a custom carried on after 1918 in the thousands of memorials that gave the war a permanent place in British cities, towns, and villages. A significant fea-

---

15. Ewa Domanska, "The Material Presence of the Past," 343.
16. Ibid., 346.

ture of these monuments was that many of them had a non-denominational form. Before the Great War, memorials were mostly based on religious and patriotic representations. Nineteenth-century monuments were mainly intended to arouse nationalism and strengthen state power. The traditional imagery, however, seemed incapable of doing justice to the Great War experiences. While many monuments did rely on conventional images and symbols, the most conspicuous and influential memorials broke new ground. As Sergiusz Michalski notes, after the First World War "metonymy replaced metaphor and allegory as the chief artistic instrument of progressive war memorials."[17]

The Tomb of the Unknown Soldier, for example, was used in nearly all warring countries and expressed the innumerable anonymous deaths in modern warfare.[18] The Unknown Soldier especially represented the missing, the approximately three million soldiers who were "blown to pieces or rotted in mud or otherwise unrecognizable."[19] The selection process of an unknown soldier went to great lengths to assure that the identity of the buried corpse would remain unknown. Britain's unknown soldier, for example, whose monument was revealed in 1920, was selected by Brigadier-General L.J. Wyatt from four unidentified bodies from four different sectors of the front.[20] The tomb, consisting of a simple black-marble stone, is located in Westminster Abbey "among the kings," as its inscription says, "because he had done good toward him and toward his house."

In the vanguard of modern memorials in Britain was the London Cenotaph. This monument, designed by Edwin Lutyens, was placed in the center of London and would develop from a temporary sculpture into the most important war monument in Great Britain. Lutyens's design deliberately broke with the nineteenth-century tradition of metaphorical representation. It laid a basis for new ways of commemoration that would influence, for instance, Maya Lin's Vietnam Veterans Memorial in Washington and the Holocaust-Mahnmal in Berlin. Lutyens was one of the most important English architects of the twentieth century. He has been responsible for more than a hundred war memorials. His designs were strongly influenced by a visit he paid to the battlefields in France. Here started, according to his biographer

---

17. Sergiusz Michalski, *Public Monuments: Art in Political Bondage 1870–1997* (London: Reaktion Books, 1998), 82.

18. Domanska's analysis of the missing human body could very well be applied to the way the Tomb of the Unknown Soldier presented the past. In this chapter, however, I have chosen to concentrate on the London Cenotaph.

19. K.S. Ingles, "War Memorials: Ten Questions for Historians," *Guerres mondiales et conflits contemporains* 167 (July 1992): 11–12.

20. Alan Borg, *War Memorials: From Antiquity to the Present* (London: Cooper, 1991), 141.

Christopher Hussey, the "train of emotion and thought for which he was to strive to find expression, with growing intensity"[21] and which culminated in the design of the London Cenotaph.[22]

Lutyens visited the French trenches in the summer of 1917 as an advisor to the Imperial War Graves Commission, the organization responsible for the war cemeteries and their monuments and memorials in Britain and on the continent. Its founder, Fabian Ware, had asked Lutyens for his ideas on the most appropriate design for these memorials. Lutyens was shocked by what he encountered during the arduous daily inspections of the hastily constructed field burials and temporary cemeteries. He came to realize the extent and magnitude of the horrors of the Western Front. In a letter to his wife, Emily, he wrote:

> What humanity can endure and suffer is beyond belief. The battlefields—the obliteration of all human endeavour and achievement.... It is all a sense of wonderment how can such things be.[23]

Lutyens characterized his impressions as "beyond imaginations and all so inexplicable that it makes writing difficult."[24] He witnessed many hastily created graves, "where men were tucked in where they fell." The sight of these graves, often marked by simple wooden crosses, made him remark, "One thinks for the moment no other monument is needed ... the only monument can be one where the endeavour is sincere to make such a monument permanent—a solid ball of bronze!"[25]

The abstract form of a ball of bronze would, in his opinion, express a timeless value. As he wrote one month later about the locations of future monuments, "the most beautiful sites should be selected not where the victories were and all that snobbery ... I do not want to put a worldly value over our dead."[26] Lutyens found it inappropriate to use the Christian

---

21. Christopher Hussey, *The Life of Sir Edwin Lutyens* (London: Antique Collectors Book Club, 1984), 372.

22. Lutyens's own reports from the frontline indicate that it seems certainly untrue that he was "detached" from the war as Adrian Gregory has recently argued. Adrian Gregory, *The Last Great War: British Society and the First World War* (Cambridge: Cambridge University Press, 2008), 255.

23. Clayre Percy and Jane Ridley, eds., *The Letters of Edwin Lutyens to His Wife Emily* (London: Collins, 1985), 349.

24. Ibid.

25. Ibid., 350.

26. Letter by Lutyens to his wife Emily from 28 August, 1917. Ibid., 354.

cross on war cemeteries. One of his first designs, the neutral Great Stone of Remembrance, was based on the stepped construction of the Parthenon in Athens. This apparently simple, rectangular stone with a sole inscription, "Their Name Liveth For Evermore," contained a geometrical structure that Lutyens would bring to perfection in the Cenotaph. It would be employed at most of the British war cemeteries on the continent.

Lutyens received the assignment for the Cenotaph in 1919 in person from British Prime Minister Lloyd George, who asked him to build a catafalque after a French example for the Peace Day Parade, a march of allied soldiers through the center of London during which the official signing of the peace treaty would be sealed.[27] The Peace Day Parade was to be held on July 19, 1919, and served the politics of commemoration the British government was instigating. The parade should stir feelings of patriotism among the population as a counterweight to "bolshevism" and the potential social unrest the authorities feared from unemployed or dissatisfied workers and disillusioned soldiers returning from the front. The Cenotaph had to contribute to the image of a "nation in mourning."[28] It should address the massive death toll of the trenches by conveying a sense that, as Lloyd George wrote, "the war was an experience where everyone sacrificed and some died, not as members of a separate group, but as citizens of a whole community."[29]

Instead of a catafalque, Lutyens proposed to build a cenotaph. In ancient Greece cenotaphs were empty graves used to honor persons whose bodies were buried elsewhere.[30] This permitted Lutyens to refrain from Christian references, because he found that troops from the whole Empire should be able to identify with the monument.[31] The design and construction of the Cenotaph in Whitehall were completed in less than two weeks. The Cenotaph was originally intended as no more than a temporary sculpture and was only one of several places of commemoration along the parade route, but it turned out to have an unexpected appeal.[32] As soon as the monument was erected on the day before the Peace Day Parade, people began to lay

---

27. Jane Ridley, *The Architect and his Wife: A Life of Edwin Lutyens* (London: Chatto and Windus, 2002), 288.

28. Gregory, *The Last Great War*, 250.

29. Lloyd George as cited in Neil Hanson, *Unknown Soldiers: The Story of the Missing of the First World War* (London: Doubleday, 2005), 276. Lloyd George also wrote: "Nations must justify mass killings." See *Unknown Soldiers*, 263.

30. Borg, *War Memorials*, 75.

31. Hanson, *Unknown Soldiers*, 273.

32. Greenberg, "Lutyens's Cenotaph," 8–9.

Figure 1.1. The Cenotaph in the days following its unveiling at the Armistice Day ceremony on November 11, 1920. "The Cenotaph covered in flowers," Mary Evans Picture Library, accessed September 20, 2018, https://www.maryevans.com. Picture No. 10942210, pictured swamped in floral tributes. © Illustrated London News Ltd./ Mary Evans.

flowers and wreaths around the memorial. These were cleared away before the parade started. After 15,000 allied soldiers had marched by to salute the dead, thousands of people again lined up to lay bouquets and wreaths until well after nightfall.[33]

---

33. Hanson, *Unknown Soldiers*, 274.

In the week after the Peace Day Parade the "pilgrimage of the poor people"[34] continued. Meanwhile a growing public clamor called for the preservation of the Cenotaph. Several members of Parliament submitted a petition to the Office of Works and the newspapers were filled with pleadings for the construction of a Cenotaph made of stone to replace the temporary one of wood and plaster.[35] As *The Times* wrote on July 21, two days after the unveiling, "The Cenotaph . . . is only a temporary structure made to look like stone, but Sir Edwin Lutyens' design is so grave, severe and beautiful that one might well wish it were indeed of stone and permanent."[36] And five days later: "no feature of the victory march in London made a deeper impression than the Cenotaph erected in Whitehall to the memory of 'The Glorious Dead' . . . it ought undoubtedly to be erected among the Monuments of London."[37] Due to the problematic location of the Cenotaph at a busy traffic junction, it was considered to move it to a less conspicuous spot at a nearby park or open space.[38] Yet according to the *Daily Mail*, the spot in Whitehall had obtained a sacred status "by the tears of many mothers"[39] and *The Times* wrote, "the desire of the great mass of the public is to see it perpetuated in its present form."[40] When the government decided to preserve the Cenotaph at its original location in Whitehall, Lutyens noted in his diary:

> It was a mass-feeling too deep to express itself more fitly than by piles of ever-fresh flowers which loving hands placed on the cenotaph day by day. Thus it was decided, by the human sentiment of millions, that the cenotaph should be as it is now.[41]

---

34. From *Review of Reviews* as cited in D. W. Lloyd, *Battlefield Tourism: Pilgrimage and the Commemoration of the Great War in Britain, Australia, and Canada, 1919–1939* (New York: Berg, 1998), 53.

35. Jenny Edkins, *Trauma and the Memory of Politics* (Cambridge: Cambridge University Press, 2003), 61.

36. *The Times*, 21 July 1919, as cited in David Cannadine, "War and Death, Grieving and Mourning in Modern Britain," in *Mirrors of Mortality: Studies in the Social History of Death*, ed. J. Wiely (London: Europa Publications, 1981), 221.

37. *The Times*, July 26, 1919, as cited in Greenberg, "Lutyens's Cenotaph," 9.

38. Edkins, *Trauma and the Memory of Politics*, 63.

39. Hanson, *Unknown Soldiers*, 275.

40. Greenberg, "Lutyens's Cenotaph," 10.

41. Lutyens's *Journal of Remembrance* as cited in Greenberg, "Lutyens's Cenotaph," 10.

On November 11, 1920, the Cenotaph, made out of Portland stone, was officially inaugurated in a ceremony that also involved the unveiling of the Tomb of the Unknown Soldier in Westminster Abbey.[42] In the week that followed, the monument was visited by no less than one million people leaving one hundred thousand wreaths.[43] A day later, *The Times* noted that "the ceremony of yesterday was the most beautiful, the most touching, and the most impressive that in all its long eventful story, this Island has ever seen."[44] During the 1920s the Cenotaph remained a place of pilgrimage and people continued to leave flowers and letters at the site, although the monument gradually became more identified with the ceremonial role it still has today.[45]

3. THE CENOTAPH AS METONYMICAL COMMEMORATION

The memorialization of the First World War is a controversial topic among historians. Modernist historians tend to regard the First World War as a traumatic event that remained anomalous in postwar societies such as Britain. These historians often refer to avant-garde art forms that departed radically from traditional cultural forms and derive the meaning of the Great War mainly from accounts of the horrifying experiences in the trenches.[46] More traditionalist historians, on the other hand, generally contest the idea of a fundamental break with pre-war society. For example, in a recent publication, Adrian Gregory resists the image of a disillusioned Britain after the war: "Depictions of Britain in the 1920s as a traumatized society, with a shattered sense of itself, should be understood for what they are: constructions to cover up a much more complex social reality of winners and losers, continuities and changes."[47] One's position in this debate would most likely influence the

---

42. The Tomb of the Unknown Soldier was intended by the Anglican Church as a counterweight to "cenotapholatry," the pilgrimages to what the church authorities saw as a pagan monument because of the lack of religious symbolism. See Lloyd, *Battlefield Tourism*, 87–88.

43. Gerald Gliddon and Timothy John Skelton, *Lutyens and the Great War* (London: Frances Lincoln, 2008), 47.

44. *The Times*, November 12, 1920, as cited in Cannadine, "War and Death," 223.

45. Lloyd, *Battlefield Tourism*, 82.

46. See for instance Paul Fussell's classic study of wartime literature, *The Great War and Modern Memory* (New York and London: Oxford University Press, 1975).

47. Gregory, *The Last Great War*, 257.

way one would account for the massive public response to the Cenotaph. Was this a spontaneous emotional outpouring of traumatized individuals, or a massive expression of patriotism stirred up by the government?

It seems obvious that there is a "traditional" top-down aspect to the Cenotaph, as the monument formed part of a politics of commemoration. Nevertheless, such a constructivist reading cannot fully account for the extraordinary appeal of the monument. The many testimonies of visitors and the thousands of letters to deceased soldiers left at the Cenotaph confirm that the memorial was experienced as a place of mourning for countless people suffering personal grief. Social surveys during the annual two-minute silence at the Cenotaph substantiate the idea that "individuals did not think of the Empire, or nations, or armies, but of individual people who were no longer there."[48] Besides the top-down aspect, in other words, it cannot be denied that there was also a bottom-up element at play in the monument, which, I would like to argue, was largely due to its *metonymical* way of commemorating.[49]

Metonymy is often seen as the counterpart of metaphor.[50] While metaphor, by "understanding and experiencing one kind of thing in terms

---

48. Interviews held by the pioneering social survey group Mass Observation. See Jay Winter, *Remembering War: The Great War Between Memory and History in the Twentieth Century* (New Haven: Yale University Press, 2006), 153–154. D.W. Lloyd connects the pilgrimages to the Cenotaph with the popularity of spiritism after the war: "The people who visited the Cenotaph also drew upon a widely held belief that the spirit or even spirits of the war dead had not been extinguished by the war or by the Armistice. The Cenotaph provided the focal point for the widespread belief or wish to believe in the continuing presence of the dead." For many, coming to the Cenotaph was meant to confirm a continuing tie with the wartime experiences. Lloyd, *Battlefield Tourism*, 62. The "presence of the dead" was also one of the arguments raised to counter the plan of moving the Cenotaph to a place where it would not interfere with the traffic.

49. In this sense, my interpretation has more affinities with the position of Jay Winter, who has resisted the idea of a fundamental break with pre-war society and attempts to go beyond the modernist-traditionalist divide by pointing to both continuities and discontinuities with pre-war society. Jay Winter, *Sites of Memory, Sites of Mourning: The Great War in European Cultural History* (Cambridge: Cambridge University Press, 1995).

50. Literature on the relation between metaphor and metonymy often refers to a text by Roman Jakobson, who as early as in 1956 pointed out a direct link between both tropes. Research on different kinds of aphasia made Jakobson conclude that the underlying structure of language and human behavior is bipolar and moves on a continuum between a metaphorical and metonymical pole, a structure that according to him could be translated to all semiotic sciences. See Roman Jakobson and Morris Halle, *Fundamentals of Language* (The Hague: Mouton, 1956), 76–82.

of another,"[51] suggests a *similarity* between entity A and entity B (A "is like" B), in metonymy a *substitution* of A with B takes place, so that B comes to *stand for* A. Consider the following examples of metonymical substitution:

> *The shoplifting* is in prison cell two.
> I love reading *Shakespeare*.
> *The Christians* invaded Iraq.

As these examples show, a metonym works as a vehicle that provides a so-called "mental access" to an underlying target entity (respectively a shoplifter, the works of Shakespeare, and soldiers of the US army). According to cognitive linguists, therefore, metaphor connects "horizontally" two distant conceptual domains, while metonymical substitution works "vertically" on the basis of contiguity within the same conceptual domain (defined as a "coherent organization of experience"[52]). Its verticality allows metonymy to not only connect concepts, but also to cut across distinct realms by connecting, for instance, real-world (nonlinguistic) referents such as things or events with words or concepts.[53]

According to Eelco Runia, the property of connecting different "levels of being" makes metonymy very relevant to philosophers of history.[54] Its verticality allows metonymy to paradoxically make things present by not presenting them. Metonymy is thus able to break into linear temporality by constituting "holes in which the past discharges into the present."[55] Standing at the basis of Runia's conception of metonymy, as in the cognitive linguistic view mentioned above, is the element of substitution.

In the Cenotaph, metonymical substitution comes about in two different ways. At a macro-level, the Cenotaph is the war memorial that *stands for* a lost generation. This contributed to the myth of the nation in grief that served the goals of the politics of commemoration. More importantly, however, on a micro-level the empty tomb emphasizes individual mortality. While the Tomb of the Unknown Soldier is dedicated primarily to the missing, the Cenotaph stands in for the graves of the fallen soldiers who, unlike for instance the American war dead, were mostly buried in war cemeteries

---

51. Lakoff and Johnson, *Metaphors We Live By*, 5.

52. Zoltán Kövecses, *Metaphor: A Practical Introduction* (Oxford: Oxford University Press, 2002), 4.

53. Ibid., 149

54. Eelco Runia, *Moved by the Past: Discontinuity and Historical Mutation* (New York: Columbia University Press, 2014), 151.

55. Ibid., 67.

on the European mainland. The official policy of the Imperial War Graves Commission stated that the repatriation of deceased soldiers was prohibited and that the war dead would be buried under uniform conditions. The fallen soldiers thus served as an ideological instrument in the hands of the state, which wanted to stress the equality of the sacrifice that was made in the service of the nation. This policy went explicitly against the wishes of many of the bereaved who wanted to have a say in the shape of headstones or the location where their relatives would be buried. The Imperial War Graves Commission received ninety letters a week with requests for the repatriation of bodies.[56] The Cenotaph was thus for many people quite literally a substitute for the graves of the war dead.

Runia sees metonymy as a "willfully inappropriate transposition" of a word belonging to context I to context II. In this way a metonym links two contexts with each other, as a result of which the metonym stands out as "just 'slightly out of place.'"[57] This juxtaposition of contexts has a disquieting effect. The Cenotaph is thus, in Runia's terminology, a "willfully inappropriate transposition" from the colossal, anonymous deaths in the trenches of World War I to postwar London. The Cenotaph put two contexts in opposition to each other: while London found itself at the Peace Day Parade in the grips of peace and patriotism, the disquieting presence of Lutyens's design put the context of war in opposition to this. The Cenotaph thus formed a disquieting presence, a *Fremdkörper* (foreign body), which explains its impact: the monument answered to the feeling that the peace celebrated by a parade took place in the shadow of a war that had barely ended. As a bereaved mother remarked, "only the heartless can want a peace day."[58] The disquieting effect of the Cenotaph was strengthened by its location in Whitehall, where many government buildings are located, including the Houses of Parliament and 10 Downing Street. From this center of power the "lost generation" had been directed into the trenches, and exactly here this generation was presented in the midst of the busy traffic, "as the stumbling block, the hindrance that reminds us of the impossibility of closure,"[59] in the words of Jenny Edkins. Jay Winter adds to this that the Cenotaph "managed to transform the commemorative landscape by making all of 'official' London into an imagined cemetery."[60]

---

56. Gregory, *The Last Great War*, 255.
57. Runia, *Moved by the Past*, 67.
58. Lloyd, *Battlefield Tourism*, 52.
59. Edkins, *Trauma and the Memory of Politics*, 66.
60. Winter, *Sites of Memory, Sites of Mourning*, 104.

The "disquieting presence" of the Cenotaph resisted the top-down structure of the politics of commemoration. It is telling that the authorities made constant efforts to subdue the metonymical aspect of the Cenotaph by proposing to attach expressions of patriotism and nationalism to the monument. During the construction of the permanent Cenotaph in 1920, for instance, Lutyens argued with the government about the British flags that were placed on both sides of the monument. Lutyens had insisted on using more symbolic flags made of stone instead of cloth because these were less likely to get dirty or be ripped apart. A memo from the Minister of Agriculture and Fishery Lord Lee of Fareham addressed to the members to the Cabinet expresses the ideological motives that inspired the refusal of Lutyens' proposal:

> Anything less calculated to inspire reverence or emotion than a petrified and raddled imitation of free and living bunting, which responds to every breeze and mood of nature, it is difficult to imagine.... I venture to plead that our national flag may be spared from such ingenuity—which special circumstances would be almost an act of sacrilege.[61]

Lutyens did, however, successfully oppose the placing of bronze sentries.[62]

Another example of the difficulties the authorities had with the disquieting aspect of the Cenotaph is that the initial plan for the unveiling of the Cenotaph intentionally excluded bereaved relatives from the ceremony, because the monument should "exalt the dignity of sacrifice without the tears," as Minister for Works Sir Alfred Mond stated. According to Mond, the Cenotaph should be conceived not as "a place to lay flowers, which seems to be commonly assumed," but as a place where Peace Day and the British victory are commemorated.[63]

Due to its metonymical form, the Cenotaph gave a historical reality a literal place in postwar London. Runia sees "presenting" the past as an important characteristic of monuments that is covered up in traditional memorials. Monuments that emphasize meaning disguise the fact that monuments are actually an interplay between two very distinct components: a monument (1) *says something* about (2) what it *stands for*.[64] For Runia, therefore, a monument forms a combination of metaphor ("giving meaning to something")

---

61. Gliddon and Skelton, *Lutyens and the Great War*, 45–46.
62. Greenberg, "Lutyens's Cenotaph," 17.
63. Sir Alfred Mond as quoted in Lloyd, *Battlefield Tourism*, 77.
64. Runia, *Moved by the Past*, 68.

and metonymy ("standing for something"). Because metaphorical "transfer of meaning" is nearly absent in the Cenotaph, attention is placed on what it stands for. The Cenotaph is not only an edifice made out of white stone; its disquieting *presence* also stresses what is ostentatiously *absent*. By this terrible *absence*—of a friend, a relative, or even an entire generation—the past is at one and the same time very much *present*.[65] Hence, the past obtains the uncanny status that Domanska referred to with regard to the missing person.

Runia conceptualizes the present past by the notion of "presence," defined as "the unrepresented way the past is present in the here and now."[66] This definition expresses presence as having to be conceived as the opposite of metaphorical meaning constructed by means of a representation. Metonymy, according to Runia, brings about a "transfer of presence" by refraining from "transfer of meaning." This implies a relation to our past where we as subjects no longer control or prefigure our object, that is, historical reality.[67] On the contrary: *we* are worked, or prefigured, by the past. That's why Runia, when discussing the role of metonymy in the work of German author W.G. Sebald, describes the trope as "a kind of 'leak' in time through which 'presence' wells up from the past into the present."[68]

4. RETHINKING THE PAST

Presence problematizes the metaphysics of modern time that underlies modern historiography. Modern historiography presupposes a linear notion of time that is embodied by the timeline, a spatial metaphor that suggests that we move "through" time "toward" the future, while leaving the past "behind" us. The object of historical research, the historical past, is hereby placed at a distance from the present and turned into an absence. Modern historical time sustains, as Michel de Certeau states, "a relation between a 'present' and a 'past' distinct from each other, one being the producer of the discourse

---

65. Eelco Runia, "De pissende pulcinella" [The Pissing Pulcinella], *De Gids* 168 (2005): 411.

66. Eelco Runia, "Presence," *History and Theory* 45 (February 2006): 1. For an evaluation of the presence debate in the philosophy of history, see Leon ter Schure, "Presence: De tegenwoordigheid van het verleden in het heden" [Presence: The presence of the Past in the Here and Now], *Tijdschrift voor Geschiedenis* 116 (2006): 230–241.

67. Eelco Runia, "Namen Noemen" [Naming Names], *Tijdschrift voor Geschiedenis* 119 (2006): 245.

68. Runia, *Moved by the Past*, 67.

and the other being what is represented by it, one the 'subject,' the other the 'object' of a certain knowledge."[69]

The construction of the historical past as "object of study" is generally hidden from view. Yet it is the conceptualization of the past as a depoliticized, "neutral" and "disinterested" field of study that permits the act of representation by the historian. De Certeau indeed perceptively remarks that historical discourse

> gives itself credibility in the name of the reality which it is supposed to represent, but this authorized appearance of the 'real' serves precisely to camouflage the practice which in fact determines it. Representation thus disguises the praxis that organizes it.[70]

By precluding the historical past from the present, the past that continues to haunt the present is suspended from historical consideration. This is the non-absent past, which manifests itself in the figure of the disappeared person.

By defying the official narrative of the war, the Cenotaph frustrated the construction of the past as object of study that normally precedes historical representation. The Cenotaph embodied a past that refused to naturally disappear from the present. It accomplished this by literally materializing the excluded past. We can even trace this back to the design of the monument. The Cenotaph has no straight lines but is composed of the surfaces of a circle. As Lutyens describes: "all its horizontal surfaces and planes are spherical, parts of parallel spheres 1801 ft. 8 in. in diameter; and all its vertical lines converge upwards to a point some 1801 ft. 8 in. above the center of these spheres."[71] The Cenotaph is thus no freestanding sculpture but forms part of a greater whole, a virtual sphere that is divided into different segments in the shape of the points of a star. In this, as Jenny Edkins points out, the Cenotaph represents what in psychoanalysis is referred to as "the real," that part of reality which has fallen out of the social order—that *needs* to be excluded to maintain this order. According to Edkins it is this reality, this repressed past, normally covered up behind social conventions and representations, that visitors of the monument are facing: "The Cenotaph, as a representation of the segment that has 'fallen out' of the whole, represents the real made—eventually—solid."[72]

---

69. De Certeau, "History: Science and Fiction," 214–215.
70. Ibid., 203.
71. *Imperial War Graves Commission*, 6th Report, 1926, as cited in Winter, *Sites of Memory, Sites of Mourning*, 104.
72. Edkins, *Trauma and the Memory of Politics*, 66–67.

Because modern historiography also needs to expel the past from the present in order to affirm itself, historians are generally antagonistic toward alternative historical temporalities that put the "distance" between past and present into question. This distance is considered necessary because modern historiography is based on the idea that growing clarity comes with the "passage" of time, which allows us to see things with greater detachment.[73] Once the absent-present relationship between the historical past and the present is disturbed, the historian can supposedly no longer assume a critical stance toward the past.

The reception of Runia's idea of presence reflects this attitude. In a critical evaluation, Keith Jenkins maintains that presence concerns not actually history per se (*historia rerum gestarum*) but merely the past (*res gestae*). Jenkins points out that the past only becomes history when the historian makes it so and that this necessarily happens through linguistic representation. For Jenkins, presence pertains to "the idealist/metaphysical corner of 'memory studies'" and contributes nothing to a better understanding of "how historical representation and therefore how 'history' (historiography) works."[74] Like many historians, Jenkins wants to stay clear of more ontological questions regarding the nature of history and historical time and wishes to focus exclusively on historical epistemology.[75] The example of the Cenotaph can make us aware, however, that ontological presuppositions about the nature of historical time precede and structure our epistemological relationship with the historical past.

In order to account for the history of the Cenotaph, the philosophy of history would need to go beyond historical epistemology. The exclusive focus by a critical philosophy of history on textual representation only reinforces the modern regime of time that underlies modern historiography and the absent past that goes with it. Rather, the philosophy of history needs an "ontological turn" that involves a more fundamental reflection on the presuppositions of modern history. This can create an awareness that modern historical time is not merely a convenient measuring instrument by which

---

73. Mark Salber Phillips, *On Historical Distance* (New Haven and London: Yale University Press, 2013), 1–2.

74. Keith Jenkins, "Inventing the New from the Old—from White's 'Tropics' to Vico's 'Topics' (Referee's Report)," *Rethinking History* 14 (2010): 243.

75. As Berber Bevernage and Chris Lorenz point out, "Although since the birth of modernity history presupposes the existence of 'the past' as its object, 'the past' and the nature of the borders that separate 'the past,' 'the present' and 'the future' until very recently have attracted little reflection within the discipline of history." Chris Lorenz and Berber Bevernage, "Breaking up Time—Negotiating the Borders between Present, Past and Future," in *Breaking up Time: Negotiating the Borders between Present, Past and Future*, ed. Chris Lorenz and Berber Bevernage (Göttingen: Vandenhoeck & Ruprecht, 2013), 9.

we can "locate" historical events in history, but that it has a political dimension as well. Berber Bevernage has shown this, for instance, with regard to transitional justice, the "collective reckoning with the legacies of human rights abuse after dictatorship or violent conflict."[76] He argues that truth commissions deal politically with the persistence of the past by managing a break with the past through modern historical discourse. Modern historical time thus serves as an antidote to memorial time, in which the past continues to haunt the present.

In chapter 2 I will further explore the relationship between modern historicity and modern historiography. For now it is enough to conclude that what seems to be, at first sight, a debate about historical epistemology in the philosophy of history ("How can the absent past be re-presented?"), in fact points to a problem of historical *ontology* ("How is the absent past produced?" "What is the nature of historical time?" "How should we conceptualize the relation between past and present?").

5. CONCLUSION

The philosophy of history has in the last decades mainly focused on questions of historical epistemology. Narrativism and representationalism have with great success problematized the historicist ideal of a historian who "wipes himself out" in his text in order to show the past "how it actually has been." It has become clear that the textual representation of the past is mediated by the historian. Historical meaning does not magically appear from the objective representation of the past. It is established by the narrative constructions of historians.

This "linguistic turn" did produce an epistemological problem: how can the historian faithfully represent the historical past when a direct access to historical reality is denied to him? If the representation of history is subjected to the historians' "aesthetic whims" (Bentley), does historiography still deserve its scientific status, or should the history departments be absorbed by the department of literary studies? And how should we make sense of the "present past"—a past that is not recognized and excluded from historical consideration and that seems to resist representation?

These epistemological debates in the contemporary philosophy of history can only be properly addressed if we take account of the ontological presuppositions regarding the nature of history and historical time within

---

76. Berber Bevernage, "Writing the Past Out of the Present: History and the Politics of Time in Transitional Justice," *History Workshop Journal* 69 (Spring 2010): 111.

modern historiography. Ontological presuppositions are important, because they provide a condition of possibility for historical writing. While postmodern philosophy of history may have *epistemologically* broken with the historicist paradigm, *ontologically* it has remained within the same, modern regime of historicity.

Critical philosophers of history generally want to stay clear of ontological questions. But while history as a science derives its authority from the historical reality that it supposedly represents, it obscures the point that historical reality is constructed as an "object of study" by distancing the past from the present. This becomes apparent at moments of a crisis of time, as the history of the Cenotaph makes clear. Does the contemporary debate about presence in the philosophy of history also point to a "crisis of time"? In order to explore whether this is the case, we will need to address the relation between historicity and historiography.

Chapter 2

Historiography, Modernity, and the Acceleration of Time

> In the twenty-five years after 1970 so much was achieved by theorists in revising the epistemological basis of historical work that they understandably lost sight of its object. The past-in-itself became an absence, a nothingness, a page on which to write, a place for dreams and images.[1]
>
> —Michael Bentley, "Past and 'Presence':
> Revisiting Historical Ontology"

> Just as speeding up a sequence of images can bring them to life in the transition from photography to film, or the acceleration of molecules can transform ice into water into steam, changes in the temporal structures of modern societies transform the very essence of our culture, social structure, and personal identity (and, of course, our experience of nature, too).[2]
>
> —Hartmut Rosa, "Social Acceleration: Ethical and Political
> Consequences of a Desynchronized High-Speed Society," in
> *High-Speed Society, Social Acceleration, Power, and Modernity*

It seems natural for us to consider ourselves as part of an all-encompassing process that we call history. Our place in history allows us to understand

---

1. Michael Bentley, "Past and 'Presence,'" 349.

2. Hartmut Rosa, "Social Acceleration: Ethical and Political Consequences of a Desynchronized High-Speed Society," in *High-Speed Society, Social Acceleration, Power, and Modernity*, ed. Hartmut Rosa and William E. Scheuerman (Pennsylvania: The Pennsylvania State University Press, 2009), 97.

"who we are" and "where we are going." It is because we see ourselves as historical beings that the study of history matters to us. History as a discipline obtains its relevance and legitimacy from the idea that our social, cultural, and political reality is shaped by historical processes.

Yet although history as a discipline is bound up with our historical being, or, in philosophical terms, *historicity*, historians rarely pay attention to the way in which historicity influences historiography. The theory of history tends to focus on questions of historical epistemology, on the status and validation of historical knowledge and modes of explanation, and disregards a more fundamental reflection on the way in which our historical being prefigures historical inquiry. A reflection on the relationship between historicity and historiography is nevertheless important because it denaturalizes our historiographical approach toward the past. It makes us aware that, just as our historicity has a history of its own, the same is true for the modes of historical inquiry that go with it.

Highlighting the way in which historicity ontologically conditions historical inquiry will allow us to gain a better understanding of the contemporary "crisis of historicity" that several commentators have registered. Since the advent of modernity in the mid-eighteenth century, historical consciousness has provided us with a way to orient ourselves in an environment in which things change at an ever-accelerating rate. The "late-modern" society that we have inhabited since approximately 1989, shaped by a political and digital revolution, has now accelerated to such a degree that it can no longer be meaningfully understood in historical terms.[3] Our "place in history" no longer matters, only the here and now. Past and future have been absorbed by the "omnipresent present" of the digital age, in which things change so frantically that "real" historical change seems to have become impossible. Within this environment, the modern concept of history is becoming obsolete and the place of history in our society and culture is increasingly being marginalized.

In this chapter I want to historicize the ontology of modern history by examining how historicity and historiography are related. I will show how mutations of our historical being affect the way in which we deal with history. This will allow me to argue that our contemporary presentistic society and culture suffer from a "crisis of historicity."

I will start in section one with an exploration of the relationship between temporality, historicity, and history through a discussion of the early Heidegger. A reading of *Being and Time* allows us to "denaturalize" history and offers us a perspective on the contingent nature of a historiographical approach of the past. Section two will specify the ontological framework of

---

3. Rosa, *Social Acceleration*, 312.

modern history. German historian Reinhart Koselleck situates the origins of the modern idea of history between 1750 and 1850, when an acceleration of time caused historical time to emancipate itself from the cycles of nature. In the third section, I argue that this acceleration of time has produced a crisis of historicity in our contemporary culture. This expresses itself in the philosophy of history by the absence of the historical past registered in chapter 1.

1. HEIDEGGER ON HISTORY AND HISTORICITY

The exclusive focus by philosophers of history on historical epistemology suggests that our primary relation with the past is cognitive and is the result of historical inquiry. This is maintained by the American philosopher of history David Carr. Carr points out that contemporary philosophy of history reduces the historical past to an object of knowledge. This, however, disregards another, primordial way in which we relate to the past. History is already tied up with our lived experience prescientifically: "in a naive and prescientific way the historical past is there for all of us . . . it figures in our ordinary view of things . . . [and] functions as background for our present experience, our experience of the present."[4]

But why would historians have to take this experiential relation with history into account? Shouldn't history be about facts, provided by historical sources and a scientific method? Carr insists that our prescientific relation with the past is important, because it allows us to gain a proper understanding of history as a discipline. We can only understand why history is of interest to us in the first place by taking into account that we are historical beings. Carr bases this insight on the ideas of the eighteenth-century Italian philosopher and historian Giambattista Vico, and, more importantly, on Wilhelm Dilthey. Citing Dilthey, Carr states that "we are historical beings first, before we are observers [*Betrachters*] of history, and only because we are the former do we become the latter."[5] We thematize history because we are historical and in order to understand "how we can obtain *knowledge* of the past" we should first address the question of "how we *relate to* the past."

Carr's thesis is sustained by the theory of history that Martin Heidegger lays out in *Being and Time*. Heidegger offers a powerful account of the ontological ground of historiographical practices. It has often been overlooked that Heidegger's analysis of human existence in *Being and Time* also includes a theory of history. An important reason why philosophers of history have

---

4. Carr, *Time, Narrative, and History*, 3.
5. Dilthey quoted in ibid., 4.

never fully processed Heidegger's ideas is no doubt that these mainly focus on the ontological basis of history. In this section I will extensively discuss Heidegger's theory of history, since this perspective on history is indispensable for showing how temporality, historicity, and historiography interrelate.

Heidegger's Fundamental Ontology

One of Heidegger's objectives in *Being and Time* is to investigate the ontological presuppositions implicit in any theory of knowledge. Although philosophers like Dilthey and Husserl had a similar agenda, Heidegger claims to operate on a more fundamental level. His objective is to formulate a *fundamental ontology*, a critical reflection on ontology as such. While Heidegger defines ontology as a reflection on the Essence of beings, fundamental ontology means reflecting on the paradigm that thematizes the Essence of beings. This prepares us for what is the objective in *Being and Time*, namely posing the *question of the meaning of being*. This question is addressed through an existential analysis of human life (*Dasein*) in general, as only human beings are able to pose and treat this question.

A fundamental ontology should reveal that the philosophical tradition has been dominated by a so-called "metaphysics of presence."[6] Metaphysics offers a limited understanding of being because it is founded on the platonic distinction between eternal essences and fleeting appearances. In modern philosophy, this objectifying tendency expresses itself in the image of humans as immutable, transcendental subjects placed in opposition to objects of knowledge. Philosophy has in this way suppressed the temporal and finite nature of human existence. In Heidegger's eyes it is important to realize that, instead of immutable essences, *time* is "the possible horizon of any understanding whatsoever of Being."[7]

Heidegger considers even his mentor Edmund Husserl as part of this philosophical tradition. Husserl's transcendental phenomenology had consisted in a proposal for a "return to things" by investigating how phenomena appear to our consciousness in perception ("beings as they show themselves"). Heidegger, however, feels that Husserl has adopted a "vulgar," objectified notion of a phenomenon, an abstraction that is separated from its ground in human existence. Heidegger expresses his criticism of Husserlian phenomenology as follows:

---

6. Not to be confused with the presence debate in the philosophy of history that was discussed in chapter 1.

7. Martin Heidegger, *Being and Time*, trans. John Macquarrie and Edward Robinson (1962; repr., Oxford: Blackwell, 2001), 1.

> Whenever a phenomenological concept is drawn from primordial sources, there is a possibility that it may degenerate if communicated in the form of an assertion. It gets understood in an empty way and is thus passed on, losing its indigenous character, and becoming a free-floating thesis. Even in the concrete work of phenomenology itself there lurks the possibility that what has been primordially 'within our grasp' may become hardened so that we can no longer grasp it.[8]

According to Heidegger, Husserl's objectification of phenomena has covered-up "what has been primarily within our grasp," namely the meaning and ground of the objectified phenomena. In order to "wrest" the meaning of Being from the phenomenological objects, phenomenology should be self-critical, in the sense that it should question its ontological presuppositions. In *Being and Time* Heidegger therefore formulates a hermeneutical phenomenology, meaning an analysis of the essential structures of Dasein, which should replace Husserl's transcendental phenomenology.

Heidegger revises the phenomenological concept of "intentionality," the notion that our consciousness is always directed at an object. According to Heidegger this definition implies and affirms a Cartesian metaphysics of subject and object. Heidegger reinterprets intentionality as a notion that expresses that Dasein is primarily involved with the world. Phenomenologically I do not in the first instance experience myself or the world but both are intertwined and given simultaneously.[9] Human beings are therefore not epistemological subjects isolated from their surroundings but are placed in the world. Knowing is not primarily an activity of subjects, but consists in a "disclosure" of the world to Dasein. This happens when human beings are absorbed in very basic, everyday activities such as

> having to do with something, producing something, attending to something and looking after it, making use of something, giving something up and letting it go, undertaking, accomplishing, evincing, interrogating, considering, discussing, determining.[10]

This basic level of meaning which precedes our theoretical understanding of the world is what Heidegger calls a *pre-ontological understanding of being*.

---

8. Ibid., 60–61.
9. Rüdiger Safranski, *Martin Heidegger: Between Good and Evil*, trans. Ewald Osers, 2nd ed. (Cambridge, MA: Harvard University Press, 1998), 154.
10. Heidegger, *Being and Time*, 83.

It is a level of everydayness that points out to us that human beings have a primordial openness to the world which preconditions any objectifying relation with the world, but which has not been taken into account by metaphysics.

Because Dasein is placed in the world it is constituted by its surroundings. It is in other words *thrown* in a certain situation determined by specific cultural, historical, or social circumstances, but also by character, gender, class, family, etc. The natural tendency of Dasein is to let itself be determined by these accidental circumstances, for instance when it gets caught up in the trivialities of everyday life. We then "abandon ourselves to the world" and live inauthentically, determined by *das Man* as an impersonal and anonymous member of the community. Inauthentic Dasein is a fragmented life, in which things simply happen to us and time passes as a succession of nows. Although everydayness cannot be escaped, it is according to Heidegger possible to momentarily resist our tendency to evade the fundamental issues of our existence.[11] In order to live authentically we must realize that our existence is essentially temporal and finite. This state, which Heidegger calls being-towards-death, allows Dasein to grasp the full significance of its existence as a whole and reveals its possibilities as a thrown being in the present. Dasein now resolutely takes on its "fate" instead of letting itself be determined by it. Heidegger considers it our responsibility to temporalize our existence by creating coherence and connectedness between past, present and future.

Although Heidegger emphasizes that his account of authenticity and das Man operates on an ontological and ahistorical level, it clearly seems to imply a critique of modern man—or, as Rüdiger Safranski puts it, of "mass culture, urbanization, unstable public affairs, the vastly growing entertainment industry, hectic everyday life, the superficial character of intellectual life."[12]

Historicity

Because Dasein's thrown condition is profoundly historical, it can also relate to its history authentically or inauthentically. Heidegger formulates his conception of history in the fifth section of *Being and Time*, where he tries to show that history as a science, like all sciences, is grounded in ontology. A scientific domain ("life," "nature," "history," etc.) is constituted according to Heidegger by certain basic concepts that "determine the way in which we get an understanding beforehand of the area of subject-matter underlying all the objects a science takes as its theme."[13] This means that we can only gain

---

11. Safranski, *Martin Heidegger*, 162–163.
12. Ibid., 161.
13. Heidegger, *Being and Time*, 30.

a proper understanding of history as a science when we take into account how it is grounded in human existence. Heidegger hereby distances himself from the positivistic tendencies of nineteenth-century historicism which prescribed that the historian should "wipe himself out" in order to show the past as it actually was. For Heidegger it is neither possible nor desirable to disconnect history from who we are.

In fact, Heidegger agrees with Dilthey that we thematize history because we are historical beings. We first have to understand what it is to *be* historical to gain access to history. This is to say that history can only be thematized because it has already been "opened up" existentially, that is "prescientifically." Heidegger adopts the notion of historicity (*Geschichtlichkeit*) from Dilthey to express this, with the difference that to Heidegger the term has an ontological instead of an anthropological or psychological significance.[14] Dilthey was famous for having established a theory of knowledge for the human sciences and history in particular. He maintained that the subject matter of the human sciences requires a radically different methodology from that of the natural sciences. The natural sciences operate on the basis of *explanation* (*Erklären*). A human science such as history, however, deals with experienced human life, which cannot be cast in abstract mathematical formulae. Because we ourselves are not external to this subject matter and participate in historical life we are able to know it from within, through our own *Erlebnis*, our lived experience. The humanities therefore operate on the hermeneutical basis of understanding (*Verstehen*).

Heidegger appreciates Dilthey's turn away from the (neo-)Kantian standpoint of the transcendental subject toward lived experience. He nevertheless finds that although the Being-question (*Seinsfrage*) is present in Dilthey's work, it is not explicitly posed because Dilthey lacked the means to do so.[15] The main reason for this is that Dilthey's search for certainty and his attempt to construct a methodology is still informed by a Cartesian logic. This prevents Dilthey from making the move that Heidegger proposes, from a regional ontology that presupposes its study object to a fundamental ontology that prepares the question of being and that analyses the prescientific existential historicity that is presupposed by historiography. Experienced life never becomes an explicit problem for Dilthey.[16] In the sections on history in *Being and Time* Heidegger sets out to "complete" the philosophical tendency inherent in Dilthey.

---

14. For a trajectory of the use of the term "historicity," see Paul Ricoeur, *Memory, History, Forgetting*, trans. Kathleen Blamey and David Pellauer (Chicago: University of Chicago Press, 2006), 370–376.

15. Robert Scharff, "Heidegger's 'Appropriation' of Dilthey before Being and Time," *Journal of the History of Philosophy* 35 (1997): 117.

16. Ibid., 121.

Historicity is a mode of temporality assuring that Dasein has coherence and self-constancy and is not made up of a mere succession of unrelated moments. It indicates that the movement by which Dasein stretches along between birth and death is a *Geschehen*, in the sense that it is embedded in an inherited historical community of which Dasein forms a part. This provides what Dilthey had called the "connectedness of life" (*Zusammenhang des Lebens*). The structure of historicity is thus, as David Couzens Hoy states, "an essential condition for Dasein's ability both to understand itself and to appropriate itself and take responsibility for its situation."[17]

For Heidegger there runs a derivative chain from temporality to historicity and from historicity to history as a discipline, which he describes as follows:

> How history can become a possible *object* for historiology [i.e., historiography] is something that may be gathered only from the kind of Being which belongs to the historical—from historicality [i.e., historicity], and from the way it is rooted in temporality.[18]

Because historicity is rooted in temporality, it is also significant to Dasein's authentic self-understanding. This is to say that, similar to temporality, we also relate to our history authentically or inauthentically. Dasein discloses its history inauthentically when it lets itself be determined by the historical circumstances in which it is thrown. It is only historical "in the very depths of its existence"[19] when it *takes on* the full burden of its "heritage" or "tradition." Heritage is not meant as a past that lies behind us and no longer affects us, but the past understood as "Dasein that has-been-there" (*dagewesenes Dasein*), a past that still influences Dasein's present situation and what Dasein will be in the future.

The authentic historical subject is capable of actively choosing its past.[20] It takes on its heritage by what Heidegger calls a "repetition" (*Wiederholung*) of past possibilities:

---

17. David Couzens Hoy, "History, Historicity, and Historiography in Being and Time," in *Heidegger and Modern Philosophy: Critical Essays*, ed. Michael Murray (New Haven: Yale University Press, 1978), 341.

18. Heidegger, *Being and Time*, 427–428. Glosses are mine.

19. Ibid., 437.

20. Howard Caygill, "Heidegger and the Destruction of Tradition," in *Walter Benjamin's Philosophy: Destruction and Experience*, ed. Andrew Benjamin and Peter Osborne (London: Routledge, 1994), 16.

> *Repeating is handing down explicitly*—that is to say, going back into the possibilities of the Dasein that has-been-there.[21]

Repetition is not merely the reconstruction of the past or its reenactment, but, as Ricoeur puts it, "a matter of recalling, replying to, retorting, even of revoking heritages."[22] It is thus "a disavowal of that which in the 'today,' is working itself out as the 'past.'"[23] By resolutely taking over the heritage that forms part of Dasein's thrown condition, possibilities of authentic existence are disclosed:

> The resoluteness in which Dasein comes back to itself, discloses current factical possibilities of authentic existing, and discloses them *in terms of the heritage* which that resoluteness, as thrown, takes over.[24]

The authentic attitude toward the past thus implies that the past is a temporalization of present and future.[25] Heidegger's notion of history resists the study of the past for the sake of the past, but points out that in history, past, present, and future are essentially united. The emphasis within this unity lies paradoxically on the future, as it is the finitude of temporality that is the hidden basis of Dasein's historicity:

> history has its essential importance neither in what is past nor in the 'today' and its 'connection' with what is past, but in that authentic historizing of existence which arises from Dasein's *future*.[26]

History should disclose the future possibilities of Dasein. As Mulhall says, "Any reclaiming of one's heritage must flow from a resolute projection into the future based on a moment of vision with respect to the present."[27]

---

21. Heidegger, *Being and Time*, 437.
22. Ricoeur, *Memory, History, Forgetting*, 380.
23. Heidegger, *Being and Time*, 438.
24. Ibid., 435.
25. Caygill, "Heidegger and the Destruction of Tradition," 16.
26. Heidegger, *Being and Time*, 438. Because of his emphasis on the future, Heidegger can be seen as a representative of the modern regime of historicity. See paragraph 2.3.
27. Stephen Mulhall, *Routledge Philosophy Guidebook to Heidegger and Being and Time*, 2nd ed. (London: Routledge, 2005), 188.

Inauthentic existence lacks the "connectedness of life" provided by authentic historicity. Dasein now understands its historicity as "world-historical," in terms of the history of the world (*Welt-Geschichte*) to which it has lost itself by forgetting questions of importance and getting caught up in the distractions of everyday life. Past, present, and future are fragmented into a series of moments, which alienates Dasein from its past and future and locks it in the present. Dasein now "understands the 'past' in terms of the 'Present' "[28] instead of its present in terms of the past. Interestingly, Heidegger presents linear clock-time ("intratemporality") as a derivation of primordial temporality, which integrates the three temporal ecstases and prioritizes the future.

In *Being and Time* an authentic realization of one's existence refers especially to the single person. The way a collective can authentically realize itself is merely alluded to. Nevertheless, man's thrown condition means that human beings are intertwined with a community and a people. This allows for the possibility that the individual person can take upon himself the destiny of a community and, in Heidegger's words, "choose his hero" from the heritage of the people. In so doing the individual person maintains a relation with society and chooses to offer his life by taking the fate of the people upon him.[29] These ideas are obviously amenable to political uses and Heidegger himself brought them into the political realm by his unfortunate support of National Socialism and choosing Hitler as his hero. Heidegger even characterized the rise of National Socialism in the terminology of *Being and Time*. He writes about Germany: "this nation, as a historical nation, must move itself and thereby the history of the West beyond the center of their future 'happening' and into the primordial realm of the powers of being."[30]

Historicity and Historiography

Heidegger's interest in historiography may come as somewhat of a surprise after having prepared the Being-question in *Being and Time*. Nevertheless, history was actually to fulfill an important function in Heidegger's project. The final and never completed section of *Being and Time* was intended as a destruction of the history of philosophy, which according to Heidegger

---

28. Heidegger, *Being and Time*, 443.

29. Safranski, *Martin Heidegger*, 208–209.

30. Heidegger, quoted in David Harvey, *The Condition of Postmodernity: An Inquiry into the Origins of Cultural Change* (Cambridge, MA: Blackwell, 1989), 208.

suffered from a progressive state of *Seinsvergessenheit*, the forgetting of the question of being.

Heidegger formulates his view on historiography with reference to Nietzsche's second Untimely Meditation, entitled *On the Use and Abuse of History for Life*. Nietzsche laments the ubiquity of history that was characteristic of the nineteenth century, claiming that the excess of historical consciousness separates human beings from life. Nietzsche especially opposes the scientific approach of history of the historicists, who study the past for the sake of the past and try to depict history "as it actually was." An objective approach to history is an illusion, according to Nietzsche. Instead, history has to be tamed and dominated, and practiced in the service of life and action.[31]

Heidegger agrees with Nietzsche that history should provide a "service to life." To Nietzsche this means that historiography should include three moments: a monumental one, an antiquarian one, and a critical one. These moments correspond respectively to future, past, and present. For Heidegger, historiography should not be merely antiquarian, because this alienates Dasein from authentic existence. An authentic approach of the past should always be "monumental," in that it takes account of the great deeds of important historical figures in order to inspire new great acts in the present. The monumental moment interprets the past in service of the anticipated future. Yet the antiquarian moment is indispensable for contrasting the past with the present. The antiquarian and the monumental—the having-been and future—have to be united in the present in the form of a critique. This critique of the present consists in a painful "detachment" from oneself and the distractions of everyday life. Heidegger hereby constructs a circular hermeneutical movement between authentic historical existence and history as a discipline, which mutually influence one another: historical truth is expounded in terms of the authentic disclosedness of the historical existence of the historian, and the historical truths that are thus revealed in turn provide an "existential interpretation" with Dasein's historicity as its theme.[32]

It is tempting to dismiss this hermeneutics as a form of subjectivism. According to David Carr, for instance, historicity has little relevance to history as a discipline because it is derived from *individual* experience.[33] Carr points out that "[Dasein's] connection to the social past arises as a function

---

31. Friedrich Nietzsche, *On the Use and Abuse of History for Life*, trans. Ian Johnston (Arlington: Richer Resources Publications, 2010).
32. Heidegger, *Being and Time*, 449.
33. Carr, *Time, Narrative, and History*, 5.

of the temporality of its own existence."[34] He finds this problematic because it neglects the social realm to which history as a discipline is directed.

Heidegger indeed shows a depreciation of the social, which is associated in *Being and Time* with the inauthenticity of das Man, and it is a common critique that being-with-others (*Mitsein*) remains underexposed in *Being and Time*. Yet Heidegger maintains that although authentic historiographical accounts cannot claim universal validity, they are still objective because they are grounded in "fateful repetition," that is, authentic temporality. Because the historian exists "in" the world and is not detached from the world, his voice discloses not only his own past possibilities but also those of larger historical forces, of his culture and generation. It is therefore not entirely justified to accuse Heidegger of opposing the individual to the social realm, because Heidegger's terminology tries to dissolve these kinds of oppositions.[35]

Heidegger's attempt to connect the ontological analysis of historicity with the ontic science of history is nevertheless problematic. The "truth" that Heidegger asks from history is not a *historiographical* but an *ontological* truth. History should provide a disclosure that, in the words of Hoy, "is the opening up of a whole context of meaning, and is not capable of being false, but only of failing to disclose."[36] Heidegger shows little interest in what the historian uses to establish historiographical truth, such as historical sources or methodology. According to Hoy, this is due to the fact that Heidegger's theory of history was meant to prepare for the destruction of the history of philosophy in the never-completed part of *Being and Time*. In other words, "[Heidegger's] description of 'authentic' historiography and its ontological

---

34. Ibid., 107.

35. David Carr maintains that "If we try to summarize what Heidegger actually means by historicity, what is perhaps hardest to see is just how it constitutes a link between the individual and the social *past*. If *knowledge* is not the original link to the past, what is?" Ibid., 108. However, by substituting "subject" with "individual" Carr threatens to interpret Heidegger's philosophy in terms of the same metaphysical vocabulary that Heidegger argues against. I agree in this respect with David Couzens Hoy, who maintains that "[An] interpretation of Dasein as a personal, private subject, an inner consciousness over against a world, incorrectly reads psychological meanings into Heidegger's ontological, philosophical analysis. Such readings confuse the ontic and the ontological: structures that constitute conditions for the possibility of empirical, psychological states are themselves taken to be such states." Hoy, "History, Historicity, and Historiography in Being and Time," 339.

36. Hoy, "History, Historicity, and Historiography in Being and Time," 350.

kind of 'truth' is more likely to be applicable to the history of philosophy, at least in his own sense of a rethinking of philosophy and its history, rather than to historiography per se."[37]

Although Heidegger's contribution to the philosophy of history may therefore not be methodological or epistemological, his theory of history *is* indispensable for showing that history as a science is conditioned by historicity. Heidegger makes us aware that we relate to history not only as an object of knowledge, but also as part of our experiential world. The field of history is, in other words, already opened up prescientifically. Heidegger shows us that this opening up is constitutive of the way we thematize history scientifically. Historicity has to be taken into account if we want to understand history as a discipline.

Ultimately, however, historicity is in *Being and Time* an ontological concept that has no empirical connotation. It merely spells out *the conditions for the possibility of* historical existence, which makes historicity comparable to a Kantian category.[38] There is a contradictory element to this ahistorical account of historicity. It is at odds with what historicity seeks to express, namely the relativity and contingency of absolute principles and ideas. While *Being and Time* seeks to historicize metaphysics, it paradoxically displays on another level, by turning historicity into a transhistorical category, an *indifference* to history. Heidegger seems to resist the ultimate implications of his own historicizing effort, namely the historical contingency of his own categories, including historicity. In order to properly understand the relation between historicity and history, I will, therefore, continue the movement inherent in Heidegger's thought by "historicizing historicity."

2. THE BIRTH OF MODERN HISTORY

A number of historians, social theorists, and philosophers have pointed out that the notion of us as historical beings, in the sense that we consider ourselves part of a general process we call History, is itself a historical phenomenon. One of the most influential accounts of the "history of history" is of course that of Michel Foucault. Foucault situates the origins of our conception of history in the nineteenth century and argues that it is bound

---

37. Ibid., 349.
38. Ibid., 345.

up with modernity. Historical thinking is the result of a transformation of the ontological plane of knowledge in the West.[39] Only after the inauguration of modernity does history start to become the principle for all possible orderings: "a profound historicity penetrates into the heart of things, isolates and defines them in their own coherence, imposes upon them the forms of order implied by the continuity of time."[40]

Foucault has drawn attention to the fact that historicity has its own history. This is also maintained by the German historian Reinhart Koselleck. While Foucault applies an archeological method, the instrument that Koselleck develops (in cooperation with Werner Conze and Otto Brunner) is called Conceptual History. Through a reading of Koselleck I will argue that our contemporary understanding of history is entangled with modernity.

Koselleck's Theory of Historical Times

Reinhart Koselleck is best known for being the principal editor of a lexicon of historical concepts, called *Geschichtliche Grundbegriffe: Historisches Lexicon zur politischen-sozialen Sprache in Deutschland* (hereafter GG). This lexicon charts the historical development of basic social and political concepts in Germany. The project was started in 1957 on the initiative of Koselleck and gradually grew in ambition and scope. Eventually the lexicon filled eight volumes, which were published between 1972 and 1997. These volumes contain 119 articles written by 109 contributors from different disciplines.[41]

Koselleck has been largely responsible for the theoretical background of the GG project. He has stressed that the concepts that are discussed in the lexicon should be considered as more than linguistic entities. Although they are cast into words, the concepts refer to a world beyond the text, governing discourse, actions, and attitudes within the whole of society.[42]

---

39. According to Foucault, our empirical knowledge is conditioned by an epistemological field that he calls an *épistème*. An *épistème* refers to the modality of things and the order of classification, before these are presented to our faculty for knowing. An *épistème* is thus a "condition for the possibility of knowledge." In *The Order of Things: Archeology of the Human Sciences* (London: Routledge, 2008), Foucault identifies two discontinuities in the *épistème* of Western culture: the first in the mid-seventeenth century, initiating the Classical Period, and the second, initiating modernity, at the beginning of the nineteenth century.

40. Michel Foucault, *The Order of Things*, xxv.

41. Niklas Olsen, *History in the Plural: An Introduction to the Work of Reinhart Koselleck* (New York: Berghahn Books, 2012), 169–170.

42. David Carr, "Reinhart Koselleck: 'Futures Past: On the Semantics of Historical Time,'" *History and Theory* 26 (1987): 197. Concepts cover a diversity of historical experiences and a multiplicity of meanings that are often contested. Tracing the history of concepts such

Basic concepts have a temporal dimension. According to Koselleck, their meaning shifts with changes in the sense of time in a society.[43] It is the task of the historian to study these transformations of temporal experience. This distinguishes history from other social sciences. The study of historical time should take place by means of a theory of history, which Koselleck calls *Historik*. *Historik* is, as Hoffmann explains, not so much a methodology as "a theory of the conditions of possible histories" that investigates "the theoretically necessary parameters that make comprehensible why histories occur, how they can take place, as well as why and how they must be investigated."[44] This theoretical dimension transforms the work of historians into proper historical research.[45]

An echo can be heard here of Heidegger, whose work made a deep impression on Koselleck during his student days.[46] Koselleck agrees with the basic premise in *Being and Time* that temporality is constitutive of human existence. In order to study historical time, the historian should investigate how past, present, and future are related. Koselleck nevertheless criticizes the abstract way in which Heidegger approaches history. For Koselleck, Heidegger's ontological interpretation of historicity lacks a practical significance.[47]

---

as "democracy," "republic," "crisis," "revolution," "citizen," or "state" serves a heuristic purpose. It maps "the dissolution of the old world and the emergence of the modern world through the history of their conceptual framing." Otto Brunner, Werner Conze and Reinhart Koselleck, *Geschichtliche Grundbegriffe: Historisches Lexikon zur politisch-sozialen Sprache in Deutschland* (Stuttgart: Klett-Cotta, 1972–1997), xiv. The articles in the lexicon show that a change of concepts took place between 1750 and 1850, a period which Koselleck calls the *Sattelzeit*. This periodization coincides more or less with the epistemic break that Foucault registers between the Classical Period and Modernity. During the Sattelzeit, the social and political vocabulary underwent an accelerated and profound change of meaning. The term *Bürger*, for instance, changed "from (*Stadt-*)*Bürger* (burgher) around 1700 via (*Staats-*)*Bürger* (citizen) around 1800 to *Bürger* (bourgeois) as a nonproletarian around 1900." Koselleck, *Futures Past*, 82.

43. Melvin Richter and Michaela W. Richter, "Introduction: Translation of Reinhart Koselleck's 'Krise,' in Geschichtliche Grundbegriffe," *Journal of the History of Ideas* 67 (2006): 346.

44. Stefan-Ludwig Hoffmann, "Koselleck, Arendt, and the Anthropology of Historical Experience," *History and Theory* 49 (2010): 219.

45. Reinhart Koselleck, *The Practice of Conceptual History: Timing History, Spacing Concepts* (Stanford: Stanford University Press, 2002), 6.

46. Olsen, *History in the Plural*, 29.

47. Koselleck: "As early as Being and Time, there is an almost complete abstracting from history. Historicity is treated as a category of human existence, yet no intersubjective or transindividual structures are thematized. Although Heidegger points the way from the finitude of *Dasein* to the temporality of history, he does not pursue it any further." Koselleck, *The Practice of Conceptual History*, 2.

He argues that Heidegger's ontology of history should itself be placed in its historical context, and that *Being and Time* has to be read as a reaction to the so-called crisis of historicism around World War I. According to Ernst Troeltsch, this crisis was a result of the idea that the study of history, which had become tremendously influential during the nineteenth century, had relativized essential norms and values and had thereby demonstrated the meaninglessness of existence.[48] As a result, philosophers, social theorists, historians, and other intellectuals struggled with the perceived limitations of knowledge and the subjective nature of all cognition concerning human behavior and social processes.[49]

In *Futures Past: On the Semantics of Historical Time*, a collection of theoretical and methodological essays about conceptual history, Koselleck investigates the nature of historical time. For him, this comes down to the question of "how, in a given present, are the temporal dimensions of past and future related?"[50] Ultimately, the principal dimension of historical time is the future. Like Heidegger, Koselleck maintains that the subject matter of history is, as Carr puts it, "not fact but possibility, not past but future; or, more precisely past possibilities and prospects, past conceptions of the future: futures past."[51]

Koselleck introduces two anthropological categories for studying the interrelation between past and future, namely "space of experience" and "horizon of expectation."[52] These categories can be seen as the anthropological equivalent of Heidegger's notion of the past as *dagewesenes Dasein* and of the future as possibility. According to Koselleck, "They are indicative of the temporality (Zeitlichkeit) of men and thus, metahistorically if you wish, of

---

48. See Iggers, *Historiography*, 30, and Allan Megill, "Was there a crisis of historicism?" *History and Theory* 36 (1997): 416.

49. Georg G. Iggers, *The German Conception of History: The National Tradition of Historical Thought from Herder to the Present* (Middletown: Wesleyan University Press, 1968), 124.

50. Koselleck, *Futures Past*, 3.

51. Carr, "Reinhart Koselleck," 198.

52. The inspiration for the concepts of experience, expectation, and horizon come from Gadamer's *Wahrheit und Methode*, which, next to Heidegger, is another important influence on Koselleck. As Olsen explains, "According to Gadamer, everybody has a limited horizon, because all horizons are bound to the temporal conditions of human finality. Yet every horizon is dynamic; it is bound to constant change, and can broaden or shrink, according to our experiences." Olsen, *History in the Plural*, 223. Zammito maintains that while both Gadamer and Heidegger moved from histories to their ontological prerequisite, historicity, "Koselleck moves in the converse direction." See John Zammito, "Koselleck's Philosophy of Historical Time(s) and the Practice of History," *History and Theory* 43 (2004): 128.

the temporality of history."[53] These categories are not derived from historical sources. They are formal, in the sense that concrete experiences and expectations cannot be derived from the categories themselves. The reason why Koselleck employs these formal categories is that they allow him to outline the *conditions of possible histories*. This means that no history can be constituted without including the experiences and expectations of the historical actors. Other formal categories can of course be thought of for the study of history. Yet to Koselleck experience and expectation are fundamental because they contain the *highest* degree of generality.[54]

Experience is "present past." It includes memories, but also the rational reworkings of past experience and unconscious modes of conduct. Expectation is "the future made present" and refers to "hope and fear, wishes and desires, cares and rational analysis, receptive display and curiosity."[55] Experience and expectation cannot be thought of independently. They presuppose one another and yet are asymmetrical and of a different order: an expectation cannot be deduced from experience and vice versa. The metaphor of space is appropriate for experience because it is, according to Koselleck, the only way in which we can speak about time.[56] It expresses that past experience is assembled into a totality "within which many layers of earlier times are simultaneously present."[57] The metaphor of the horizon is appropriate to expectation because a horizon always retreats; it is thus emblematic for the projected future of a certain present. Experience and expectation allow us to investigate historical time: "it is the tension between experience and expectation which, in ever-changing patterns, brings about new resolutions and through this generates historical time."[58]

The Acceleration of History

The anthropological categories of experience and expectation allow Koselleck to register the emergence of modernity. Koselleck argues that in the premodern

---

53. Koselleck, *Futures Past*, 258.

54. Ibid., 256–257.

55. Ibid., 259.

56. According to Bergson, thinking and speaking about time in terms of space is our way of dealing with the elusiveness of time. This allows us to control temporal processes, but also distorts the nature of time as duration. For Bergson's treatment of time, see chapter 4.

57. Koselleck, *Futures Past*, 260.

58. Ibid., 262.

world, roughly before 1750, the future was imagined as a continuation of the past so that past experiences could provide lessons for the future.

Koselleck illustrates this by referring to a painting by Albrecht Altdorfer from 1529, entitled *Alexanderschlacht*. This painting displays in great detail the Battle of Issus in 333 B.C., between Alexander the Great and the Persians. The anachronisms in the painting are illustrative of the premodern experience of time. The Persians resemble the Turks, who attempted to capture the city of Vienna in the same year that the painting was made, while Alexander resembles emperor Maximilian of the Holy Roman Empire. According to Koselleck, "the event that Altdorfer captured was for him at once historical and contemporary . . . The present and the past were enclosed within a common historical plane."[59]

Alexanderschlacht projects an eschatological horizon of expectation. In the premodern world in which Altdorfer lived, the church retained a firm grip on the organization of time by prophesying that the Last Judgment was approaching. Thus the future remained bound to the past.[60] As both Maximilian and Alexander were part of an ongoing struggle between Christ and the Antichrist, they could be considered as contemporaries inhabiting the same space of experience.

The continuity between experiences and expectations, Koselleck argues, had consequences for the way that history was perceived. For two millennia, history had had the role of being a teacher for life, or, in the words of Cicero, *historia magistra vitae*. History was considered a reservoir of examples that could provide lessons for the future, and the writing of histories had primarily a didactical function. Many of Machiavelli's writings, for instance, embody the exemplary function of past experiences. In his *Discourses* (1520), Machiavelli evokes the example of Ancient Rome with the objective of learning from its success in order to repeat it.[61]

When almost three hundred years later Friedrich Schlegel came across *Alexanderschlacht*, the organization of past, present, and future had completely changed. Schlegel was astonished by the work, which he distinguished both

---

59. Ibid., 10.

60. Ibid., 264.

61. *Historia magistra vitae* reverberates in the *Discourses on the Ten Books of Titus Livy* (written probably between 1515 and 1519), when Machiavelli writes, for example, "Hence, if Florence had not been forced by necessity or conquered by passion, and had read or learned the ancient habits of the barbarians, she would not have been deceived by them at this and many other times, for they have always been of one sort and have under all conditions and with everybody shown the same habits." Niccolò Machiavelli, "Discourses on the First Decade of Titus Livius," in *The Chief Works and Others I*, trans. Allan Gilbert (Durham and London: Duke University Press, 1989), 522.

from his own time and from the antiquity it represented. Schlegel displayed a critical-historical distance with respect to the painting that was inconceivable to Altdorfer and his contemporaries. As Koselleck notes: "there was for Schlegel, in the three hundred years separating him from Altdorfer, more time (or perhaps a different mode of time) than appeared to have passed for Altdorfer in the eighteen hundred years or so that lay between the Battle of Issus and his painting."[62]

What happened in the three hundred years that separated Altdorfer and Schlegel? According to Koselleck, there has been an alteration in the European sense of time since around 1750. This has caused expectations to distance themselves evermore from previous experience.[63] A first change in the premodern horizon of expectation was brought about by the Reformation and the religious wars in Germany. The Peace of Augsburg subordinated religious affiliation to worldly authorities. Suddenly it was no longer the church that controlled the future but politicians, who were more concerned with the temporal rather than the eternal. During the seventeenth century prophecies about the future were replaced by a sense that the future could be manipulated through political calculation and rational forecast.[64] The relatively stable environment of absolutist European politics, however, still bound prospective futures to past experience.

The plane of Christian expectations fundamentally ruptured only in the eighteenth century, under the influence of progress. The philosophy of progress provided a typical eighteenth-century mix of rational calculation and salvational expectation. Koselleck mentions several developments that contributed to the idea of progress, such as the Copernican Revolution, new technologies, geographical discoveries, and changes in the social order as a result of industrial development and the influence of capital. Expectations of the future now became detached from all previous experience.

The idea of progress was bound up with a *temporalization* of history. The *Sattelzeit* (saddle time), the period between 1750 and 1850, is characterized by the discovery of a specifically *historical* temporality. In the premodern world, the sense of time was still grounded in the rhythms of nature. Harvests were determined by weather and natural circumstances, skills were passed on from generation to generation, and in the cities guild regulations assured fixed social structures. Within this reality there was an "almost seamless transference of earlier experiences into coming expectations."[65] In the

---

62. Koselleck, *Futures Past*, 10.
63. Ibid., 263.
64. Ibid., 17.
65. Ibid., 264.

Sattelzeit or *Neuzeit*, however, historical time emancipates itself from nature and gains a quality of its own:

> Time is no longer simply the medium in which all histories take place; it gains a historical quality . . . history no longer occurs in, but through, time. Time becomes a dynamic and historical force in its own right.[66]

The temporalization of history means that the future approaches us with ever-increasing speed. Modernity is characterized by an *acceleration* of historical time which continually brings into play new and unknown factors. The future thereby gains an unknown quality, and expectations diverge and remove themselves from all previous experience. The future promised to be different and better than the past: "Progress . . . combined experiences and expectations, both endowed with a temporal coefficient of change."[67] The increasing difference between past and present means that lived time is being experienced as a rupture. The present becomes a permanent period of transition. This indeed becomes characteristic of the experience of modernity.

Koselleck's account of the emergence of historical temporality confirms Bruno Latour's association of modernity with a "modern Constitution." By means of this metaphor, Latour emphasizes that the moderns divide the world into two ontologically distinct zones: that of human beings (Culture) and that of nonhumans (Nature). The Constitution prescribes that Nature has always existed "out there" and that man is only "discovering" its hidden secrets. It also guarantees that only human beings construct society and therefore freely determine their own destiny.[68] In order for the Constitution to function, the scientific representation that is aimed at the discovery of the laws of nature on one hand, and political representation that should establish the emancipation of humanity on the other, should not be confused.

The domain of Culture is the domain of change and history, while Nature functions according to fixed laws and is unhistorical. Latour points out that the modern Constitution separates and purifies the domains of

---

66. Ibid., 236.

67. Ibid., 266.

68. Latour, *We Have Never Been Modern*, 30. Latour maintains that, although the moderns do not recognize this, the dichotomy of Nature and Culture paradoxically enables the proliferation of hybrids, of phenomena in which Nature and Culture are entangled. The modern Constitution simultaneously constantly does what it prohibits itself to do. You only have to look in the newspaper to become aware that the modern Constitution is a myth and that we have in fact never been modern.

Nature and Culture by means of a modern conception of time. The arrow of modern-historical time turns the asymmetry between Nature and Culture into an asymmetry between past and future: "The past was the confusion of things and men; the future is what will no longer confuse them."[69]

The asymmetry between a premodern past and a modern future is sanctioned by a new conception of history that emerges under the influence of the acceleration of historical time. During the eighteenth century, *Historie*, referring to the exemplary account of past events, is replaced by the term *Geschichte*, which encompasses both historical events *and* their representation. Koselleck maintains that this semantic change allows for a notion of history as a general concept to emerge. The plural form of "*Geschichte*" is gradually condensed into a "collective singular" that absorbs singular events in a universal process of historical becoming. It now becomes possible to refer to "history pure and simple," or simply to "History."[70]

This substantive notion of history is attributed a logic according to which historical events unfold. There is a sense that History contains a "secret or evident plan to which one could feel responsible, or in whose name one could believe oneself to be acting."[71] This logic becomes an object of reflection. In the same years that History as a collective singular starts to manifests itself, between 1760 and 1780, the notion of a "philosophy of history" surfaces which is concerned with the study of "universal" or "world" history.[72]

This new concept of history means the end of *historia magistra vitae*: "History, processualized and temporalized to constant singularity, could no longer be taught in an exemplary fashion."[73] A famous statement by Tocqueville succinctly illustrates the demise of *Historie*: "As the past has ceased to throw its light upon the future, the mind of man wanders in obscurity."[74] According to the modern concept of history, counsel is to be expected not from the past but from the future that has yet to be made. The open future paradoxically allows for the possibility—even necessity—of planning, and philosophies of history start to determine the direction and goal of History.

With the formulation of philosophies of history, the role and status of the political in modernity is reconceptualized. Hartmut Rosa points out that,

---

69. Ibid., 71.
70. Koselleck, *Futures Past*, 33.
71. Ibid., 35.
72. Ibid., 36.
73. Ibid., 268.
74. Ibid., 31.

by defining the direction and goal of the perceived movement of history, philosophies of history become constitutively tied to the idea of political movement:

> society becomes a task of political organization within time in accordance with the principles of social development. The category of social and political progress, as 'the first genuinely historical category of time,' constitutes the key concept for this expectation of goal-directed historical movement.[75]

The idea of progress manifested itself, for instance, in the narrative of the Enlightenment.[76] According to the Enlightenment philosophers, the accumulation of knowledge and the rationalization of social organization would provide liberation from the irrationalities of myths, superstitions, and religion that had chained humanity for ages.[77] This provides an example of the way in which counsel is now expected from the future instead of the past.[78] The consequence of the emphasis on the future is a depreciation of the past from which the moderns tried to move away. The moderns sought an active break with history and tradition because they saw the past as synonymous with backwardness, irrationality, and superstition.

Simultaneously, this progressive historical temporality produced a dissociation of the past from the present. The dissociated past could subsequently become an object of historical knowledge. The philosophy of progress is thus the basis for modern historiography; as Zammito puts it, progress "privileged the unknown future over against the past, but at the same time it *estranged*

---

75. Rosa, *Social Acceleration*, 257. Rosa points out that modern political groups often identify themselves significantly as *movements*. This claims that politics in modernity have become "the pacesetter for societal development in the context of the (classical) modern experience of history." Both conservative and progressive political movements have integrated the "irreversibility of historical development" and "conservative and progressive often designate different *speeds*, rather than genuinely different directions." (258)

76. According to Dan Edelstein, the Enlightenment was essentially a self-reflexive historical narrative adopted by contemporaries that revolved around the notion of an age characterized by a "philosophical spirit." The Enlighteners, according to Edelstein, thus continually opposed a "modern" present to an "ancient" past. Dan Edelstein, *The Enlightenment: A Genealogy* (Chicago: The University of Chicago Press, 2010). I discuss Edelstein's account of the Enlightenment in chapter 7.

77. Harvey, *The Condition of Postmodernity*, 12.

78. For a Bergsonian critique of the Enlightenment's idea of progress, see chapter 7.

the past in a radical way, rendering this sense of its inevitable otherness a core to the practice of disciplinary history."[79]

While in *The Order of Things* Foucault presents a periodization of history as a succession of *epistèmes*, Koselleck emphasizes that his theory of historical time is in fact a theory of multiple temporalities.[80] In particular in his later work—most notably *Zeitschichten* (2002)—Koselleck draws attention to the fact that there really is not a single historical temporality, but a multiplicity of historical times that exist simultaneously. He calls this "the simultaneity of the nonsimultaneous in our history."[81] Historical time is, according to Koselleck, always multilayered and consists of different tempi of historical change, each with a different duration and origin.[82] These multiple temporalities are politically synchronized, as we will see in the following section, by means of the modern concept of History which functions as a "collective singular." Koselleck argues that historical research has to take the historical layers of time into account, because these form a condition for the possibility of history as a discipline. As an example, he mentions Fernand Braudel's model of multiple historical durations. The multiplicity of historical times does not conflict with Koselleck's account of the Sattelzeit. The Sattelzeit should rather be considered as a period in which the multiplicity of historical time first manifests itself.[83]

3. CRISIS OF THE MODERN REGIME OF HISTORICITY

The French historian François Hartog has argued that the modern "regime of historicity" has been operative between, symbolically, 1789 and 1989.[84] A

---

79. Zammito, "Koselleck's Philosophy of Historical Time(s)," 127.

80. John Zammito and Helge Jordheim argue that many Anglophone readings of Koselleck wrongfully present Koselleck's theory of historical time(s) as a periodization. Jordheim sees Koselleck's approach even as "a theory developed to defy periodization." See Zammito, "Koselleck's Philosophy of Historical Time(s)" and Helge Jordheim, "Against Periodization: Koselleck's Theory of Multiple Temporalities," *History and Theory* 51 (2012): 151.

81. Koselleck, *The Practice of Conceptual History*, 8.

82. Zammito, "Koselleck's Philosophy of Historical Time(s)," 125.

83. As Koselleck's biographer Niklas Olsen puts it, "The theory of historical times as described in *Zeitschichten* is not to be viewed as a rupture in Koselleck's historical thinking, but rather as a shift of interest that encompassed new ways of approaching and evaluating certain themes and issues." Olsen, *History in the Plural*, 228.

84. Hartog, *Regimes of Historicity*, 104.

regime of historicity expresses a certain temporal experience and designates how, at different times and places, the categories of past, present, and future are articulated. It is therefore a condition of possibility for historical writing.[85]

To Hartog, regimes of historicity are especially useful for helping us reach a better understanding of moments of crisis in time—when "the way in which past, present, and future are articulated no longer seems self-evident."[86] According to Hartog we are currently living in such a crisis, which expresses itself in a prevailing "presentism": "As a historian who tries to be attentive to his time, I have, like many others, observed how the category of the present has taken hold to such an extent that one can really talk of an omnipresent present."[87]

Characteristic for the modern regime of historicity was that the past and the present were illuminated by a "view from the future." Hartog notes that since the fall of the Berlin Wall, the category of the future has lost its appeal. There is no longer a sense of historical progress marked by a hopeful expectation toward the future; the future is no longer a source of enlightenment but, if anything, has turned into a threat, a location of uncertainty and disaster. With the waning of a view from the future we now find ourselves trapped in a *présent perpétuel*, an omnipresent present that has drawn the past and the future into itself:

> [The] future is not a radiant horizon guiding our advancing steps, but rather a line of shadow drawing closer, which we ourselves have set in motion. At the same time we seem to be caught on the treadmill of the present and ruminating upon a past which simply won't go down.[88]

In this section I will explore whether we really are currently living in a "crisis of historicity," and if so, how we can make sense of it. What does this imply for the role of history in our culture?

In order to answer these questions, I will have to combine Koselleck's conceptual approach of modernity and modern historicity with philosophical and social theories of modernity. Conceptual history is an excellent tool

---

85. Hartog states that "depending on the way relations between the past, the present, and the future are configured, certain types of history are possible and others are not." Ibid., 16–17.
86. Ibid., 16.
87. Ibid., 8.
88. Ibid., 191.

for registering the origins of the modern experience of time and history. Yet what remain underexposed are the processes that *bring about* conceptual changes. Koselleck does not explain *why* history has accelerated since the Sattelzeit. He refers to a number of historical events—the religious wars in Germany, the Copernican Revolution, scientific and technological progress—but he offers no theoretical framework to account for the underlying forces behind conceptual change.[89]

The "fundamental logic" behind conceptual changes is important, because experiences of space and time are not isolated phenomena. Concepts of time and space are "basic categories of human existence" (Harvey) that cannot be understood independently from the material processes that bring them about.[90] This raises the question of which material practices and processes we should ascribe the acceleration of historical time in modernity to. Answering this question, so I argue, allows us to understand the contemporary crisis of historicity and the place of history in our society and culture.

"All that is solid melts into air"

Peter Conrad has remarked that modernity is about "the acceleration of time, and also the dispersal of places."[91] This has created a universe in which "all that is solid melts into air" (Berman, Marx). Modernity unites all of mankind in a "unity of disunity." It "pours us all into a maelstrom of perpetual disintegration and renewal, of struggle and contradiction, of ambiguity and anguish."[92] In modernity there is, as David Harvey states, an "overwhelming sense of fragmentation, ephemerality, and chaotic change."[93]

This ephemerality highlights the dual nature of the modern condition, which is a state of *creation by destruction*. Living a modern life promises

---

89. As Espen Hammer writes, Koselleck "does not . . . seek to identify the fundamental logic leading to the uprooting of traditional time-consciousness. As a student of semantic alteration, he delimits his research methodologically from any kind of serious engagement with the impacting causes; thus, like much of the hermeneutic tradition from which it springs, his work might be said to suffer from a certain idealistic prejudice." Espen Hammer, *Philosophy and Temporality from Kant to Critical Theory* (Cambridge: Cambridge University Press, 2011), 44.

90. Harvey: "it is only through the investigation of the latter that we can properly ground our concepts of the former." Harvey, *The Condition of Postmodernity*, 204.

91. Peter Conrad, *Modern Times, Modern Places* (New York: Alfred A. Knopf, 1999), 9.

92. Marshall Berman, *All That is Solid Melts into Air: The Experience of Modernity* (New York: Penguin Books, 1982), 15.

93. Harvey, *The Condition of Postmodernity*, 11.

excitement, growth, and transformation, but simultaneously it involves the constant threat of chaos and the destruction of one's identity and known environment. It is not possible to withdraw oneself from the condition of modernity. The modern is all-encompassing because everyone is involved in it. The transitoriness of modernity makes it hard for modern subjects to value their own past and to preserve a sense of historical continuity. It is only from within the maelstrom of change that the meaning of history can be understood.[94]

The maelstrom of modernity can, according to Harvey, be understood in terms of successive waves of "time-space compression" that have occurred since the eighteenth century. Through a speed-up in the pace of life we have overcome spatial barriers, to the extent even that "the world sometimes seems to collapse inwards upon us."[95] According to the sociologist Hartmut Rosa, the feeling that history, culture, and society—even time itself—accelerates is indeed a constitutive trait of modernity. In his work on social acceleration, Rosa presents an analytical framework that allows us to understand the acceleration of history that Koselleck has registered.

Rosa distinguishes three analytically as well as empirically distinct categories of social acceleration:

1. Technological acceleration—a speeding-up of processes of transportation, communication, and production.[96] Technological acceleration has had tremendous social consequences and has brought about a time-space compression. An important motor for technological acceleration and innovation is the capitalist mode of production, because capitalism functions according to a logic whereby "time is money."

2. Acceleration of social change—an acceleration *of* society, encompassing attitudes and values, fashions, social relations, groups, classes, and social languages, but also social practices and habits.[97] These change at an ever-increasing rate, bringing about a "contraction of the present": the space of experience and horizon of expectation become increasingly incongruous, as the decay rate of reliable experiences and expectations

---

94. Ibid., 11–12.
95. Ibid., 240.
96. Rosa, "Social Acceleration," 82.
97. Ibid., 83.

increases.[98]

3. Acceleration in the pace of life—the feeling that modern life speeds up and the experiencing of a "lack of time." This manifests itself in a social tendency to compress actions and experiences: to do more in less time.[99]

It may seem strange that technological acceleration coincides with an increase in the pace of life. Shouldn't new technologies lead to *more* spare time and hence a *deceleration* of life? Rosa explains this paradox through the "acceleration cycle" that characterizes late-modern "acceleration societies." The acceleration cycle describes how the three categories of acceleration are causally connected in a feedback loop:

technological acceleration
↓
acceleration of social change
↓
acceleration of the pace of life
↓
technological acceleration
. . .

New technologies bring about social changes—new social practices, communication structures and forms of life, etc., bringing about a contraction of the present. An increase in the pace of life is subsequently inevitable, because

---

98. Hermann Lübbe, "The Contraction of the Present," in *High-Speed Society, Social Acceleration, Power, and Modernity*, ed. Hartmut Rosa and William E. Scheuerman (Pennsylvania: Penn State University Press, 2009), 159–160. Rosa argues that "change in these two realms—family and work—has accelerated from an intergenerational pace in early modern society to a generational pace in 'classical' modernity to an intragenerational pace in late modernity." Rosa, "Social Acceleration," 84.

99. The increase in the pace of life is, according to Rosa, sustained by the dominant cultural ideal of the fulfilled life: that we should realize as many options as possible during our lifetime. This ideal is the equivalent on earth of religious ideas about eternal life: "Acceleration serves as a strategy to erase the difference between the time of the world and the time of our life. The eudaimonistic promise of modern acceleration thus appears to be a functional equivalent to religious ideas of eternity or eternal life, and the acceleration of the pace of life represents the modern answer to the problem of finitude and death." Ibid., 91.

one cannot withdraw from social life. People are forced to accommodate social acceleration because otherwise they face marginalization.[100] The social answer to the scarcity of time is, again, technological innovation, and the acceleration cycle starts anew.

Like Harvey, Rosa notes that social acceleration is not a steady process but one that evolves in waves. A wave of acceleration, often brought about by a new technology or new form of socio-economic organization, is followed by a rise in the discourse of acceleration, "in which cries for deceleration in the name of human needs and values are voiced but eventually die down."[101] The history of modernity consists of successive periods of time-space compression that have been experienced as moments of crisis in time and history—moments indeed, when, as Hartog expresses it, "the way in which past, present, and future are articulated no longer seems self-evident."[102] These are intellectually and culturally processed through philosophical reflection and artistic expression. Modernist and avant-garde art-forms, for instance, can be considered as a way for coping with modern currents of creative destruction.[103]

Because the condition of modernity is all-encompassing and inescapable—that, in the words of Rimbaud, *Il faut être absolument moderne*—the modern subject has no option but to find a way to cope with the maelstrom of modernization. The project of the Enlightenment, for instance, with its faith in reason, science and progress, can be considered as an affirmation of the creative aspect of modernity, while Romanticism, with its melancholy for that which lies in the past and is permanently lost, braces itself for the destructive character of modern change.

In a similar way, the historical consciousness of the nineteenth century that is embodied by German historicism can be seen as a way of coping with modernity's creative destruction.[104] According to the historicists, we can understand "who we are" by looking at our history. As long as we can take the past as a model for present and future in the narratives about our individual and collective origins, there are no difficulties with this. These do arise, however, when the acceleration of history turns the past into something alien

---

100. Rosa calls this the "slippery-slope phenomenon," which he derives from capitalist production: "the capitalist cannot pause and rest, stop the race, and secure his position, since he either goes up or goes down; there is no point of equilibrium because standing still is equivalent to falling behind, as Marx and Weber pointed out." Ibid., 88.

101. Ibid., 78.

102. Harvey, *The Condition of Postmodernity*, 16.

103. Ibid., 260–283.

104. For a more extensive discussion of German historicism, see chapter 6.

more quickly, in which case a "scientifically disciplined historical consciousness" is needed in order to appropriate one's past. As Hermann Lübbe puts it: "Historical culture, then, is a specifically modern culture whose necessity increases with the dynamism of modern civilization."[105]

In this sense, the point of departure of historicism is profoundly modern. The premise of the historicist worldview is that the past is dissociated from the present, a "foreign country" as it were, and this allows for the possibility of transforming the past into an object of scientific study. Only the *historian* is able to *re-present* the past. To this end, the historian, according to the German historicist Leopold von Ranke, would have to "wipe himself out" in order to show the past "how it actually had been."

The historicists dealt with the disruptive maelstrom of modernity by establishing historical continuity through their writings. An illustration of how history coped with the discontinuity, ephemerality, and fleeting nature of the modern condition is the way in which nineteenth-century historians processed the most significant discontinuity of their time, the French Revolution. Nineteenth-century historians made desperate attempts to fit the Revolution within a narrative of historical continuity; their multi-volume histories are a testament to this effort.[106]

Nevertheless, the French Revolution could not so easily be absorbed by a linear narrative. This teaches us that historiography is not merely a scientific practice, it is also, and maybe even foremost, a cultural practice and a way of giving meaning to a present that finds itself in a perpetual state of flux. Historians try to construct meaning from within this temporal change, which, as I will argue in the next section, sheds a new light on the absent status of the historical past in the contemporary philosophy of history.

Presentism

In the last decades something strange seems to be going on within our historical consciousness. From different perspectives, our contemporary, late-modern culture (originating roughly from around 1989) has been diagnosed with a "crisis of historicity." We seem to live in a culture that no longer finds its moorings in its past or in its future, but first and foremost in its present, to the extent even where the present seems omnipresent. François Hartog

---

105. Lübbe, "The Contraction of the Present," 163.
106. As Peter Fritzsche points out, "in the two decades that followed [the French Revolution], liberal historians strained mightily to impose structure, pattern, and necessity onto the French Revolution and to narrate the great event in terms of a unifying and rational process." Fritzsche, *Stranded in the Present*, 46.

recently raised the question of whether we are not witnessing the formation of a *presentistic* regime of historicity that has replaced the modern regime.[107]

A first diagnosis of presentism and a crisis of historicity was given through the discourse on postmodernity in the 1980s. Postmodernism registered a shift in the modernist experience of time and history since the 1970s, when postmodernism first manifested itself in a variety of cultural fields such as art and architecture, philosophy, anthropology, political science, and theology, and also in the philosophy of history.

A significant feature of postmodernism was its total acceptance of the fragmentation, ephemerality, discontinuity, and chaotic change that characterized the condition of modernity. Contrary to modernist cultural forms, postmodernists did not try to transcend these conditions in order to find the "eternal and immutable" elements in it: "Postmodernism swims, even wallows, in the fragmentary and the chaotic currents of change as if that is all there is."[108] Jean-François Lyotard, for instance, defined postmodernity as "the end of grand narratives"—that is, all-explaining accounts of history, such as the Enlightenment belief in progress, the Christian myth of salvation, or the Marxist doctrine of historical materialism.[109] In the philosophy of history, the postmodern turn was instigated by the publication of Hayden White's *Metahistory* (1973). White's book discredited speculative accounts of history by focusing on the way that "grand narratives" about history are first and foremost narrative constructions by historians.

The Marxist theorist Fredric Jameson has argued that the postmodern consists in both a "new depthlessness" and a "new culture of the image or the simulacrum."[110] He illustrates this by comparing two paintings: Van Gogh's well-known painting of peasant shoes, which is a product of high modernism, and Andy Warhol's *Diamond Dust Shoes*.

While the first can be read hermeneutically and placed within a certain historical context, Warhol's work does not allow for a hermeneutic gesture. *Diamond Dust Shoes* represents a flatness and superficiality that, according to Jameson, highlights the commodity fetish in late capitalism. Furthermore, the painting expresses a new emotional tonal ground that he characterizes as a "waning of affect." The depthlessness of postmodernity can be experienced in architectural design but expresses itself also in contemporary theory.

---

107. Hartog, *Regimes of Historicity*.

108. Harvey, *The Condition of Postmodernity*, 44.

109. Jean-François Lyotard, *The Postmodern Condition: A Report on Knowledge*, trans. Geoff Bennington and Brian Massumi (Manchester: Manchester University Press, 1984).

110. Fredric Jameson, *Postmodernism, or, the Cultural Logic of Late Capitalism* (New York and London: Verso, 1991).

"Depth models" of explanation such as hermeneutics, dialectics, the Freudian model of latent and manifest, existentialism, and semiotics have gone out of fashion. We can discern a similar development in the philosophy of history: narrativist theories of history are less concerned with the "depth" relation between historical reality and the historical representation, but focus more on the way that historical meaning is created by means of narrative constructions in the present.

The shift from modernism to postmodernism should, according to Jameson, be conceived as a shift from questions of *time* to a logic of *space*. The spatial logic of postmodernity affects the organization of time and temporality. The relation between past, present, and future is fragmented due to a "breakdown in the signifying chain" (Lacan) that constitutes meaning. Instead of the traditional relation between signifier and signified, the postmodern logic produces meaning as an effect of a series of unrelated, material signifiers. This fragmentation makes a coherent temporal experience of past, present, and future impossible and produces a schizophrenic identity. Experience falls apart into "a series of pure and unrelated presents in time."[111] The present is now all there is and "comes before the subject with heightened intensity, bearing a mysterious charge of affect, here described in the negative terms of anxiety and loss of reality, but which one could just as well imagine in the positive terms of euphoria, a high, an intoxicatory or hallucinogenic intensity."[112]

The extended present also has consequences for the status of the past. Jameson notes a weakening of historicity in both the public and private domain. The notion of the past as a retrospect indispensable for our orientation on a collective future has disappeared. Instead, the past has become a collection of images, a "multitudinous photographic simulacrum." As Jameson says, "In faithful conformity to poststructuralist linguistic theory, the past as 'referent' finds itself gradually bracketed, and then effaced altogether, leaving us with nothing but texts."[113] This provides an adequate description of what we have identified as the perceived absence of the historical past in the philosophy of history.

According to Jameson it is important to realize that postmodernism is not merely a cultural style that one can reject or embrace. More importantly, postmodernism is a periodizing concept, a "cultural logic" that has something to say about *res gestae*, the specific socio-political circumstances that we find

---

111. Ibid., 27.

112. Ibid., 27–28.

113. Ibid., 18.

ourselves in.[114] Rosa indeed argues that "we can say that late modernity is nothing other than modern society accelerated (and desynchronized) beyond the point of possible reintegration."[115] He maintains that the modern concept of history as "collective singular" has become increasingly problematic.

Rosa argues that, "contrary to widespread opinion, modernity has not just established a single, unitary form of abstract, linear time that synchronizes its various subsystems."[116] It has also resulted in a "functional differentiation" that has created a series of "almost autopoietic subsystems," such as the economy, science, law, politics, the arts, etc. Each of these subsystems has its own temporality. Because there is "no integrating temporal authority," this results in an "increasing temporal desynchronization."

In classical modernity, this integrating temporal authority was provided by politics. Rosa points out that the modern concept of history as collective singular was a way to politically manage the acceleration of historical time. The different subsystems of society were integrated in a goal-directed movement of history that was marked by a notion of historical progress. Rosa registers that in late-modern "acceleration societies," the political project of enlightened modernity, which consisted in the deliberate political shaping of our form of life and society, has become obsolete. On a personal level, this expresses itself in a "situational" form of identity. While in classical modernity personal identities were long-term projects that assumed the form of a Bildungsroman, late-modern identities have become situational. Social structures change so fast that life can no longer be planned in accordance with a line that runs from past to future.[117]

In addition to personal identity, politics has also become situationalist. It reacts to pressures, instead of developing a progressive vision of its own. Political decisions no longer actively steer acceleratory social developments, but have become defensive and deceleratory. The structural problem of the disappearance of politics is, according to Rosa, the fundamental inability of the political subsystem to accelerate. Because of the complexities of late-modern societies, political decision-making on the one hand requires more time, while on the other the acceleration of surrounding systems, such as the economy or technology, in fact *decreases* the time that is given to politics. There is a constant threat that political decisions are outdated once they are

---

114. Adam Roberts, *Fredric Jameson* (London and New York: Routledge, 1991), 111.

115. Rosa, "Social Acceleration," 97.

116. Ibid., 104.

117. Late-modern identity in this sense resembles "premodern forms of existence in which people had to cope with unforeseen contingencies on a day-to-day basis without being able to plan for the future." Ibid., 100.

finally reached. As a result, political decision-making is shifted toward other, faster arenas, such as the legal system (juridification), the economy (privatization), or individual responsibility (deregulation).[118]

Both individually and politically, a sense of directed historical movement has been replaced by "an overwhelming sense of directionless change."[119] This has caused a perception that history has come to an end. A "view from the future" seems no longer possible. The present has become all there is, "something immense, invasive, and omnipresent, blocking out any other viewpoint, fabricating on a daily basis the past and the future it needed."[120] Now that the present has extended into future and past there is no more historical time, because this was set in motion by a *tension* between the space of experience and the horizon of expectation.[121]

Hartog describes two symptoms of presentism. The first is "the present's immediate self-historicization."[122] History has to be made here and now—a task that was originally of the future. In a desperate attempt to escape the presentistic regime of historicity, important contemporary events such as 9/11 are immediately accompanied by reflections on their historical significance. The luxury of historical distance can no longer be given to historians now that the present extends into the future.

While the self-historicization of the present is an indication of a "presentistic future," we also have a presentistic relation to our past. Another symptom of, and response to, the current crisis of time is the enormous proliferation of heritage since the 1990s. It seems as if everything can be declared heritage—not only monuments or cultural and historical sites, but also landscapes, animals and plants, know-how, languages, folk traditions, and even the gene pool.[123] In the Netherlands recently "consumer fireworks" have been declared cultural heritage.[124] The proliferation of heritage shows how "confidence in progress has given way to a desire to preserve and save."[125] Without direction from the future, however, it has become impossible to determine the difference between what belongs to the past and what pertains to history. Therefore *everything* is preserved, a tendency that acquires

---

118. Ibid., 106.
119. Ibid., 101.
120. Hartog, *Regimes of Historicity*, 185.
121. Ibid., 203.
122. Ibid., 193.
123. Ibid., 182–183.
124. "Consumentenvuurwerk is cultureel erfgoed."
125. Hartog, *Regimes of Historicity*, 185.

its urgency from the acceleration of time: "through the imperative to act quickly, before it is too late, before evening falls and the light fades to a darkness that may be total."[126]

4. CONCLUSION

Our reflection on contemporary presentism places the current crisis in the philosophy of history in a new light. The "absent past" does not primarily represent an *epistemological* crisis—which is maintained by many analytic philosophers of history who work in the tradition of narrativism—but points first and foremost to a crisis of historical ontology. More specifically, the presentism of narrativism indicates a crisis of the modern regime of historicity.

Historicity has a history of its own. The modern regime of historicity has produced a concept of history as collective singular. Through this notion of history, we have been able to deal with the maelstrom of modernity that was brought about by the acceleration of historical time. It has allowed us to politically shape our collective future and to make sense of our past.

In late-modern societies, however, history no longer takes up the central role for our collective self-understanding. History can no longer be conceptualized as a collective singular that integrates multiple temporalities. Late-modern societies have accelerated beyond the point of reintegration. Despite frantic changes, history seems to have come to a standstill. The crisis of the modern regime of historicity expresses itself as the impossibility of a "view from the future." Its place has been taken by an "omnipresent present" that has drawn past and future into itself.

The challenge that a new, presentistic regime of historicity faces is, as Hartog puts it, to "restore some form of communication between present, past, and future, without allowing the tyranny of any of them."[127] To a thinker such as Latour this means that we have to paradoxically stop being modern, which requires a recognition that we in fact have never been modern. This entails the recognition that the modern Constitution is a modern myth. To reverse the marginalization of history and to restore its role as a provider of meaning and orientation, it is necessary to develop a historical ontology that can connect with late-modern presentism—similar to the way in which the modern concept of history as collective singular provided meaning, direction, and a sense of the future in classical modernity.

---

126. Ibid., 191.

127. François Hartog, "Time, History and the Writing of History: The *Order* of Time," *KVHAA Konferenser* 37 (1996): 111.

We can learn in this respect from previous moments of crisis of the modern regime of historicity, as occurred at the beginning of the twentieth century, around World War I.[128] During this period, historians, philosophers, artists, and writers such as Braudel, Benjamin, Proust, Péguy, and also Heidegger and Henri Bergson, assessed a crisis of the modern regime of historicity by formulating new concepts of time and history. Although their efforts did not result in the end of the modern regime, they may help us to account for and overcome our contemporary crisis of historicity. This may lead us to conclude that the contemporary crisis of time also provides new opportunities to open up and rethink our relation to history and time.

---

128. Ibid., 96.

CHAPTER 3

BERGSON AND THE CRISIS OF THE MODERN REGIME OF HISTORICITY

> Then as now, rapid changes in technology, globalization, communication technologies and changes in the social fabric dominated conversations and newspaper articles; then as now, cultures of mass consumption stamped their mark on the time; then as now, the feeling of living in an accelerating world, of speeding into the unknown, was overwhelming.[1]
>
> —Blom, *The Vertigo Years*

Like our own times, the decades between 1880 and 1920 were characterized by a crisis of the modern regime of historicity. This expressed itself in various attempts to invent new concepts of history and to define new temporalities.[2] One of the most influential thinkers in this respect was the French philosopher Henri Bergson. Bergson's philosophy of time formed part of a broader cultural reaction to a reconfiguration of time and space. The environment in which Bergson formulated his ideas was marked by a sense that life and society were speeding up as a consequence of new technologies. Against this background "Bergsonism" became a cultural phenomenon with artistic and political reverberations.

---

1. Blom, *The Vertigo Years*, 2.
2. Hartog, "Time, History and the Writing of History," 104.

1. TIME AND SPACE

As discussed in chapter 1, the London Cenotaph derived its appeal to a large extent from the way in which its metonymic form embodied the profound disruption of historical continuity that was brought about by the First World War. According to the historicist worldview of the nineteenth century, the present was conceived as the outcome of a continuous historical process. The war experiences, however, could no longer be meaningfully understood in terms of what came before. This produced a crisis of the modern regime of historicity, which manifested itself as a widespread feeling of being cut off from the pre-war period and a sense of uncertainty toward the future. In the fragmented present that this crisis brought about, everything seemed to happen all at once and faster than ever before.

The first global war only became possible once the world had been united through new technologies, methods of communication, and means of transportation. These brought about a time-space compression that affected the basic structure of human experience and expression. Stephen Kern identifies the sheer *swiftness* with which events unfolded in the aftermath of the assassination of Franz Ferdinand in Sarajevo as one of the causes of World War I:

> In the summer of 1914 the men in power lost their bearings in the hectic rush paced by flurries of telegrams, telephone conversations, memos, and press releases; hard-boiled politicians broke down and seasoned negotiators cracked under the pressure of tense confrontations and sleepless nights, agonizing over the probable disastrous consequences of their snap judgements and hasty actions.[3]

Traditional diplomacy, Kern points out, could not cope with the volume and speed of electronic communication, reports of newspapers that sparked public anger, and the dynamics of massive mobilizations throughout Europe facilitated by the railway system. Gertrude Stein maintained that the fighting of the war, moreover, meant a reconfiguration of spatiality. She compared the battlefield to a Cubist composition: without beginning or end and with no center, where every corner was as important as another.[4] Walter Benjamin noted how a generation that lived "the most monstrous events in the history of the world" paradoxically returned not richer but poorer in communicable experience from the front. With the technological developments that resulted in the Great War, argued Benjamin, a new form of poverty had descended

---

3. Kern, *The Culture of Time and Space*, 260.
4. Ibid., 288.

on mankind, a poverty of *experience*: "never has experience been contradicted more thoroughly: strategic experience has been contravened by positional warfare; economic experience, by the inflation; physical experience, by hunger; moral experiences, by the ruling powers."[5]

The material foundations of this "new kind of barbarism" lay in a number of innovations that are associated with the Second Industrial Revolution.[6] The decades around 1900 saw the invention of, among other things, the telephone, the wireless telegraph, the airplane, the automobile, electricity, the X-ray, and the cinema.[7] In the economic realm the first capital markets and an international credit system were created. During 1847 and 1848 reckless speculation and overproduction had caused the first real capitalist crisis of over-accumulation, which brought the question of the representation of temporal and spatial forms to the foreground.[8]

The First World War thus not only marked a sharp discontinuity with the pre-war period, but also underlined a number of radical transformations in the experience of time and space in the decades leading up to the war. It emphasized the importance of finding new and adequate ways to represent and process these transformations. The modernist aesthetics of the prewar decades can be considered a response to these new temporal and spatial experiences. As Harvey states, "neither literature nor art could avoid the question of internationalism, synchrony, insecure temporality, and the tension within the dominant measure of value between the financial system and its monetary or commodity base."[9] However, not only artists, but also economists, psychologists, and scientists formulated new conceptions of time and space. New disciplines and theories emerged, such as psychoanalysis, Taylorism, and the theory of relativity. In general, temporality prevailed in these accounts over spatiality, and becoming over being. In philosophy also, time and space became important themes. The most influential philosophical reflection on the subject in these years came from the French philosopher Henri Bergson (1859–1941).

---

5. Benjamin, "Experience and Poverty," 732.

6. As I argued in chapter 2, I do not want to suggest a technological determinism in which the acceleration of time in modernity is traced back exclusively to the invention of new technologies. Sandra Ramírez speaks in this respect of the "coconstitución de tecnica y formas de vida" [co-constitution of technology and life-forms]. Sandra Lucía Ramírez, *Conocimiento y formas de vida: Elementos para la construcción de espacios públicos en cuestiones científico-tecnológicas* [Knowledge and Forms of Life: Elements for the Construction of Public Spaces in Scientific-Technological Questions] (Mérida: Universidad Nacional Autónoma de México, 2011), 50–52.

7. Kern, *The Culture of Time and Space*, 1.

8. Harvey, *The Condition of Postmodernity*, 264.

9. Ibid., 262–263.

2. THE CLOCK

While during the nineteenth century people were confronted with an acceleration of time, the public sphere was being simultaneously regulated by clock-time. The homogenization and "spatialization" of time served a concrete purpose in the context of the increasing speed of modern life. It allowed for an integration of the "space of experience" and "horizon of expectation," which had increasingly broken apart in modernity. Spatial time, as Richard Glasser points out, could satisfy a "general need for security" as it directed future possibilities into a restricted number of channels. He notes that "this conception of things, which determined the future both as regards time and space with the greatest exactitude, might be symbolized as a railways system and a timetable."[10]

Though the mechanical clock had already been invented in the Middle Ages, until the end of the nineteenth century there still existed a variety of local and regional times. The new railway system required the synchronization of these multiple times.[11] This was facilitated by the telegraph, which allowed for long-distance communication and the possibility of transmitting exact schedules for every stop on the line.[12] Eventually, Greenwich Mean Time was adopted as the standard for global public time. The homogenization of time also created the conditions for a temporal speed-up. The experience of mechanical transportation made contemporaries speak of a "destruction of space by time" and of a world that became increasingly smaller. Written down on the walls of Grand Central Station in New York was the text "The Devourer of Space and Time."[13]

The clock did not simply keep track of time but was also a regulator of public life. It imposed time discipline and obedience.[14] For this reason, argued Lewis Mumford, "the clock, not the steam-engine, is the key-machine of the modern industrial age."[15] Homogeneous time allowed for a stricter

---

10. Richard Glasser, *Time in French Life and Thought* (Manchester: Manchester University Press, 1972), 194.

11. Peter Peters, *De haast van Albertine: Reizen in de technologische cultuur: naar een theorie van passages* [Albertine in a Hurry: Travel in Technological Culture: Towards a Theory of Passages] (Amsterdam: Uitgeverij De Balie, 2003), 98–99.

12. D.S. Landes, *Revolution in Time: Clocks and the Making of the Modern World* (Cambridge, MA: Belknap Press, 1983), 285.

13. Peters, *De haast van Albertine*, 80.

14. Landes, *Revolution in Time*, 6–7.

15. Lewis Mumford, *Technics and Civilization*, 7th ed. (London: Routledge and Kegan Paul, 1955), 14.

regulation of the industrial production process.¹⁶ This became nowhere more apparent than in the production method created by the American engineer Frederick Taylor called "scientific management," which aimed to increase the efficiency of factory work. By breaking up the labor of a worker into a series of standardized operations, Taylor succeeded in transforming qualitative worktime into a quantitatively measurable process. The principles of scientific management were put into practice in the Ford factories, where for the first time assembly lines were used to increase mass production.

Marxist theorists like Georg Lukács criticized Taylorism for reducing workers to no more than isolated and abstract atoms. To Lukács, scientific management confirmed his conviction that the capitalist homogenization of time strengthened the process of capitalist reification.¹⁷ Taylorism, states Lukács, drains temporality of its

> qualitative, variable, flowing nature; it freezes into an exactly delimited, quantifiable continuum . . . in short, it becomes space. In this environment where time is transformed into abstract, exactly measurable, physical space, an environment at once the cause and the effect of the scientifically fragmented and specialized production of the object of labour, the subjects of labour must likewise be rationally fragmented.¹⁸

Writers, artists, and philosophers came to experience the homogenization of time increasingly as a straitjacket. They began to emphasize the heterogeneity and fluidity of subjective time as a means to escape from the pressures of a rationalized public space. New literary genres emerged, such as the stream-of-consciousness novel. In his novel *In Search of Lost Time* (*À la recherche du temps perdu*, also translated as *Remembrance of Things Past*) (1913–1927), Marcel Proust revolutionized the realist, objective notion of time by replacing the omniscient narrator with a subjective, first-person one.¹⁹ A clearly defined historical time (from the Dreyfus Affair to World War I) is merely the background to the exploration of a more profound memorial time of the main character Marcel. In Kafka's *The Trial* (1914–1915), protagonist Josef

---

16. On the relation between industrialization and time discipline, see E.P. Thompson, "Time, Work-Discipline, and Industrial Capitalism," *Past and Present* 38 (1967): 56–97.
17. Martin Jay, *Downcast Eyes: The Denigration of Vision in Twentieth-Century French Thought* (Berkeley: University of California Press, 1993), 196.
18. Georg Lukács, *History and Class Consciousness: Studies in Marxist Dialectics*, trans. Rodney Livingstone (Cambridge, MA: MIT Press, 1971), 90.
19. Sowerwine, *France since 1870*, 100.

K. struggles with the official public time, while Joyce's *Ulysses* explores the heterogeneity of time by narrating a single day in the life of Leopold Bloom.[20]

In the visual arts, subjective time was explored by the Impressionists, who tried to capture on their canvases a momentary impression lifted from the sequence of linear time. Artistic explorations like these were sustained by developments in physics, where in 1905 the special theory of relativity was formulated by Einstein. This radically changed the absolute concepts of time and space that had dominated Enlightenment thought. According to Newton, time had been a container-like principle that organized events in the external world as a succession with mathematical properties. Erasing the "antique dimensions of time and space" by fusing them in a relativistic continuum of space-time inspired many artists, including, for example, the Italian futurists and their obsession with speed.[21]

3. BERGSON

During the nineteenth century, time increasingly came to be experienced as a transformative *force*. As a result, Kant's notion of time as a homogeneous, atomistic, and universal *medium* was questioned.[22] One of the most influential challenges came from Henri Bergson.

---

20. Kern, *The Culture of Time and Space*, 15–17.
21. Conrad, Modern Times, Modern Places, 14.
22. In the Critique of Pure Reason (1781), Kant argues that time and space are "merely a subjective condition of our (human) intuition." Immanuel Kant, The Critique of Pure Reason, trans. J.M.D. Meiklejohn (Reno, NV: Everyman Paperbacks, 1991), 51. Together they constitute two forms of intuition that we impose on reality in order to make sensory experience possible. While space is, according to Kant, the pure form of external intuition, time orders inner sense and is more comprehensive because it is the a priori condition of all phenomena. Time also differs from space because it constitutes sense-impressions as a succession, while space implies a simultaneity of objects. Temporal succession proceeds in a mathematical fashion that can be grasped through calculus. Kant furthermore argues that time is "one," because different times can all be reduced to time in its pure form. Because time is an "invisible" framework that has no shape or form and is devoid of empirical content, we represent its course by the spatial image of a line that progresses to infinity (50). Hence Kant's conception of time as homogeneous, universal, and atomistic. As a theoretician of time Kant holds an ambivalent position. On the one hand he discusses the centuries-old problem of how we should understand the "time of the universe." Like Aristotle, Augustine, and Newton, he adopts the metaphor of the geometrical point by assigning mathematical properties to temporal succession. However, Kant also makes a decisive move towards a phenomenal approach of time, without actually adopting a phenomenological position himself. Kant makes, as David Couzens Hoy points out, "the first step beyond a metaphysics of time and toward a phenomenology of temporality." David Couzens Hoy, *The Time of Our Lives: A Critical History of Temporality* (Cambridge, MA: MIT Press, 2009), 6–7.

Bergson was born in Paris in 1859 and came from a Jewish family with a Polish musician as a father and an English mother. As a child, he lived in France, London, and Geneva.[23] He attended the École Normale Supérieur, together with Émile Durkheim, where he studied philosophy. In 1889 Bergson published his doctoral thesis *Time and Free Will,* followed in 1896 by *Matter and Memory.* In 1892, he married Louise Neuburger, a second cousin of Marcel Proust. After teaching at various *lycées* in Paris, Bergson became a professor at the École Normale in 1898 and was appointed to the Collège de France in 1900. In these years, he became hugely popular among a wide audience, especially after the publication of *Creative Evolution* in 1907. After becoming a member of the prestigious Académie Française in 1914, Bergson traded his academic career for a career in politics. He undertook various diplomatic missions to the United States during World War I. In the 1920s he worked at the League of Nations. He became president of the International Committee on Intellectual Cooperation and he received the Nobel Prize for Literature in 1927. Plagued by arthritis, Bergson was forced to retire, but he did publish one last book: *The Two Sources of Morality and Religion.* At the end of his life, Bergson refused the exemption from anti-Semitic regulations that was offered to him by the Vichy government and stood in line to register as a Jew. Only a few weeks later, in January 1941, Henri Bergson died.[24]

One of Bergson's main objectives was to reveal how the philosophers from the seventeenth and eighteenth centuries participated in shaping a modern and mechanistic worldview based on a spatialized conception of time. According to Bergson, the *duration* of time is thereby confused with the *measurement* of duration. This is problematic, because this fixates temporal movement and change.[25]

One of Bergson's targets in his first major work, *Time and Free Will,* is Kant's transcendental philosophy. Suzanne Guerlac even states that "every

---

23. Canales, *The Physicist and the Philosopher,* 23.

24. In his last years, Bergson inclined towards Catholicism, about which he wrote in his will: "I would have become a convert, had I not foreseen for years a formidable wave of anti-Semitism about to break upon the world. I wanted to remain among those who tomorrow were to be persecuted." See "Henri Bergson: French philosopher," Encyclopaedia Britannica, accessed October 15, 2014, http://www.britannica.com/biography/Henri-Bergson.

25. In a letter from 1908 to his friend William James he describes how, as a philosophy student, he came to realize the contingency of the atomistic time of science while reading the work of Herbert Spencer, who frequently made use of mechanistic categories: "It was the analysis of the notion of time, such as it appears in mechanics or physics, which revolutionized all of my ideas. I realized to my great amazement *that scientific time has no duration.*" (Italics added.) Keith Ansell-Pearson, John Mullarkey, and Melissa MacMahon, ed., *Henri Bergson: Key Writings* (New York: Continuum, 2002), 362.

move of the argument [in *Time and Free Will*] follows a contour of Kant's thought, turning it inside out, or on its head."[26] According to Bergson, Kant did not objectively reflect the structure of experience and the understanding. The "forms of intuition" do not have a synthetic *a priori* quality but are a construction of our intellect, stimulated by the surge of modern science. While Kant pretended to distinguish time, as the form of inner sense, from space, the form of external objects, he actually projected space onto time by envisioning time as a line of successive "moments" that can be counted. As Bergson notes with regard to this image, "When we evoke time, it is space which answers our call."[27]

It is not only Kant, however, but the entire history of philosophy that shows an obsession with space. Bergson is one of the first philosophers to recognize the performative quality of the homogenization and spatialization of time. He argues that this has actively constituted our being in the world and has alienated us from our surroundings. The concept of time implicit in the developing sciences during the Second Scientific Revolution has, according to Bergson, affected our sense of freedom and led to the rise of determinism. In *Time and Free Will*, Bergson poses the question of "whether the insurmountable difficulties presented by certain philosophical problems do not arise from our placing side by side in space phenomena which do not occupy space."[28] What Bergson is actually asking from us is to start to *think in time*, requiring a huge effort because we are naturally inclined to think spatially and to favor permanence over change.

4. BERGSONISMS

Suzanne Guerlac notes that both too much and too little has been said about Bergson:

> Too much, because of the various appropriations of his thought. Too little, because the work itself has not been carefully studied in recent decades.[29]

---

26. Suzanne Guerlac, *Thinking in Time: An Introduction to Henri Bergson* (Ithaca: Cornell University Press, 2006), 44.

27. CM, 4.

28. Henri Bergson, *Time and Free Will: An Essay on the Immediate Data of Consciousness* (*Essai sur les données immédiates de la conscience*, 1889), trans. F.L. Pogson (1913; repr., Mineola, NY: Dover Publications, 2001) (hereafter TFW), xix.

29. Guerlac, *Thinking in Time*, 13.

It is indeed important to distinguish Bergson's philosophy from its popular versions that came up after 1900, when Bergson became an important public figure in France. Bergson's twice-weekly public lectures at the Amphithéâtre VIII of the Collège de France drew a huge and diverse crowd, among whom were many members of the intellectual elite and the bourgeois high society of the salons. Famous were the so-called "five o'clock Bergsonians," who would send out their servants in advance to occupy their seats in the lecture hall.[30] The French author Charles Péguy described the crowd he encountered at one of Bergson's lectures:

> I saw elderly men, women, young girls, young men, many young men, Frenchmen, Russians, foreigners, mathematicians, naturalists, I saw there students in letters, students in science, medical students, I saw there engineers, economists, lawyers and priests . . . I saw there poets, artists, I saw there M. Sorel, I saw there Charles Guieysse and M. Maurice Kahn, I saw there Emile Boivin, who takes notes for someone in the provinces; they descend from the Cahiers, from Pages libres . . . they come from the Sorbonne and I think the Ecole Normale; I saw there well known bourgeois types, socialists, anarchists.[31]

Mystical pilgrimages were even undertaken to Bergson's summer home in Switzerland, "where locks of his hair at the local barbers were treated as holy relics."[32] When his work was translated into English, Bergson became an international celebrity. His visit to Columbia University in 1913 supposedly caused one of the first traffic jams on Broadway.[33] La Belle Époque, the decades preceding World War I in France, is known for its optimistic attitude toward the future. The inauguration of the Eiffel Tower at the Paris Exhibition of 1889 celebrated the new urban, industrial, and technological age. It expressed a great confidence that scientific modernization would assure progress for humanity and eventually unravel all of the world's mysteries. The intellectual climate in France was in sync with this mentality and was predominantly rationalistic, materialistic, and positivistic. But there were also many people who experienced the rationalization of public life, the capitalist

---

30. Grogin, *The Bergsonian Controversy in France*, 123.

31. Péguy as cited in Mark Antliff, *Inventing Bergson: Cultural Politics and the Parisian Avant-Garde* (Princeton, NJ: Princeton University Press, 1993), 4.

32. Grogin, *The Bergsonian Controversy in France*, ix.

33. Thomas V. Quirk, *Bergson and American Culture: The Worlds of Willa Cather and Wallace Stevens* (Chapel Hill: University of North Carolina Press, 1990), 1.

Figure 3.1. "Listening at the window to the course by M. Bergson," Collège de France, February 1914. "On écoute aux fenêtres le cours de M. Bergson." *Excelsior. Journal Illustré Quotidien*, February 14, 1914. Bibliothèque nationale de France, accessed September 30, 2018, https://gallica.bnf.fr.

homogenization of time, and the determinism of a mechanistic culture as oppressive. It was mainly to these people that Bergsonism appealed.[34]

The popularization of Bergsonism especially thrived after the publication of *Creative Evolution* in 1907. In this work, Bergson translates his theory of

---

34. Grogin, *The Bergsonian Controversy in France*, ix.

duration into a theory of life. He argues that evolution is the expression of a creative mode of time, an *élan vital* that is analogous to the duration of consciousness. Bergson became the most important representative of a broad anti-mechanistic current that propagated spiritualist ideas that emphasized the principles of life—intuition, freedom, and creativity—as opposed to "Cartesianism" and mechanistic science.[35] Bergson's ideas have also been associated with a broader occult revival in pre–World War I Europe. This involved an interest in the unconscious and supernatural and (para)psychological phenomena. Bergson, for instance, participated in hypnotic sessions during the 1880s that would have a lasting influence on his thought.[36] Many scientists and thinkers were convinced that the twentieth century would bring a new Copernican Revolution, but of the human psyche this time.[37] Scientific research of "psychical phenomena" was institutionalized in numerous societies, the most important of which was the Society for Psychical Research, which had Bergson as its president in 1913.[38]

The Bergsonian conception of time and space also shaped the aesthetic and social theories of the modernist avant-garde. Bergsonism influenced *Du Cubisme* (1912), the first theoretical treatise about Cubism by Albert Gleizes and Jean Metzinger, who presented the Cubist imagery as emerging from the durational flux of the artist's consciousness. A Cubist painting represented, according to the authors, a qualitative approach of space and tried to evoke an intuitive response in the viewer.[39] Futurism, Symbolism, and J.D. Fergusson's Rhythmism also referred to Bergson in their resistance to bourgeois notions of quantitative and rationalized space and time.[40]

This Bergsonian aesthetics also had a cultural and political aspect. Although the works that Bergson published before World War I did not primarily address social or political issues, it was thought that Bergson's

---

35. Three spiritualist philosophers had a great influence on Bergson: Felix Ravaisson, Jules Lachelier, and Emile Boutroux. Ibid., 11–16.

36. Henri F. Ellenberger, *The Discovery of the Unconscious: The History and Evolution of Dynamic Psychiatry* (New York: Basic Books Inc., 1970), 168. In an early article, Bergson discusses his experiments with hypnosis. He notes how subjects under hypnosis are capable of extending their perception. These experiments would have a lasting influence on Bergson's thought. Henri Bergson, "De la simulation inconsciente dans l'état d'hypnotisme," *Revue Philosophique* 22 (1886): 525–531.

37. Grogin, *The Bergsonian Controversy in France*, 45–46.

38. This society still exists. See the website of the Society for Psychical Research, accessed September 30, 2018, http://www.spr.ac.uk.

39. Antliff, *Inventing Bergson*, 48–53.

40. Ibid., 168.

philosophy had a political meaning that could be deduced from its principles.[41] Bergsonism was attacked by the nationalistic and anti-Semitic right-wing movement Action Française, which resisted all foreign, and especially Jewish and Germanic, influences on French culture. According to Charles Maurras, one of the leaders of the Action Française, the philosophy of the "Jewish rhetorician" Bergson was a "feminine romanticism" that had no place in the French nation.[42]

Bergsonian notions were nevertheless embraced by both the right and left of the political spectrum. Conservative and religious thinkers saw in Bergsonism a critique of the modern industrial age, which had robbed society of spiritual values. *Creative Evolution*, with its emphasis on mobility and becoming, could, however, just as well be read as an affirmation of the dynamic change and innovation of modernity. On the far left, the syndicalist movement aimed at replacing liberal democracy with a socialist corporatist state and associated Bergsonian intuition and creativity with Marxism. In his *Reflections on Violence* (1908), the anarcho-syndicalist Georges Sorel criticized intellectualized forms of Marxism and explored the dynamic and revolutionary force of myth as opposed to "static" utopia. To Sorel, the development of socialism should be compared with a biological evolution that could be grasped only intuitively. The "myth of the general strike" would instantaneously be intuited by the proletariat and invoke revolutionary action and class warfare that would destroy the capitalist system.[43]

Bergson's organic model of temporality thus became part of a broader resistance against industrial capitalism, which was seen as imposing an oppressive regime of quantified time. Mark Antliff argues that in this context the lack of a historical dimension in Bergson's critique of the homogeneous time of capitalism became problematic. To Bergson, the quantification and rationalization of time was not so much a sociohistorical construct as the result of a natural tendency inherent in the process of life. To many Bergsonians this implied that the alternative to the modern and capitalist temporal regime was a more "natural" state that they sought in a premodern and pre-industrial

---

41. Ellen Kennedy, "Bergson's Philosophy and French Political Doctrines: Sorel, Maurras, Péguy and de Gaulle," *Government and Opposition* 15 (January 1980): 75. Kennedy notes, "The difference between what Bergson stood for and favoured in politics and what others thought his philosophy implied for politics is most striking and points to the difficulties inherent in taking practical advice from metaphysical arguments." (76)

42. Grogin, *The Bergsonian Controversy in France*, 187.

43. Ibid., 88–93. For a recent comparison between Marx and Bergson, see Gregory Dale Adamson, *Philosophy in the Age of Science and Capital* (London and New York: Continuum, 2002).

social order. This favored an essentialist and naturalist conception of the nation state. As Antliff notes,

> What is occurring in the criticism of the Bergsonian avant-garde is a merger of three time frames: the cadence of human time, the rhythmic pattern of time in nature, and the variable temporal systems invented by particular cultures throughout their historical development. The Bergsonists claim that the rhythm of nature, in the guise of the élan vital, is synonymous with the creative duration of the artist's subjective experience and the creative élan of the nation. Thus the nation takes on the characteristics of the artist, it has a 'body' and an intuitive consciousness. . . . When the time of artistic creativity, peasant labor, or modern society is declared organic, the socially relative time of human culture becomes a naturalized absolute, with a time frame of cosmic proportions.[44]

The homogenization of time could thus be conceived as a danger to the "roots" of the nation. For this reason, Grogin claims that despite Bergson's allegiance to democracy, "there was in the period before [World War I] no greater intellectual assault upon the rationalist bases of French democracy than Bergsonian vitalism."[45] According to Antliff there even runs a line from prewar vitalism to the reactionary and nationalistic movements that emerged after 1918. Fascism, for instance, propagated a regionalist politics of "blood and soil" on the basis of an organic definition of the nation, which it opposed to the internationalism of capitalism and liberalism. This also allowed them to project the "rootlessness" and mobility of international capital onto the Jewish people, who could consequently be conceived of as a threat to the nation's health.[46]

Although Bergson can obviously not be held responsible for the reception of his ideas, these interpretations should be taken into account in any attempt to actualize Bergsonism. Antliff, for instance, stresses the need to historicize the pre–World War I critique of capitalism, especially because the "disparaging of rationalist modes of social organization . . . continues as a central preoccupation of the contemporary discourse on modernism and the Marxist dialogue on time."[47] This is particularly necessary in cases when

---

44. Antliff, *Inventing Bergson*, 174.
45. Grogin, *The Bergsonian Controversy in France*, 88.
46. Antliff, *Inventing Bergson*, 178–179.
47. Ibid., 170.

an organicist model of time is adhered to. The historicization of organic and mechanical temporal models has, according to Antliff, been taken up by a number of contemporary theorists, such as Michel Foucault, David Harvey, and Martin Jay, who relate temporal regimes to sociohistorical instead of biological conditions. Yet these authors have disregarded the role of Bergsonism as part of "the widespread reaction against the temporal hegemony of industrial capitalism."[48]

After World War I the popularity of Bergsonism rapidly declined. Numerous reasons have been cited for this, such as the fact that Bergsonism was always a popular philosophy and never established an academic tradition with doctoral students who would eventually occupy key positions in the academic world; that Bergson became fused with the popular appropriations of his philosophy; that Bergson withdrew from academic teaching after 1914; and that other themes started to dominate the philosophical agenda during the Interbellum. The dispute in 1922 between Einstein and Bergson on the nature of relativity, which Bergson arguably lost, is also mentioned as a reason for Bergson's decline into oblivion.[49] In 1985 the Polish philosopher Leszek Kolakowski stated that "it is true that sometimes somewhere someone is writing a dissertation on 'Bergsonism,' but in all honesty we can say that contemporary philosophers, both in their research as in their teachings, are as good as indifferent towards his legacy."[50] And yet soon after Kolakowski wrote these words the status of Bergson began to change, mainly under the influence of the French philosopher Gilles Deleuze, who adopted many Bergsonian concepts. In the last decades Bergson has been going through a revival in which philosophers are also returning to Bergson's original texts. As John Mullarkey put it in 1999, "many now believe that the neglect of [Bergson's] work is both unfair to him and irresponsible to philosophy."[51]

5. CONCLUSION

Though Bergson's historical situation often remains implicit in his writings, we have seen that Bergsonism incorporates many themes that were simultaneously addressed by artists, cultural critics, scientists, politicians, and economists

---

48. Ibid., 178.

49. On the debate between Einstein and Bergson, see Canales, *The Physicist and the Philosopher*.

50. My translation. Leszek Kolakowski, *Bergson*, trans. H. van den Haute (Kampen: Klement, 2003), 17.

51. John Mullarkey, "Introduction: La Philosophie nouvelle," 1.

around 1900. Bergson's response to the reconfigurations of time and space, brought about by the process of modernization, was highly original, and is now being discovered in the contemporary revaluation of Bergson.

The revival of Bergsonism might also be fueled by the fact that we are once again experiencing a crisis of the modern regime of historicity. The *neue Unübersichtlichkeit* ("new indistinctiveness," Habermas) of our times resembles in many ways the Vertigo Years (Blom) preceding the outbreak of World War I that reverberate in Bergson's philosophy. As Philipp Blom argues,

> The Vertigo Years had much in common with our own day, not least their openness: in 1910 and even in 1914, nobody felt confident of the shape the future world would have, of who would wield power, and what political constellation would be victorious, or what kind of society would emerge from the headlong transformation . . . With the collapse of the Soviet empire, some of the openness and uncertainty of the Vertigo Years have reappeared, and today it is much more difficult to say what the future will bring for our societies.[52]

If such a comparison has any ground, this raises the question as to what extent Bergsonism—as a response to the modern condition—can contribute to overcoming the contemporary crisis of the modern regime of historicity.

Contemporary accounts of Bergsonism approach Bergson's philosophy often from either a historical or a philosophical-analytical perspective. The historical studies present Bergsonism as a historical phenomenon and tend to reduce Bergson's ideas to the social, cultural, and political context of the Belle Époque. Examples of this are the works by Grogin, Antliff, Quirk, and Gillies. These approaches somewhat neglect the philosophical relevance of Bergson's ideas. The many philosophical-analytical studies of recent years, on the other hand, focus on either the outdated status of Bergson's philosophy (Kolakowski's *Bergson*) or its relevance to contemporary debates (such as Mullarkey's *Bergson and Philosophy* or Deleuze's *Bergsonism*). These philosophical works put less emphasis on the historical conditioning of Bergsonism.

In the following chapters, however, I will show that a contextualization of Bergsonism does not diminish its philosophical originality. In fact, the philosophical relevance of Bergsonism *is bound up* with it being a reaction to a crisis of the modern regime of historicity. Bergsonian ideas should not be studied in isolation from the historical and cultural matrix out of which they evolved, either by treating them exclusively as contributions to specific

---

52. Blom, *The Vertigo Years*, 3.

philosophical and scientific debates or by "historicizing" Bergsonism altogether and treating it as a historical curiosity. The value of Bergson as a historical thinker—which is the subject of this book—comes to the fore once we recognize that Bergson's arguments, especially the problems that he addresses, arise from the historico-cultural milieu in which they were introduced.[53]

---

53. This approach is similar to Janik and Toulmin's approach of Wittgenstein. See Allen Janik and Stephen Toulmin, *Wittgenstein's Vienna* (New York: Simon and Schuster, 1973), 27.

CHAPTER 4

A WORLD MADE OUT OF TIME

> We live in time, it bounds us and defines us, and time is supposed to measure history, isn't it? But if we can't understand time, can't grasp its mysteries of pace and progress, what chance do we have with history—even our own small, personal, largely undocumented piece of it?[1]
>
> —Julian Barnes, *The Sense of an Ending*

> I want to show that behind the prejudices of some, the mockery of others, there is, present and invisible, a certain metaphysic unconscious of itself,—unconscious and therefore inconsistent, unconscious and therefore incapable of continually remodelling itself on observation and experience as every philosophy worthy of the name must do.[2]
>
> —Henri Bergson, *Mind-Energy: Lectures and Essays*

Bergson's philosophy has often been dismissed for its speculative and incoherent nature. Critics point to the vagueness of concepts like "intuition," "duration," and "*élan vital*," which lack a clear-cut definition and seemed to take on a slightly different meaning with each new work. According to these critics, Bergson's literary and metaphorical style obscures a lack of philosophical rigidity and foundation for his ideas. As Bertrand Russell put it, "Like advertisers, [Bergson] relies upon picturesque and varied statement, and on apparent explanation of many obscure facts."[3]

---

1. Julian Barnes, *The Sense of an Ending* (London: Cape, 2011), 60.
2. Henri Bergson, *Mind-Energy: Lectures and Essays* (*L'Énergie spirituelle*, 1919), 1920, trans. H. Wildon Carr (London: Henry Holt and Company, 1920) (hereafter ME), 77.
3. Russell, *A History of Western Philosophy*, 799.

The non-systematic nature of Bergsonism may be best illustrated by the transformations that Bergson's key concept, duration, went through. In Bergson's earlier work, especially *Time and Free Will*, duration refers to the temporal succession of psychological states, which is contrasted with material processes. In making this distinction, Bergson suggests that there is a fundamental difference between the lived experience of time and the "spatial" temporality of matter. Yet in subsequent works, duration is no longer reserved for the psychological realm but is developed into an ontology. Duration becomes "the very stuff of reality,"[4] and Bergson sketches an enduring universe made up of different "rhythms of duration."

Some critics even go so far as to argue that Bergsonism is actually made up of two very different philosophers. The Polish philosopher Leszek Kolakowski, for instance, argues that the "Bergson-Cartesian" who propagates a version of the cogito contradicts the "Bergson-cosmologist" who presents the universe as the product of a divine and creative *élan*. Kolakowski finds that there are insurmountable contradictions between these two "Bergsons": "one cannot be simultaneously Descartes and Schelling."[5]

Bergson himself seems not to have been bothered by these inconsistencies. He even stated that with each new work he wanted to make an effort to forget his previous positions.[6] As Vladimir Jankélévitch put it, "Bergson writes each of his books oblivious of all the others, without even worrying about the inconsistencies that might at times result from their succession."[7] An important reason for this is that Bergson turns against the tendency of philosophers to construct systems of thought. We should never start by describing the systematic unity of the world, argues Bergson, because "who knows if the world is actually one?"[8] It is only *experience* that can inform us whether such a unity exists.

---

4. CE, 272.

5. Kolakowski, *Bergson*, 132.

6. The non-systematic nature of Bergsonism is actually bound up with its philosophical contents. An early interpreter of Bergson, H. Wildon Carr, perceptively remarks about Bergsonism that "one of its most important conclusions is that the universe is not a completed system of reality, of which it is only our knowledge that is imperfect, but that the universe is itself becoming." Herbert Wildon Carr, *Henri Bergson: the Philosophy of Change* (London: Jack, 1911), 11–12. On the non-systematic nature of Bergsonism see also John Mullarkey, *Bergson and Philosophy* (Notre Dame, IN: University of Notre Dame Press, 2000), 4–5.

7. Vladimir Jankélévitch, *Henri Bergson*, trans. Nils F. Schott (Durham: Duke University Press, 2015), 1.

8. CM, 19.

This emphasis on experience may seem strange for a philosophy that has often been put aside as metaphysical speculation—a label that undoubtedly contributed to Bergson's oblivion in the second half of the twentieth century, when the general trend in philosophy was antagonistic toward metaphysics. Nevertheless, it is significant that no matter what shape Bergson's philosophy of duration takes on, whether it is applied to psychology, psychophysics, evolutionary biology, or morality and religion, Bergson always purports to take his point of departure in experience. If there is a unifying characteristic of Bergson's oeuvre, it seems that it has to be sought not primarily on the level of the philosophical content, but in a methodology based on experience that is consistently applied throughout his work. Indeed, Bergson himself declared that his philosophy was based on an "intuition of duration" that is laid out in his first work, *Time and Free Will*.[9]

Before I discuss the implications of Bergsonism for the theory of history in the following chapters, I will first in this chapter introduce Bergsonism as primarily a philosophy of experience. Contrary to what other interpreters such as Kolakowski maintain, I will argue that Bergsonism does not consist of two contradictory philosophies, one phenomenological and directed at the subjective experience of time, the other naturalistic and ontological in nature. These limited readings obscure a perspective on Bergsonism as a whole. The coherence of Bergsonism lies instead in its empiricism, or what Bergson calls the *intuition of duration*.

Section one is dedicated to the defining notion of what Bergson means by experience, namely intuition. By contrasting Bergsonian intuition with Kant's notion of experience as laid out in the *Critique of Pure Reason*, I will show that intuition does not appeal to a vague mysticism, but firmly roots Bergson's project in the history of philosophy. Intuition should be understood as an extension of our ordinary experience. Sections two and three will trace how intuition opens a window onto duration. I will identify the transformation of duration throughout Bergson's oeuvre and maintain that there is in fact a unity in Bergsonism, namely a consistent effort to explore the *intuition of duration*.

1. INTUITION

The central place of experience in Bergson's philosophy expresses itself in its methodology, which would eventually be called "intuition." Bergson found

---

9. Jean Hyppolite, "Various Aspects of Memory in Bergson," trans. Athena V. Colman, in Leonard Lawlor, *The Challenge of Bergsonism. Phenomenology, Ontology, Ethics* (New York: Continuum, 2004), 112. Bergson maintains that "to think intuitively is to think in duration." CM, 22.

that "of all the terms that designate a mode of knowing, [intuition] is still the most appropriate."[10] Bergson first wrote about intuition as a philosophical method in the essay *Introduction to Metaphysics* from 1903, after he had already published important works like *Time and Free Will* (1889) and *Matter and Memory* (1896).[11] The late introduction of the method of intuition nevertheless did not imply a fundamental reorientation of his philosophy. The appeal to an immediate access to reality as another way to acquire knowledge besides the intellect also figures in Bergson's early work. The term "intuition" might not have been the happiest choice. With a sense of understatement Bergson would later remark that it led to "a certain confusion" after it was introduced.[12] Intuition suggested a religious and spiritual affinity that was ridiculed by rationalist philosophers such as Bertrand Russell, who jibed, "in the main intellect is the misfortune of man, while instinct is seen at its best in ants, bees, and Bergson."[13]

Contrary to what these hostile interpretations suggest, Bergsonian intuition was certainly not primarily intended as a move toward some vague spiritualism or religious aesthetic—quite the contrary. By appealing to intuition Bergson wanted to root his project in the history of philosophy and enter into debate with the modern philosophers, especially Kant. Nor was intuition meant to be anti-intellectual. More than once Bergson stressed that intuition is not superior to intellectual knowledge. Both provide us with different but complementary *kinds* of knowledge. Each opens up one half of the "totality of things" and is therefore "equally precise and certain."[14] This does not mean that intuition and intellect should operate in isolation. Bergson maintains that science, which revolves around intellectual knowledge, cannot function properly without the guidance of intuition. Bergson wanted to re-establish the relationship between science and metaphysics, which had been broken down by Kant in the *Critique of Pure Reason*.[15] The method of

---

10. CM, 18.

11. Deleuze, *Bergsonism*, 13.

12. Bergson explains: "Because a Schelling, a Schopenhauer and others have already called upon intuition, because they have more or less set up intuition in opposition to intelligence, one might think that I was using the same method. But of course, their intuition was an immediate search for the eternal! Whereas, on the contrary, for me it was a question, above all, of finding true duration." CM, 18.

13. Bertrand Russell as cited in Mary Ann Gillies, *Henri Bergson and British Modernism* (Montreal: McGill-Queen's University Press, 1996), 34.

14. CM, 30.

15. Ansell-Pearson, *Philosophy and the Adventure of the Virtual*, 116.

intuition, states Bergson, wants to "escape from the objections which Kant had formulated against metaphysics in general, and its principal object is to remove the opposition established by Kant between metaphysics and science, by taking account of the new conditions in which science works."[16]

These "new conditions" refer to the growth of life sciences in the nineteenth century, especially psychology and biology. Bergson examines whether these sciences, which are non-mathematical, can nevertheless give us knowledge.[17] In this sense, a parallel can be drawn with the German historicists of the nineteenth century, who wanted to create a science of the human world, as the natural sciences had done for the natural world. According to the historicists, science should not only be about universal laws but should also take the particularity of things into account.[18] In a similar way, Bergson reaches the conclusion that psychological and biological "facts of life" cannot be translated into the mechanistic categories of the mathematical sciences that had shaped the scientific revolution of the seventeenth and eighteenth centuries.

Newton had compared the universe to a gigantic machine that functions according to mechanical laws. The implication of this metaphor was that all of reality could eventually be understood by means of mathematical calculations. The important sciences from the eighteenth century, such as physics and astronomy, therefore all had a mathematical basis. Mathematics was considered to be the ultimate foundation for scientific knowledge. According to these mathematical formulae, time had no real impact. From the perspective of seventeenth- and eighteenth-century dynamics, the laws of motion reduced temporality essentially to the eternal interactions of particles, meaning that time was considered reversible.[19]

Bergson criticizes Kantianism for its adherence to the mathematical sciences of the eighteenth century. He argues that the *Critique of Pure Reason*

---

16. Henri Bergson, *Mélanges*, ed. André Robinet (Paris: Presses Universitaires de France, 1972) (hereafter ML), 493. Trans. Keith Ansell-Pearson.
17. A.D. Lindsay, *The Philosophy of Bergson* (London: Dent, 1911), 12.
18. In chapter 6 I will provide a reading of Bergsonism as a "nonmodern historicism."
19. Ilya Prigogine and Isabelle Stengers state that contemporary physics, as in the classical tradition, also denies the efficacy of time: "Classical dynamics seems to express in an especially clear and striking way the static view of nature. Here time apparently is reduced to a parameter, and future and past become equivalent. It is true that quantum theory has raised many new problems not covered by classical dynamics but it has nevertheless retained a number of the conceptual positions of classical dynamics, particularly as far as time and process are concerned." Ilya Prigogine and Isabelle Stengers, *Order out of Chaos: Man's New Dialogue with Nature* (Toronto: Bantam Books, 1984), 11.

incorporates crucial aspects of the mechanistic worldview that had established itself under the influence of Newtonian physics. When Kant wants to found his philosophical investigation of pure reason on a scientific basis, he is—not surprisingly—guided by the contemporary prevalence of mathematical universalism.[20] This leads Kant to the doctrine that an examination can only be considered scientific to the extent that it is mathematical.[21]

The "Copernican Revolution" in the *Critique* entails that phenomenal reality functions according to mechanistic principles. This signifies that reality can only be known to the extent that we perceive it mechanistically. This reverberates in Kant's mechanistic conception of time and space. Time and space as homogeneous media are according to Kant *a priori* forms that allow for sensuous experience. This implies that we can only know things to the extent that they can be considered as discrete points on a timeline.[22]

The three central questions in the *Critique* also display the primacy of mechanical and mathematical principles: "How is pure mathematics possible?" "How is pure physics possible?" and "How is pure metaphysics possible?" After having affirmed the possibility of pure mathematics and pure physics, Kant denies the possibility of pure metaphysics because it does not fulfil the conditions of the mathematical sciences. Metaphysics refers to the noumenal reality that lies beyond the phenomenal realm that is presented to us in experience. Because science only applies to the phenomenal realm of possible experience, metaphysics is naturally excluded. An access to the metaphysical reality of the "thing in itself" would require a special faculty of knowing, a superior "intellectual intuition," which Kant holds does not exist.[23] If reason does fall for the temptation of directing itself to metaphysical issues for which it is not equipped, it produces antinomies, which are inherently contradictory statements that are never-ending because both thesis and antithesis can be sustained with clear and irrefutable proof. An example is the thesis "The world has, as to time and space, a beginning," and its antithesis, "The world is, as to time and space, infinite."[24]

---

20. Bergson: "Kant took for a reality this dream of certain modern philosophers: much more, he thought that all scientific knowledge was only a detached fragment, or rather a projecting stone of universal mathematics. The main task of the *Critique*, therefore, was to lay the foundations of this mathematics, that is, to determine what the intelligence should be and what should be the object in order that an unbroken mathematics might bind them together." CM, 166.

21. Lindsay, *The Philosophy of Bergson*, 16.

22. Ibid.

23. CM, 116.

24. Immanuel Kant, *Prolegomena to Any Future Metaphysics*, trans. Paul Carus (Boulder: NetLibrary, 1997), 59.

While Kant pretended to explore pure reason, Bergson argues that he actually defined the *a priori* conditions for a very specific *kind* of knowledge: "If you read the *Critique of Pure Reason* you see that Kant has criticized, not reason in general, but a reason fashioned to the habits and exigencies of the Cartesian mechanism or the Newtonian physics."[25] According to Bergson, Kant's definition of science is too limited. It is, for instance, not possible to found psychology and biology on a mechanical basis. Organic change confronts us with a temporality that cannot be adequately represented in mathematical terms. The main reason for this is that mechanistic time cannot take the unicity and individuality of living organisms into account. This does not mean that psychology or biology is impossible, but only that they have their own standards and methods. A.D. Lindsay argues that in addition to Kant's inquiry after the possibility of mathematics and physics, Bergson asks how psychology and biology are possible. He answers: "Only because knowledge is not exhausted in mathematical analysis, because over against the discursive understanding stands the more immediate intuitive knowledge."[26] Lindsay notes that in addition to Kant's critique of the understanding, Bergson now investigates the possibility of biology and psychology by providing a "critique of intuition."[27]

Biological and psychological "facts of life" show us that the transcendental structure of the mind should not be approached as "given" as Kant supposed. Bergson argues that "it is not enough to determine, by careful analysis, the categories of thought; we must engender them."[28] We have to take the evolutionary background of our cognitive apparatus into account. This will make clear that our intellect does not have an *epistemological* function. It was not constituted to produce "truthful" knowledge about reality, but to provide us

---

25. ML, 493. Trans. A.D. Lindsay.

26. Lindsay, *The Philosophy of Bergson*, 17.

27. Alexander Dunlop Lindsay was one of the few proponents of Bergsonism in Great Britain and also one of the first to relate Bergsonism to history. Lindsay was a teacher and mentor of the universal historian Arnold Toynbee (1889–1975) and is credited by Christian Kerslake for creating the space for Toynbee's Bergsonian historiography. Kerslake argues that in his *A Study of History*, published in twelve volumes between 1934 and 1961, "Toynbee in effect brought about a fusion of Bergsonism with a type of historiography rooted in the education of the classics offered at Oxford and Cambridge in the late nineteenth and early twentieth centuries. Rejecting both empiricist and Marxist approaches to historiography, his historiographical inspirations came from classical historians (Polybius), from Edward Gibbon's *Decline and Fall of the Roman Empire*, from Oswald Spengler's *Decline of the West*, and, by his own acknowledgement, from the Bible." Kerslake, "Becoming against History," 19.

28. CE, 207.

with "useful" knowledge. The mechanistic inclination of the understanding that Kant lays out in the *Critique* has facilitated our evolution. It has allowed human beings to act upon matter and to thereby take control of their material environment. Bergson argues that this evolutionary approach can bring the Kantian project a step further. Kant considered, according to Bergson, three alternatives for a theory of knowledge: either the mind is determined by things as the rationalists maintain; things are determined by the mind as the empiricists claim; or "between mind and things we must suppose a mysterious agreement,"[29] and it is in response to this last option that Kant develops his transcendental philosophy. By now placing the transcendental structure in an evolutionary perspective, argues Bergson, a fourth possibility opens up: "This alternative consists, first of all, in regarding the intellect as a special function of the mind, essentially turned toward inert matter; then in saying that neither does matter determine the form of the intellect, nor does the intellect impose its form on matter, nor have matter and intellect been regulated in regard to one another by we know not what pre-established harmony, but that intellect and matter have progressively adapted themselves one to the other in order to attain at last a common form."[30]

According to Bergson, matter and intellect have a "double genesis." They have evolved in a process of mutual adaptation of the one toward the other that has given our cognitive apparatus and our perception of matter its current form.[31] For this reason, Bergson stresses the need to connect a theory of knowledge with a theory of life. If we disconnect the two, we will get the impression that the mind coincides with the intellect.[32] We will then, as Ansell-Pearson states, "blindly accept the concepts—of matter, of life, of time, etc.—that the understanding has placed at our disposal."[33] We will start thinking from pre-existing frames that are indeed mechanistic in nature. This, according to Bergson, is what happens in the *Critique of Pure Reason*.

By placing the understanding against an evolutionary background, Bergson revises Kant's division of the real into a phenomenal and noumenal realm. Instead, Bergson sees epistemological questions in terms of the relation between parts and wholes.[34] What Kant calls phenomena are merely "partial"

---

29. CE, 205.

30. CE, 206.

31. Bergson: "intellect and matter have progressively adapted themselves one to the other in order to attain at last a common form." CE, 206.

32. CE, 206.

33. Ansell-Pearson, *Philosophy and the Adventure of the Virtual*, 117.

34. As Ansell-Pearson puts it, "Instead of ending up with a split between appearance and reality, or between phenomenon and noumenon, we approach epistemological issues in terms of the relation between parts (our partial perspective on the real in accordance

views that are cut out from the moving continuity of the real in accordance with mechanistic principles, for the purpose of action.[35] The Bergsonian approach has interesting similarities with what Thomas Metzinger has recently called the "egotunnel"—a metaphor that he introduces to express that our conscious model of reality is a "low-dimensional projection of the inconceivably richer physical reality surrounding and sustaining us."[36] Metzinger hereby confirms Bergson's evolutionary thesis that our senses have been developed for reasons of survival, and not to adequately depict the "enormous wealth and richness of reality in all its unfathomable depth."[37]

Bergson's evolutionary theory of mind reopens the question of the possibility of metaphysics. As Ansell-Pearson puts it, "Once the understanding is situated within the evolutionary conditions of life it is possible to show how the frames of knowledge . . . can be enlarged and gone beyond."[38] Metaphysics is not the domain that lies *beyond* our experience, but a reality to which we can gain access by transgressing the pragmatic framework into which our cognitive apparatus has evolved. The possibility of metaphysics requires no "special faculty" that radically differs from both consciousness and sensuous experience.[39] Bergson's conception of metaphysics implies that we do not have to go beyond sensory experience:

---

with our vital needs of adaptation) and a mobile whole (the moving continuity of the real)." Ansell-Pearson, *Philosophy and the Adventure of the Virtual*, 117.

35. Bergson: "as for the thing, as intelligence understands it, it is a cutting which has been made out of the becoming and set up by our mind as a substitute for the whole." CM, 22. I will discuss Bergson's holism in further detail in chapter 6.

36. Thomas Metzinger, *The Ego Tunnel: The Science of the Mind and the Myth of the Self* (New York: Basic Books, 2010), 6.

37. Ibid. Metzinger therefore maintains that the "ongoing process of conscious experience" is not so much an "image" or representation of reality as it is a tunnel *through* reality, hence the metaphor of the "egotunnel." An egotunnel is a "consciousness tunnel" with the feature of having evolved the property of creating a "robust first-person perspective," in the sense of a "subjective view of the world' (12).

38. Ansell-Pearson, *Philosophy and the Adventure of the Virtual*, 117.

39. Mullarkey, *Bergson and Philosophy*, 159. As Bergson states in *Matter and Memory*: "Our knowledge of things would thus no longer be relative to the fundamental structure of our mind [my note: as Kant proposes], but only to its superficial and acquired habits, to the contingent form which it derives from our bodily functions and from our lower needs. The relativity of knowledge may not, then, be definitive. By unmaking that which these needs have made, we may restore to intuition its original purity and so recover contact with the real." Henri Bergson, *Matter and Memory* (*Matière et mémoire*, 1896), trans. Nancy Margaret Paul and W. Scott Palmer (1912; repr., Mineola, NY: Dover Publications, 2004) (hereafter MM), 241.

in order to reach intuition it is not necessary to transport ourselves outside the domain of the senses and of consciousness. Kant's error was to believe that it was.[40]

Bergson ends up with a peculiar combination of metaphysics and empiricism. Intuition simply requires a removal of the inhibitions of our perception and memory, which will allow for an extended, deepened, widened experience of reality, an experience that transgresses the pragmatic limitations of our reflective consciousness.[41] Intuition thus exists, in the words of Mullarkey, as the *perception* of metaphysical reality.[42] Intuition is a form of radical empiricism that, instead of "rising above" our perception of things, proposes to "plunge into it" and "insert our will into it," which will "expand our vision of things."[43] Mullarkey compares intuition to a kind of "mind expansion technique" that opens the doors of perception to "altered states of consciousness and experience." Bergson, however, does not resort to drugs to accomplish this, as for instance does Aldous Huxley in *The Doors of Perception* (1954). Bergson considers intuition to be a native resource of the mind, as Mullarkey states, "in an attempt to change our place in reality rather than escape from it. . . . Hence, intuition can act as a resource, the excavation of which can lead to new inventions, art forms, theories and emotions."[44] Bergson's own philosophical works are examples of this, as we will see in the next sections.

Bergson's empirical notion of intuition provides the basis for a metaphysics of duration that turns "traditional" metaphysics on its head: instead of an eternal realm behind a world of fleeting appearances, Bergson will argue that a direct grasp of the whole of reality reveals to us duration and change behind a world that appears to us as stable.

2. THE DISCOVERY OF PURE DURATION

In his early work, Bergson does not yet appeal to intuition as a philosophical method. *Time and Free Will* nevertheless already evokes experience, which becomes clear from the subtitle of the English edition: *An essay on*

---

40. CM, 105.
41. CM, 110.
42. Mullarkey, *Bergson and Philosophy*, 159.
43. CM, 110.
44. Mullarkey, *Bergson and Philosophy*, 160.

the immediate data of consciousness. Bergson's early psychological investigations are founded on an *immediate* experience. This immediacy is, as we have seen, not the same as ordinary experience. It requires an *effort* to transcend the pragmatic framework of our experience in order to investigate the true nature of states of consciousness.[45] This mode of operation reveals something about the nature of time. The mechanistic inclination of our mind tends to immobilize temporal change for pragmatic purposes by confusing time with space. It considers temporal succession as a series of discrete elements placed side by side in homogeneous space. The lived experience of time, however, shows that the true nature of time is *duration*. In *Time and Free Will*, Bergson attempts to explore the nature of this duration in its pure form. He concludes that conscious states are of a fundamentally different nature than material processes and provide us with a radically different temporal regime than matter: "while the material point, as mechanics understands it, remains in an eternal present, the past is a reality perhaps for living bodies, and certainly for conscious beings."[46]

In *Time and Free Will* Bergson turns against the influence of the mechanistic worldview in psychology. At the end of the nineteenth century, experimental psychology was dominated by associationist psychology.[47] The associationist conception of the mind held that there is no difference between a psychological and a physical process and that both are mechanical in nature. This implied that our consciousness is a succession of discrete and causally connected psychological states that are placed side by side in a temporal series.[48] Bergson maintains that while mechanistic theories may be appropriate for understanding material processes, they are unfit for the "realm of life."[49] In *Time and Free Will* Bergson points to the dangers of mechanistic theories of mind. Associationism may lead to psychological determinism and deny the essence of human beings, namely their freedom.

---

45. Bergson certainly does not propose to take the "evidence of experience" as facts. Through the method of intuition he questions the construction of our ordinary experience. Experience is treated not as evidence but as what needs to be explained. This opens up the possibility of a historicization of experience. I will come back to this in the conclusion to this chapter.

46. TFW, 153.

47. Guerlac, *Thinking in Time*, 76–77.

48. Examples of associationist thinkers are John Locke, David Hume, John Stuart Mill, and Bertrand Russell. William G. Barnard, *Living Consciousness: The Metaphysical Vision of Henri Bergson* (Albany: State University of New York Press, 2011), 46.

49. TFW, 153.

The Immediate Data of Consciousness

The first elaboration of duration is based on an investigation of psychological states. In the first chapter of *Time and Free Will* Bergson notes how we tend to regard psychological states as "intensive magnitudes." We think that a psychological state can be measured despite its inextensive nature and that "states of consciousness, sensations, feelings, passions, efforts, are capable of growth and diminution."[50] We are, for instance, inclined to distinguish different *degrees* of anger that relate to one another as "container to contained." According to Bergson, however, it is misleading to translate the qualitative transformations of emotional states into quantitative and measurable units.

One way to make conscious states measurable is by relating the intensity of a sensuous experience to its external causes. Psychophysicists like Gustav Fechner (1801–1887) and Joseph Delboeuf (1831–1896) argued that it is possible to measure the intensity of the sensation of light by the quantity of luminous sources. External factors would therefore allow for a quantitative treatment of a qualitative phenomenon like luminous sensation. A similar argument is, according to Bergson, often brought forward when we think about the color black: "We have grown accustomed, through the combined influence of our past experience and of physical theories, to regard black as the absence, or at least as the minimum, of luminous sensation, and the successive shades of grey as decreasing intensities of white light." But in reality, "black has just as much reality for our consciousness as white."[51]

The attempts by "quantifiers" like the psychophysicists are, according to Bergson, nothing but a mathematical trick which translates qualitative difference, a *difference in kind*, into quantitative difference, a *difference in degree*. But in truth, argues Bergson, "there is no point of contact between the unextended and the extended, between quality and quantity."[52] A conscious state does not increase or decrease, but rather undergoes a succession of changes that result in qualitative differences between, for instance, different *kinds* of anger. This is also illustrated by the supposed increase of an aesthetic sensation. Its increasing intensity in reality consists of *different* feelings. It is "this qualitative progress which we interpret as a change of magnitude, because we like simple thoughts and because our language is ill-suited to render the subtleties of psychological analysis."[53]

---

50. TFW, 1.
51. TFW, 53–54.
52. TFW, 70.
53. TFW, 13.

Bergson argues that the dualism of quantity and quality implies that we can distinguish two different forms of multiplicity. Firstly, there is the *discrete* multiplicity of material objects, which can be expressed numerically; a number always implies space, because it presupposes distinct units that can be counted by placing them side by side in a homogeneous medium. The second form of multiplicity is the continuous or *virtual* multiplicity of states of consciousness, which proceed in time and consist of a *duration*.[54] A numerical interpretation of states of consciousness requires a symbolical representation by our reflective consciousness, by which we "refract" time through space. This basically means that we project the spatial relations of matter onto states of consciousness by placing them side by side in space. Time is now equated with space: "when we speak of time, we generally think of a homogeneous medium in which our conscious states are ranged alongside one another as in space, so as to form a discrete multiplicity."[55] In reality, however, time has nothing to do with space: "time, conceived under the form of a homogeneous medium, is some spurious concept, due to the trespassing of the idea of space upon the field of pure consciousness."[56] Time or duration, the virtual multiplicity of states of consciousness, is according to Bergson an exclusive feature of consciousness and fundamentally differs from the discrete multiplicity of spatial relations in the material world.

The Self, Language, and Consciousness

Bergson argues that our ideas, perceptions, sensations, and emotions occur under two aspects that correspond with two different levels of our personality. There is the *superficial self*, which consists of distinct and well-defined states that are analogous to a discrete multiplicity. The superficial self is clear and precise and adapted to the requirements of social life.[57] Yet the superficial self is merely a shadow of our duration, a projection into homogeneous space ("refraction") of our *fundamental self*, which is a virtual multiplicity of psychical states that melt into one another and that is "confused, ever changing, and inexpressible, because language cannot get hold of it without

---

54. While Bergson uses the term "continuous" multiplicity, Deleuze associates this continuous multiplicity with virtuality. To Deleuze, the virtual is the most important concept of Bergson's philosophy. There will be more on Deleuze's interpretation of Bergsonism as a philosophy of the virtual in chapter 6.
55. TFW, 90.
56. TFW, 98.
57. TFW, 139.

arresting its mobility or fit it into its common-place forms without making it into public property."[58]

Bergson illustrates these two levels of our personality with a description of the impression that an encounter with a new city leaves on us:

> When e.g. I take my first walk in a town in which I am going to live, my environment produces on me two impressions at the same time, one of which is destined to last while the other will constantly change. Every day I perceive the same houses, and as I know that they are the same objects, I always call them by the same name and I also fancy that they always look the same to me. But if I recur, at the end of a sufficiently long period, to the impression which I experienced during the first few years, I am surprised at the remarkable, inexplicable, and indeed inexpressible change which has taken place.[59]

Without realizing it we come to experience the city differently over a period of time. We are not aware of this because our language fixates reality:

> We instinctively tend to solidify our impressions in order to express them in language. Hence we confuse the feeling itself, which is in a perpetual state of becoming, with its permanent external object, and especially with the word which expresses this object.[60]

During our life, the crust of the superficial self that overlays our fundamental self will thicken.[61] This has an important social function, because people would not be able to interact if they would continually have to rephrase and nuance their impressions and experiences. Language reinforces this process of socialization by "fixating" our experiences. This in turn influences the way we experience things: "the word with well-defined outlines, the rough and ready word, which stores up the stable, common, and consequently impersonal element in the impressions of mankind, overwhelms or at least covers over the delicate and fugitive impressions of our individual consciousness."[62]

---

58. TFW, 129. By "public property" Bergson means that through reflection duration is in a way "disowned" and turned from something highly personal into something public. In this way duration loses its particularity.

59. TFW, 129–130.

60. TFW, 130.

61. TFW, 138.

62. TFW, 132.

Deep feelings such as love or melancholy lose their life and color when we try to capture them in words.[63]

During the course of our lives, the fundamental self gradually disappears from sight. We increasingly identify ourselves with the public identity that has formed itself in our contact with the outside world. Our duration is hereby more and more relegated to an unconscious existence. Similar to Freud, Bergson maintains that socialization contributes to the formation of the unconscious. Socialization estranges us from ourselves. It obscures our true identity and makes us lose contact with ourselves.

It is nevertheless possible to regain contact with our lived duration. This can for instance be achieved through art. A poetic use of language that proceeds not through "naming" but by "suggestion" is able to restore contact with our duration.[64] If a "bold novelist" tears aside the "cleverly woven curtain" of our fundamental self and "shows us under this appearance of logic a fundamental absurdity, under this juxtaposition of simple states an infinite permeation of a thousand different impressions which have already ceased to exist the instant they are named, we commend him for having known us better than we knew ourselves."[65] Also the metaphors that Bergson himself frequently employs to designate duration can be seen as tools for articulating his intuitive metaphysics.[66]

Regaining a sense of duration is not reserved only for artists but can also be established through our immediate consciousness. This immediacy does not correspond with our ordinary experience. Bergson emphasizes that it requires an *effort* to go beyond our reflective consciousness in order to grasp duration: "Let us ask consciousness to isolate itself from the external world, and, by a vigorous effort of abstraction, to become itself again."[67] We will initially be confronted with the superficial encrustment of our personality that consists of clear-cut and juxtaposed perceptions and memories, and the motor habits that are bound to these perceptions and memories. Beneath this "superficial congelation," however, we find the virtual multiplicity of our duration:

---

63. Bergson: "This influence of language on sensations is deeper than is usually thought. Not only does language make us believe in the unchangeableness of our sensations, but it will sometimes deceive us as to the nature of the sensation felt." TFW, 131.

64. Guerlac, *Thinking in Time*, 72–73.

65. TFW, 133.

66. Iris van der Tuin, "'A Different Starting Point, a Different Metaphysics': Reading Bergson and Barad Diffractively," *Hypatia* 26 (Winter 2011): 28.

67. TFW, 90–91.

> a flow comparable to no other flowing I have ever seen. It is a succession of states each one of which announces what follows and contains what precedes.[68]

This is a first account of an "extended experience" that Bergson would develop in later works into his method of intuition.

The "effort of abstraction" reveals duration in its pure form. It shows us that the virtual multiplicity of our lived experience of time has nothing to do with space. Instead, pure duration can be compared to music. Succession in music consists not of a series of distinct tones, but of notes that melt into one another: "We can thus conceive of succession without distinction, and think of it as a mutual penetration, an interconnection and organization of elements, each one of which represents the whole, and cannot be distinguished or isolated from it except by abstract thought."[69] When we listen to music, we notice how each note brings about a qualitative change in the musical phrase as a whole. This highlights the most significant aspect of duration, namely a *survival of the past*: "both the past and the present states form an organic whole."[70] While spatial time implies that a new state is a rupture with preceding states, duration is a continuous emergence of unforeseeable novelty *because* the past is prolonged in the present. In chapter 5 I will explore the relevance of the survival of the past for the philosophy of history.

Freedom

A feature of the background to Bergson's intervention in the new science of psychology and his investigation of lived time is the dynamic of industrial modernity. Bergson argues that the advances in science and the process of industrial modernization and mechanization emphasize the natural, geometrical tendency of the reflective consciousness toward spatialization and homogenization. Bergson warns of the dangers of applying the mechanistic principles to the realm of life, for this does not merely produce a misconceived theory of mind but in a broader sense objectifies human beings. Guerlac even argues that "the moral and political consequences of this [mechanistic] perspective were to be viciously played out in the two world wars of the twentieth century."[71]

---

68. CM, 137.
69. TFW, 101.
70. TFW, 100.
71. Guerlac, *Thinking in Time*, 42–43.

The influence of the mechanistic worldview was also felt in psychology. Associationist psychologists maintained that psychological reality could be understood analogously to physical processes, namely by mechanistic explanations, in terms of the elementary movements of molecules or atoms that behaved according to fixed laws, and that answered to the principle of the conservation of energy. The associationists denied the existence of a substantive "self." Instead, they argued that the self consists of a collection of isolated and fragmented mental "atoms" that, like beads on a thread, are associated with each other according to psychological laws. Change consists, according to the associationist logic, merely in a rearrangement of mental atoms that theoretically can return to their original position, which makes creation impossible.[72] Mental processes could be understood in a similar way, as a chain of psychological states that determine one another, so that we can for instance say that a conscious state or action is *caused by* preceding states of consciousness. By reconstructing these causal relations between conscious states, it would even be possible to predict future actions.

Bergson admits that the mechanical logic of cause and effect might be applicable to acts that spring from the superficial self. The superficial self is responsible for the majority of our insignificant, everyday actions that are performed more or less automatically, such as reflexes and habits.[73] Yet freedom is exercised within duration, the "dynamic progress in which the self and its motives, like real living beings, are in a constant state of becoming."[74] These are actions performed by our fundamental self. Bergson's distinction between a superficial self and a fundamental self has interesting parallels with the difference between our "intuitive self" and "conscious and rational self" that Daniel Kahneman makes in his bestselling 2001 book *Thinking, Fast and Slow*.[75] Duration acts as a *creative force* that escapes the law of the conservation

---

72. As Bergson remarks about mechanistic models, "time cannot bite into it; and the instinctive, though vague, belief of mankind in the conservation of a fixed quantity of matter, a fixed quantity of energy, perhaps has its root in the very fact that inert matter does not seem to endure or to preserve any trace of past time." TFW, 152–153.

73. TFW, 168.

74. TFW, 183.

75. In *Thinking, Fast and Slow*, psychologist Daniel Kahneman distinguishes two imaginary individuals (or "systems") in our brain, to account for the dual way in which we think and to highlight how we make our choices. These individuals have their own capabilities and limitations. Most of our thought and actions are generated by the fast, intuitive, and emotional system 1. This individual works fast and automatically, with little or no effort. It constantly generates impressions, associations, intentions, and feelings for system 2, which is our conscious, rational self. While system 1 works fast, system 2 is associated

of energy. In the realm of life, it is therefore absurd to suppose that things can return to their original position and that we can go back to the past: "while the material point, as mechanics understands it, remains in an eternal present, the past is a reality perhaps for living bodies, and certainly for conscious beings."[76]

We act out our freedom at important moments in our lives: "It is at the great and solemn crisis, decisive of our reputation with others, and yet more with ourselves, that we choose in defiance of what is conventionally called a motive, and this absence of any tangible reason is the more striking the deeper our freedom goes."[77] Bergson gives the example of making an important decision. We may receive advice and ideas from friends that little by little form a thick crust that covers up our own sentiments:

> But then, at the very minute when the act is going to be performed, something may revolt against it. It is the deep-seated self rushing up to the surface. It is the outer crust bursting, suddenly giving way to an irresistible thrust. Hence in the depths of the self, below this most reasonable pondering over most reasonable pieces of advice, something else was going on—a gradual heating and a sudden boiling over of feelings and ideas, not unperceived, but rather unnoticed.[78]

The decision springs from a natural evolution that took place at an unconscious level. It is significant that we are often unable to give a reason or a motive for such actions. Free actions spring from the *whole* of our personality, which is the equivalent of the *whole* of our past. This leads to the paradoxical thesis that the extent to which we appeal to the past is what determines our freedom, innovation, and creation.

And yet our reflective consciousness is not equipped to conceive of freedom because it places itself outside of duration. In its reconstruction of an action, it will follow its natural inclination and substitute the dynamic

---

with "slow thought." It monitors system 1 and comprises a conscious attention for mental efforts. Kahneman argues that the two systems constantly interact; while our "experiencing self" (system 1) does the living, the remembering self (system 2) keeps score and makes the choices. Kahneman's distinction may not precisely reflect Bergson's account of the superficial and fundamental self, but it does underwrite the timeliness of Bergson's psychological categories. Daniel Kahneman, *Thinking, Fast and Slow* (New York: Farrar, Straus and Giroux, 2011), 19–30.

76. TFW, 153.

77. TFW, 170.

78. TFW, 169.

process of duration with a material symbol, by translating time into space. Once this reconstruction is completed, it can argue that, given this set of antecedents, the action could not have taken place otherwise and therefore could have been foreseen. But what the determinist forgets here, argues Bergson, is that we can only know the antecedents in retrospect, after the final act was completed. While the act was in the making, it was not yet known, and therefore neither were its antecedents. Bergson concludes that "when we ask whether a future action could have been foreseen, we unwittingly identify that time with which we have to do in the exact sciences, and which is reducible to a number, with real duration, whose so-called quantity is really a quality, and which we cannot curtail by an instant without altering the nature of the facts which fill it."[79]

Duration can only be conceived when we *identify* or *sympathize* with the movement that brings about the free action. The problem is that this identification seems to be inexpressible. Once we try to put this into words we are breaking up the flow of duration, converting what is a virtual multiplicity into a discrete multiplicity and immobilize time by refracting its progress through space. Bergsonian intuition is an attempt to overcome this paradox and to explore the philosophical possibility of *thinking in duration*.

Interestingly, Bergson's analysis of the workings of our reflective consciousness is confirmed by contemporary research in social psychology, which shows that explanations of our actions are often constructed ex post facto. In *Time and Free Will*, Bergson argues that a person who is made to perform certain actions under hypnosis is inclined to fabricate reasons afterwards that explain why he acted the way he did. Social psychologist Timothy Wilson confirms Bergson's thesis. His *Strangers to Ourselves* (2002) investigates the significance for our behavior of the so-called "adaptive unconscious," which he defines as "mental processes that are inaccessible to consciousness but that influence judgments, feelings, or behavior."[80] On the basis of much empirical evidence, Wilson and his colleague Nisbett formulated the thesis that (1) "Many human judgments, emotions, thoughts, and behaviors are produced by the adaptive unconscious" and (2) "Because people do not have conscious access to the adaptive unconscious, their conscious selves confabulate reasons for why they responded the way they did."[81]

---

79. TFW, 197–198.

80. Timothy Wilson, *Strangers to Ourselves: Discovering the Adaptive Unconscious* (Cambridge, MA: The Belknap Press of Harvard University Press, 2002), 23.

81. Ibid., 106. Wilson sees three nineteenth-century theoreticians as "fathers" of the contemporary *adaptive unconscious*: William Hamilton, Thomas Laycock, and William Carpenter. Wilson: "They observed that a good deal of human perception, memory, and action

3. DURATION AS PHILOSOPHY OF LIFE

The meaning of duration radically changes in Bergson's next two important books, *Matter and Memory* (1896) and *Creative Evolution* (1907). Duration develops from a limited, psychological notion into an all-encompassing metaphysical concept in the context of a philosophy of life. The dualism of mind and matter in *Time and Free Will* dissolves into a "dynamic monism" (Čapek) that implies that both mind *and* matter are durational. Duration now is "the very stuff of reality"[82] and in *Creative Evolution* Bergson maintains that "the universe endures."[83]

How should we interpret this shift from psychology to metaphysics and a philosophy of life? Does this represent a radical break within Bergson's oeuvre? There have been a number of theorists who indeed maintain that the metaphysics of duration is inconsistent with psychological duration.[84]

Bergson himself, in any case, certainly did not think that his philosophy contained inherent contradictions. He declared on several occasions that the unifying principle of his philosophy was the *intuition of duration*.[85] A number of theorists have therefore pointed out that the dualism of mind and mat-

---

occurs without conscious deliberation or will, and concluded that there must be 'mental latency' (Hamilton . . .), 'unconscious cerebration' (Carpenter's term), or a 'reflex action of the brain' (Laycock's term)." (10) Bergson seems to have been familiar with the work of Hamilton. In TFW he refers twice to John Stuart Mill's *Examination of Sir Hamilton's Philosophy* (1865), in which Hamilton's conception of consciousness is being discussed.

82. CE, 272.

83. CE, 11.

84. Several interpreters have argued that Bergson's introduction of intuition in 1903 marks a fundamental break within his oeuvre. F.C.T. Moore, for instance, finds the "later" Bergson too speculative. As a "generalized principle of metaphysics," intuition allowed Bergson, according to Moore, to apply his philosophy of duration to *any* subject, including evolution and physics (in *Creative Evolution* (1907) and *Duration and Simultaneity* (1922)). F.C.T. Moore, *Bergson: Thinking Backwards* (Cambridge: Cambridge University Press, 1996), 7. This thesis does disregard, however, that an appeal to "immediate experience" had already formed the basis for Bergson's first work, TFW. In this respect see Jan Bor, *Bergson en de onmiddellijke ervaring* [Bergson and Immediate Experience] (Meppel: Boom, 1990). More than a fundamental break, I would argue that *Introduction to Metaphysics* should therefore be considered as a systematization of an approach that was already implicitly present in Bergson's early work.

85. Hyppolite, "Various Aspects of Memory in Bergson," 112. In MM, 236, Bergson suggests that the dualism of (psychological) duration and matter has to be seen as an abstraction that allowed him to study duration in its pure form.

ter in *Time and Free Will* should be conceived as merely a preparation for Bergson's metaphysics of duration. Gilles Deleuze, for instance, maintains that "the question 'Do external things endure?' remained indeterminate from the standpoint of psychological experience" and that to Bergson, "Psychological duration [was] only a clearly determined case, an opening onto an ontological duration."[86] To Deleuze, the *virtual multiplicity* of duration is for this reason the unifying principle of Bergsonism.

The French philosopher Jean Hyppolite also argues that the presentation of pure duration and pure matter in *Time and Free Will* prepares for the *unification* of these notions in Bergson's later writings. According to Hyppolite, *Time and Free Will* "discovers" duration by an "effort of abstraction" that can be compared to Descartes' discovery of the cogito in the *Meditations*. Pure duration is thereby isolated from space and matter, "with which it is ordinarily mixed." Yet this dualism of mind and matter dissolves when duration is subsequently put back into the world, where it is brought into relation with the concrete material circumstances in which we exercise our freedom.[87] Freedom is now *incarnated*. As Hyppolite puts it, "In *Matter and Memory*, we are no longer considering merely pure and undivided duration, but the relationship of this duration to things; this is why the role of the body is central in it."[88] Absolute freedom, which coincides with pure duration, is impossible in this concrete manifestation. While the pure duration of *Time and Free Will* was far removed from the world, the "incarnated" duration of *Matter and Memory* is described as a "certain measure of indetermination connected to the complexity of an organic system."[89] The focus on organic systems prepares, according to Hyppolite, for the thesis of *Creative Evolution*, namely that life obtained, in the form of the human body, an instrument of freedom from matter.

Metaphysics of Duration

In the fourth chapter of *Matter and Memory*, Bergson exchanges the dualism of mind and matter that was posed in *Time and Free Will* for what Čapek calls a "dynamic monism." While Bergson introduced pure duration in *Time and*

---

86. Deleuze, *Bergsonism*, 48–49.
87. Hyppolite, "Various Aspects of Memory in Bergson", 114–115. *Matter and Memory* deals, according to Hyppolite, with the problem of the *"insertion of our freedom into material being."*
88. Ibid., 115.
89. Ibid., 116.

Free Will by radically opposing psychological duration to material processes, he argues in *Matter and Memory* that matter or extensity taken in itself, that is, independent from space, also has duration.

As in *Time and Free Will*, Bergson again resorts to immediate experience to develop his theory of matter.[90] In *Time and Free Will* Bergson had argued

---

90. I am well aware that the line of argument in this chapter forces me to a limited reading of *Matter and Memory* that does not do justice to the complexity and sophistication of the book. A vital and very original element of *Matter and Memory* is, for instance, Bergson's theory of perception and the body. In the opening line Bergson summarizes the objective of *Matter and Memory* as follows: "This book affirms the reality of spirit and the reality of matter, and tries to determine the relation of the one to the other by the study of a definite example, that of memory." MM, vii. This seems to imply a dualism, but Bergson immediately states that this dualism is different from the more traditional philosophical dualism of realism vs. idealism. In order to reframe the relation between body and mind, Bergson argues that matter is an "aggregate of images." An image is on the one hand "more than that which the idealist calls a *representation*" and on the other hand "less than that which the realist calls a *thing*" (vii) as it is placed halfway between thing and representation. One image has a special meaning for me within the aggregate of images, which is my own body. My body is not a "producer of representations" placed at a distance from the world, but is part of the world, an image that "acts like other images, receiving and giving back movement." (5) The only difference with other images is that my body can withdraw itself from the lawlike manner according to which images interact; it can "choose, within certain limits" and thereby "add something new to the universe and to its history." The operations of my body as "centre of action" within the world are "probably suggested to it by the greater or less advantage which it can derive from the surrounding images," and therefore the images that surround my body display those aspects from which my body can profit. In other words, while matter is an aggregate of images the *perception* of matter is "*these same images referred to the eventual action of one particular image, my body.*" (8) This means that perception in its pure form coincides with the world as aggregate of images, and hence that there is no dualism of mind and body. Yet pure perception is purely theoretical; concrete perception adopts my body as its center and limits itself in relation to the body's double faculty of performing actions and feeling affections. I do not perceive the whole of reality, but only the real to the extent that it is relevant to me. This explains that there are pragmatic limitations to my perception—limitations that, in accordance with the theory of perception, can be overcome through intuition. This also explains Bergson's interest in "psychical phenomena" such as telepathy, which he saw as states of perception that transgress the pragmatic boundaries of concrete perception. Psychical phenomena could serve as empirical evidence for his theory of intuition. Concrete perceptions are supplemented by memory. It is the actualization of memory-images from pure memory that gives us our freedom and the ability to bring about the new through our actions (Bergson's theory of memory will be discussed in chapter 5). Concrete perception is therefore always located between a hypothetical pure present (pure perception) and a hypothetical pure past (pure memory). This leads to an intermediate position between realism and idealism. The dualism of mind and body should

that freedom can only be conceived by replacing ourselves in duration, and in *Matter and Memory* he asks, "Is a method of this kind applicable to the problem of matter?"[91] Can we seize the durational tendency in matter, in a similar way to how we can bring ourselves back to pure duration? Hereto matter, or, *extensity*, will have to be detached from homogeneous space. Bergson considers geometrical space as merely a symbolic "mental diagram" by which we organize extensity in support of action.[92] Space has the characteristic that it can be subdivided indefinitely, figures can be carved out from it arbitrarily, and movement can only appear in it as a "multiplicity of instantaneous positions."[93]

The mental diagram of space distorts our view of extensity. This diagram can, however, be pushed aside. By means of *immediate knowledge* or *intuition* it is possible to transcend space "without stepping out from extensity."[94] We have to place ourselves at the "*turn* of experience"—a point before our immediate experience is "reduced" to what is useful in it.[95] Thus we may "restore to intuition its original purity and so recover contact with the real."[96] Immediate knowledge shows us that many difficulties, problems, and contradictions that have haunted philosophy "are mainly the result of the symbolic diagrams which cover it up, diagrams which have for us become reality itself, and beyond which only an intense and unusual effort can succeed in penetrating."[97] This also holds, as we will see, for the dualism of mind and matter.

Bergson draws four conclusions from the intuition of matter:

---

be conceived not in "spatial" terms but in duration: "*Questions relating subject and object, to their distinction and their union, should be put in terms of time rather than of space.*" (77) This opens up the possibility of an ontology based on a multiplicity of *rhythms of duration*.

91. MM, 244.

92. Bergson: "Such is the primary and the most apparent operation of the perceiving mind: it marks out divisions in the continuity of the extended, simply following the suggestions of our requirement and the needs of practical life. But, in order to divide the real in this manner, we must first persuade ourselves that the real is divisible at will. Consequently, we must throw beneath the continuity of sensible qualities, that is to say, beneath concrete extensity, a network, of which the meshes may be altered to any shape whatsoever and become as small as we please: this substratum which is merely conceived, this wholly ideal diagram of arbitrary and infinite divisibility, is homogeneous space." MM, 278.

93. MM, 245.

94. MM, 245.

95. MM, 241.

96. MM, 241.

97. MM, 245.

I. "Every movement, in as much as it is a passage from rest to rest, is absolutely indivisible."[98] Bergson argues that the mixture of space and duration produces false philosophical problems. An example Bergson mentions repeatedly are the paradoxes formulated by Zeno of Elea in the fifth century B.C. One of these paradoxes describes a race between Achilles and the tortoise, and states that Achilles will never overtake the tortoise he races because each time he arrives at the point where the tortoise was moments before, the tortoise will already have moved further. According to Bergson, the confusion here is that we equate the movements of Achilles and the tortoise to the space that is traversed. But, asks Bergson, "how can something moving coincide with something immobile?" Achilles and the tortoise would only "be" at a certain point in space when they would stop, but then we would no longer be dealing with their movements. Bergson argues that the solution to the paradox is given to us by our immediate intuition of movement, which teaches us that movements in themselves are indivisible and do not coincide with the points that are traversed in an underlying space.

II. Therefore, "there are *real* movements."[99] As the example of Achilles has shown, movement is a concrete and *absolute* reality. Movement cannot be treated symbolically in, for instance, mathematical terms, because such a mathematical approach treats movement as *relative* to underlying homogeneous space. Bergson sympathizes more with the physicist's perspective, which is concerned with concrete changes occurring in the *whole* of the universe.[100] In order to conceive of absolute movement, it is necessary to let go of the view of matter as a discontinuity of distinct and independent objects, because this leads us only to relative change: we have to approach change in the *whole* of matter. We catch a glimpse here of the holistic nature of Bergson's philosophy of duration, which I will explore in further detail in chapter 6.

III. Hence the third conclusion: "All division of matter into independent bodies with absolutely determined outlines is an artifi-

---

98. MM, 246.
99. MM, 254.
100. MM, 254.

cial division."[101] Immediate intuition shows us material extensity as a moving continuity, "in which everything changes and yet remains."[102] It is the requirements of *life* that create the "irresistible tendency to set up a material universe that is discontinuous, composed of bodies which have clearly defined outlines and change their place, that is, their relation with each other. . . . Our needs are, then, so many search-lights which, directed upon the continuity of sensible qualities, single out in it distinct bodies."[103] Theories of matter that regard atoms as the elementary particles of matter are the result of the practical inclination of our mind. Bergson points to the latest developments in nineteenth-century physics, which show that "beyond" the atom are lines of force, tension, and energy.[104] He finds it telling that this image corresponds with our immediate intuition: matter has the characteristics of movement, matter is a "flow."[105] Montebello and Lapidus point out that Bergson's conception of matter has been influenced by the scientific developments of his time.[106] Already in the 1860s, electromagnetic physics suggested that matter was not made up of solid bodies, but of "waves and light, indivisible energy and continuous flow."[107]

---

101. MM, 259.

102. MM, 260.

103. MM, 260–262.

104. MM, 265–266.

105. Milič Čapek points out that Bergson's theory of matter was often ignored by his contemporaries, and he attributes this to its revolutionary character. In 1896, the year when *Matter and Memory* was published, the "classical corpuscular-kinetic view of nature" still remained unchallenged: "The view that matter and its spatio-temporal framework eventually would be stripped of their classical, mechanistic features, which yielded so easily to pictorial models, was at that time looming on a very distant horizon, indeed—and only in a few and heretically daring minds." According to Čapek, Bergson anticipated the general direction which science would follow in the subsequent decades, because he had "an unusual insight into the inadequacies of the accepted conceptual scheme." Čapek, *Bergson and Modern Physics*, x–xi.

106. Montebello and Lapidus write, "Although it wasn't until 1924 that particles of matter such as electrons were also considered as possessing wave-like properties, and people began to speak of waves of matter, as early as the 1860s, atomic matter was considered to dissolve into immaterial fields of force." Pierre Montebello and Roxanne Lapidus, "Matter and light in Bergson's 'Creative Evolution,'" *SubStance* 36 (2007): 93.

107. Ibid.

IV. "Real movement is rather the transference of a state than of a thing."[108] With this thesis Bergson attacks the mechanical conception of movement. Movement should not be conceived from the point of view of objects placed in homogeneous space that has movement added to it. By arguing that matter equals movement, and after having claimed that movement is a qualitative process in itself, Bergson can conclude that matter, like consciousness, is durational. This is decisive for transcending the dualism of mind and matter.[109]

With these conclusions Bergson has revised the commonsense notion of matter as a collection of objects placed in homogeneous space. Extensity in itself, not refracted through space, is in reality movement and therefore has duration.[110] The movements of matter are analogous to the continuity of psychological duration, and for this reason we can obtain a vision of the true nature of extensity through immediate intuition: "try first to connect together the discontinuous objects of daily experience; then resolve the motionless continuity of their qualities into vibrations on the spot; finally fix your attention on these movements, by abstracting from the divisible space which underlies them and considering only their mobility (that undivided act which our consciousness becomes aware of in our own movements): you will thus obtain a vision of matter, fatiguing perhaps for your imagination, but pure, and freed from all that the exigencies of life compel you to add to it in external perception."[111]

Bergson argues that many of modern philosophy's controversies, such as that between materialism and idealism, result from a mistaken metaphysical dualism of mind and matter. While materialists subordinate the mind to matter and the idealists hold the reverse position, Bergson can now argue that mind and matter are united in that they are *both* durational in nature. The difference between mind and matter amounts to different *rhythms of duration*: "In reality there is no one rhythm of duration; it is possible to imagine many different rhythms which, slower or faster, measure the degree of tension or

---

108. MM, 267.

109. Guerlac formulates it enthusiastically: "Bergson now implies that the heterogeneity he identified with duration in the Essai (and limited to consciousness and to the inner experience of sensation) pertains to matter itself!" Guerlac, *Thinking in Time*, 163.

110. Bergson: "Matter thus resolves itself into numberless vibrations, all linked together in uninterrupted continuity, all bound up with each other, and travelling in every direction like shivers through an immense body." MM, 276.

111. MM, 276–277.

relaxation of different kinds of consciousness, and thereby fix their respective places in the scale of being."[112] These rhythms are a kind of pulsation with which the past prolongs itself in the present. Matter or extensity on the one hand, and mind and consciousness on the other, are on a scale of increasing tension. Bergson thus replaces the metaphysical dualism of mind and matter by a dualism of matter and *memory*. Bergson's theory of memory will be discussed in greater detail in the next chapter.

Now that Bergson has established extensity as duration, the implication is that matter has a rudimentary form of memory of its own. This memory, however, amounts to a *repetition* of the past, and for this reason physical processes are not creative but predictable: "To reply, to an action received, by an immediate reaction which adopts the rhythm of the first and continues it in the same direction, to be in a present and in a present that is always beginning again,—this is the fundamental law of matter: herein consists *necessity*."[113] Past and future of matter are given in the here and now and the physical world therefore answers to natural laws.

Higher on the "scale of being" we find durations with higher tensions. These durations are able to free themselves from necessity because of the extent to which the past prolongs itself in the present.[114] The human mind, for instance, is able to bring about change and novelty and a change in the rhythm of duration because of the input of memory. Hence it is the participation of the past that makes up the difference between mind and matter/extensity. As the share of the past increases, freedom, which is the change that is brought about within a lawful reality, also increases. As Guerlac writes, "Freedom implies a change in rhythm from the rhythm of matter."[115]

Simultaneously, however, Bergson emphasizes that the solidification of the real, which is brought about by our perceptual apparatus by means of a refraction of duration through space, is a necessary prerequisite for free action. In order to establish real changes, an act of *Verdinglichung*—the act of "making something into a thing"—is a necessary precondition:

> Homogeneous space and homogeneous time are then neither properties of things nor essential conditions of our faculty of knowing them: they express, in an abstract form, the double work of solidification and of division which we effect on the moving

---

112. MM, 275.
113. MM, 279.
114. MM, 279.
115. Guerlac, *Thinking in Time*, 164.

continuity of the real in order to obtain there a fulcrum for our action, in order to fix within it starting-points for our operation, in short, to introduce into it real changes. They are the diagrammatic design of our eventual action upon matter.[116]

The Élan Vital

In *Matter and Memory* Bergson cleared the way for a broader application of the concept of duration, and thereby for the introduction of a notion of creative time in the sciences of life. By showing that duration pertains not only to the human mind but also to matter, Bergson can declare in *Creative Evolution* that "the universe endures"[117] and that within the universe it is "life" that brings about creative change, because only in the living the past survives.[118] Life inserts freedom in material necessity.[119] The evolution of a living being, according to Bergson, "implies a continual recording of duration, a persistence of the past in the present, and so an appearance, at least, of organic memory."[120] As in conscious states, the evolution of life has also to be understood from "*all* the past of the organism . . . its heredity—in fact the whole of a very long history."[121]

In *Creative Evolution* Bergson wants to approach "life in general" as a concrete fact instead of an abstract concept that would encompass all kinds of life-forms. An organism (plant, animal, or human) is, according to Bergson, "an excrescence, a bud"[122] of an underlying *élan vital*, which is the continuous progress of "a current passing from germ to germ through the medium of a developed organism."[123] Bergson constantly equates the duration of evolution with psychological duration: "the more we fix our attention on this continuity of life, the more we see that organic evolution resembles the evolution of a consciousness, in which the past presses against the present

---

116. MM, 280.

117. CE, 11.

118. Bergson: "Wherever anything lives, there is, open somewhere, a register in which time is being inscribed." CE, 16.

119. Wahida Khandker, "The Idea of Will and Organic Evolution in Bergson's Philosophy of Life," *Continental Philosophy Review* 46 (2013): 58.

120. CE, 19.

121. CE, 20.

122. CE, 27.

123. CE, 27.

and causes the upspringing of a new form of consciousness, incommensurable with its antecedents."[124]

The notion of the *élan vital* has given rise to many misinterpretations of Bergson's philosophy. It gave him the name of being a vitalist who proclaimed the existence of an immaterial "life force" that drives the evolution of species forward. The *élan vital*, however, does not refer to some mysterious "vital fluid." The analogy with psychological duration emphasizes, as Mullarkey points out, that the *élan vital* presents us first and foremost with a mode of *time*, and only secondarily with a theory of life. By means of the image of the *élan vital* Bergson introduces "a philosophy of creative time into the science of life."[125]

The *élan vital* is therefore an analogy that allows Bergson to think about life.[126] It has the character of a hypothesis but has its basis in immediate experience.[127] In a later work, *The Two Sources of Morality and Religion* (1932), Bergson emphasizes "the distinctly empirical character of our conception of the 'vital impetus.' "[128] The image of the *élan vital* can, according to Bergson, account for a number of empirical facts that mechanistic explanations of evolution have been unable to explain. The *élan vital* is in this sense a product of Bergson's method of "true empiricism," which he would develop into his method of intuition.[129] Bergson maintains that we can apply our intuition to the "facts of life" because there is a fundamental similarity between the duration of life and our consciousness. As Bergson expresses it in a lecture from 1908: "One of the objects of Creative Evolution is to show that All is . . . of the same nature as the I, and that one grasps it by a more and more complete immersion in oneself."[130] In *Creative Evolution* Bergson ultimately thinks of life as consciousness, and thereby also transforms

---

124. CE, 27.

125. Mullarkey, *Bergson and Philosophy*, 63.

126. The *élan vital* is an analogy, as Ansell-Pearson points out. According to Bergson, life can only be thought *analogically*. Ansell-Pearson, *Philosophy and the Adventure of the Virtual*, 137.

127. See CE, 54 and 87.

128. Henri Bergson, *The Two Sources of Morality and Religion* (*Les Deux sources de la morale et de la religion*, 1932), trans. R. Ashley Audra and Cloudesley Brereton (1935; repr., Notre Dame, IN: University of Notre Dame Press, 2006) (hereafter TS), 112.

129. As Ansell-Pearson states, "Bergson's effort [is] to cultivate a 'superior' empiricism. It exists to remind us of our ignorance and to encourage us to go further with our inquiry into the real free[dom] of pre-formed ideas and immediate intuitions." Ansell-Pearson, *Philosophy and the Adventure of the Virtual*, 139.

130. ML, 774. Cited in Montebello and Lapidus, "Matter and light," 91.

our understanding of individual human consciousness, by placing it at the periphery of organic evolution.[131]

By introducing a notion of creative time in the science of life, Bergson resists both mechanistic and finalistic theories of evolution that had been developed since Darwin's *The Origin of Species* (1859). According to Bergson, radical mechanism assumes that time has no efficacy. It "implies a metaphysic in which the totality of the real is postulated complete in eternity, and in which the apparent duration of things expresses merely the infirmity of a mind that cannot know everything at once."[132] The mechanists make the same mistake as the determinists with regard to free will. They reconstruct the evolutionary process with "fragments of the evolved" and thereby treat evolution as analogous to the way in which a machine is built up, namely as an association of parts that is brought about by external circumstances.[133]

Although Elizabeth Grosz has recently pointed to the similarities between the conceptions of life, evolution, and becoming in the work of Darwin and Bergson, Bergson himself saw Darwinism as an example of such a mechanistic theory of evolution.[134] In Bergson's eyes, Darwin presented evolution as a mechanical process of natural selection, a series of accidental variations of which those that were best adapted to the natural environment would survive.[135] Bergson argues, however, that Darwin's idea of accidental variation cannot explain why the same organs have developed in parallel lines of evolution. A complex organ like the eye, for instance, has developed in an identical manner in both humans and animals. Bergson writes:

> An accumulation of accidental variations . . . requires therefore the concurrence of an almost infinite number of infinitesimal causes. Why should these causes, entirely accidental, recur the same, and in the same order, at different points of space and time?[136]

---

131. Khandker, "The Idea of Will and Organic Evolution," 59.

132. CE, 39.

133. CE, 88.

134. Grosz points out that, like Bergson and Nietzsche, Darwin also links life to the movement of time. In Darwin's work, Grosz argues, "life is now understood, perhaps for the first time in the sciences, as fundamental becoming, becoming in every detail. Darwin makes it clear, indeed a founding presupposition, that time, along with life itself, always moves forward, generates more rather than less complexity, produces divergences rather than convergences, variations rather than resemblances." Elizabeth Grosz, *The Nick of Time: Politics, Evolution and the Untimely* (Sydney: Allen and Unwin, 2004), 7.

135. Kolakowski, *Bergson*, 80.

136. CE, 56.

Examples such as that of the eye suggest that there is a *directionality* in evolution. These directions cannot be merely explained with reference to external conditions that serve as mechanical "causes." Experience teaches us that they are only accounted for by the hypothesis of an "inward impulse" that "passes from germ to germ through individuals, that carries life in a given direction, towards an ever higher complexity."[137]

This directionality nonetheless does not imply that evolution is a teleological process. Bergson can agree with finalistic theories of evolution like vitalism, to the extent that these maintain that evolution is driven by a directional tendency, but he finds the finalistic thesis that evolution is the unfolding of a predestined plan to be unacceptable. This notion of a predestined plan is, according to Bergson, nothing but an inverted mechanism, because it adopts the mechanistic hypothesis that "*all is given.*"[138] But when all is given, "if there is nothing unforeseen, no invention or creation in the universe, time is useless again."[139] There would merely be an ordering and reordering of parts, that leaves no space for true change and the creation of new forms.[140]

The development of the eye can, according to Bergson, only be explained by the hypothesis of an "original impetus"—an *élan vital*—that moves life forward. What strikes us with regard to the eye is the contrast between, on the one hand, the *complexity* of its structure and on the other the *simplicity* of its function:

> The mechanism of the eye is, in short, composed of an infinity of mechanisms, all of extreme complexity. Yet vision is one simple fact.[141]

But while the *simplicity* belongs to the eye itself, its *complexity* is dependent on the external views that we take on it.[142] As Bergson concludes, "the eye, with its marvelous complexity of structure, may be only the simple act of

---

137. TS, 113. Ansell-Pearson points out, however, that "other explanations of convergent evolution are equally, if not more, credible." Ansell-Pearson, *Philosophy and the Adventure of the Virtual*, 135.

138. CE, 39.

139. CE, 39.

140. Bergson's time-philosophy emphasizes, "as always," according to Mullarkey "the unforeseeable and indeterminate creation of novelty, and this [is] no less true in his application of that theory to evolution." Mullarkey, *Bergson and Philosophy*, 63.

141. CE, 88.

142. CE, 89.

vision, divided *for us* into a mosaic of cells, whose order seems marvelous to us because we have conceived the whole as an assemblage."[143] It is merely our external, mechanistic perspective that represents the evolution of an organ such as the eye as a machine of enormous complexity made up of a multiplicity of parts.

We can only properly understand evolution when we start to "think in duration" by relying on our immediate intuition. This will teach us that the evolution of an organism is a simple and *indivisible* movement. Bergson says, "Nature has had no more trouble in making an eye than I have in lifting my hand."[144] Yet in reality the evolutionary movement does meet with resistance, because it has to bring about change within organic matter. Bergson compares the process by which nature constructs the eye with the movement of a hand through compressed iron filings that offer resistance proportionately as the hand goes forward. At a certain moment the hand will have exhausted its movement and the iron filings will be arranged in a certain way. Now suppose that the hand were invisible. Spectators would then look for the reason of the arrangement in the filings themselves. The mechanists "will account for the position of each filing by the action exerted upon it by the neighboring filings,"[145] while finalists "will prefer to think that a plan of the whole has presided over the detail of these elementary actions."[146] But the truth is that there was merely the simple and indivisible act of the hand that passed through the filings.[147] The relation of vision to the visual apparatus is analogous to this example: "According as the undivided act constituting vision advances more or less, the materiality of the organ is made of a more or less considerable number of mutually coordinated elements, but the order is necessarily complete and perfect."[148]

This analogy also underlines that evolution is not an association of separate parts into wholes. Evolution has to be considered as a whole, instead of a collection of parts: "The whole of the effect is explained by the whole of the cause, but to parts of the cause parts of the effect will in no way correspond."[149] Life itself operates as a "special cause" on matter and the

---

143. CE, 90.
144. CE, 91.
145. CE, 94.
146. CE, 94.
147. CE, 94.
148. CE, 95.
149. CE, 94.

coordination of the parts will remain a mystery as long as we reconstruct evolution in terms of an association of parts. By simply looking at the way in which an embryo develops, we become aware that life proceeds not by association and addition of parts like human technology, but by dissociation and division of unities that were also themselves a product of previous dissociations and divisions.[150] Life is, as Mullarkey puts it, "an ongoing creation formed through the cascading dissolution of earlier, provisional and relative unities."[151]

Evolution is not a gradual and continuous process, as for instance the metaphor of the "tree of life" suggests. Such an image is merely the result of a retrospective reading that projects the evolutionary process into homogeneous space and time and which eliminates real duration. Instead, Bergson compares the dissociation and division of life to an exploding shell, "which suddenly bursts into fragments, which fragments, being themselves shells, burst in their turn into fragments destined to burst again, and so on for a time incommensurably long."[152] The movement of evolution is not continuous because the course of the *élan vital* is determined by two contradictory tendencies. We can see this occurring in the exploding shells that break into fragments because the explosive force of the powder is resisted by the metal of the shell. In a similar way "life breaks into individuals and species"[153] because the *creative* tendency of life, the *élan vital*, is resisted by the opposite tendency of matter toward *repetition*.[154] Organisms are therefore "unstable unities," because they are the material manifestation of a tension of two opposing tendencies.[155] Mullarkey characterizes these tendencies as "modes of movement," that are "nothing more substantial than time itself."[156]

---

150. CE, 89.

151. Mullarkey, *Bergson and Philosophy*, 64.

152. CE, 98.

153. CE, 98.

154. Life "strives to introduce into [matter] the largest possible amount of indetermination and liberty" CE, 251.

155. According to Mullarkey such an image corresponds with the contemporary understanding of living organisms as "far-from-equilibrium dissipative structures." Mullarkey, *Bergson and Philosophy*, 66.

156. Ibid. Bergson: "In reality, life is a movement, materiality is the inverse movement, and each of these two movements is simple, the matter which forms a world being an undivided flux, and undivided also the life that runs through it, cutting out in it living beings all along its track." CE, 249.

The "explosion" of the shells shows that, because of the resistance of matter, these organic forms are created by *discontinuous* leaps.[157] It is like the sudden movement of the hand that plunges into the iron filings and that causes an instantaneous readjustment.[158] The hypothesis of the *élan vital* reveals that adaptation is in fact a response of life to *problems* that are set by external, material conditions.[159]

We must distinguish the opposite *tendencies*—of life toward creation and of matter toward repetition—from *actual* living and material forms.[160] Mullarkey stresses that there are two different types of life and matter: virtual and actual. On an actual level matter is external to life, while on a virtual level matter and life imply one other. Actualized life is life in its *organic form*, while life as a *virtual potentiality* has to be conceived as a "type of organization." The same goes for matter, which in its actual form constitutes the *obstacles that resist actual life*, while matter in a virtual and unrealized state consists of a *tendency* that is internal to life as a principle of organization. As Mullarkey explains, "the actual forms of both life and matter are dissociated from each other and cause further dissociations, but the virtual forms are held together in a tension that is confusingly also called life or *élan vital*."[161] As virtual tendencies, matter and life make up the *élan vital*, which works on the actualized forms of life and matter.[162]

---

157. The *discontinuity* of creation contrasts with the *continuity* of pure duration that Bergson established in TFW. The obvious difference between evolution and the pure duration of psychological states, however, is that the duration of evolution is no longer *pure*, but deals with the *real and effective* duration that is essential for life—in other words, it has to realize itself within the opposing tendency towards repetition of matter. This highlights that pure duration is merely an abstraction, an ideal type that had to be established before Bergson could investigate duration in its concrete manifestations in, for instance, *Matter and Memory* and *Creative Evolution*.

158. TS, 116.

159. TS, 113.

160. Life's movement of dissociation is what Mullarkey calls the "condition of possibility" of any organic form. These tendencies are contained within life as a type of organization that is the condition of possibility of evolution.

161. Mullarkey, *Bergson and Philosophy*, 81. Ansell-Pearson makes a similar point: "It is as if Bergson is asking us to think on two different planes, equally real, at one and the same time: on the plane of a pure virtual in which the tendencies of life have not yet been actualized and so exist in terms of an intensive fold (a monism): and on the plane of an actualization in which there are only divergent lines with forms of life, such as animal and plant, becoming closed on themselves, constituting an unlimited pluralism." Ansell-Pearson, *Philosophy and the Adventure of the Virtual*, 96.

162. The virtual will be further explored in chapter 6, where I will interpret Bergson's philosophy of life as a nonmodern form of historicism.

Instinct, Intellect, and Intuition

The *élan vital* forms the basis for an evolutionary epistemology. This makes clear that intuition is derived from Bergson's philosophy of duration. Bergson's theory of life highlights how intuition allows us to gain contact with other durations. Life has developed into three main "directions," namely toward plant life, instinct (animals), and intelligence (humans). These lines do not differ in *degree*, in the sense that humans are "higher developed animals," but emphasize different tendencies of one and the same original vital impetus. Because life proceeds by dissociation and division, we may assume that these lines of evolution have emerged by dissociation from a simple reality, an original impetus, in which both movements were virtually contained. This common origin implies that the characteristics of the other tendencies of life are, in a latent and rudimentary form, also present in other lines of evolution. Animal instinct, for instance, is perceptible in man as the soft flickering of intuition.

The first important bifurcation in evolution has been, according to Bergson, that between plants and animals. Plants directed themselves to the conservation of energy from the sun, by forming organic matter from the inorganic. This dismissed them from the necessity of movement and feeling, and caused consciousness to die out in plants. Animals, on the other hand, developed in the direction of an increasing mobility, because the energy that the animal obtained from plants was transformed in explosive movements.

Furthermore, the animals fell apart in two different tendencies, one toward instinct and one toward intelligence, because both could not be intensified in one and the same species. Intelligence and instinct have a practical function and are therefore defined by Bergson in terms of the use and fabrication of instruments. Intelligence is directed to the use and fabrication of artificial instruments, while instinct is tied up with the use and fabrication of organic instruments, that is, instruments that form part of the organism itself. They are both, according to Bergson, different solutions for one and the same problem, namely, how to overcome the resistance of the material tendency toward repetition. But there is also an important difference. The organic instrument of the animal has a specific and specialized function and implies a spontaneous, immediate action on matter. Because there is no moment of choice or doubt, consciousness is not, or is hardly, developed in animals. This is different for intelligence, which is designed for the construction of artificial instruments. As these can be constructed at will for a variety of purposes, human beings have been able to control their material environment. Human development is no longer determined by problems that contingently arise from its natural environment. Instead, human beings can take their evolution into their own hands by constructing and solving their own problems.

The development of consciousness in the form of the intellect has provided human beings with an unprecedented mobility. Only in humans has consciousness succeeded in overcoming the limitations of matter. The difference between consciousness in humans and animals is described by Bergson as follows (italics added):

> Now, in the animal, invention is never anything but a variation on the theme of routine. Shut up in the habits of the species, it succeeds, no doubt, in enlarging them by its individual initiative; but it escapes automatism only for an instant, for just the time to create a new automatism. The gates of its prison close as soon as they are opened; by pulling at its chain it succeeds only in stretching it. With man, consciousness breaks the chain. In man, and in man alone, it sets itself free. *The whole history of life* until man has been that of the effort of consciousness to raise matter, and of the more or less complete overwhelming of consciousness by the matter which has fallen back on it.[163]

We already see here that "history" is to Bergson limited not only to "human history" as the modern connotation of the term prescribes, but to the history of life as a whole.[164]

In humans, consciousness has succeeded in escaping the "prison house" of matter by turning the same matter into an "instrument of freedom," one that prevails over the determinism of nature. Consciousness has given humans the possibility of free choice, free from the regularity to which other organisms are condemned. The evolutionary lines of plants and animals have been useful companions to humanity, in which the *élan vital* could dispose of surplus. In humans the creative tendency of the *élan vital* has been able to realize itself, and in this sense humanity is, according to Bergson, the crown of creation. While consciousness in plants and animals has been canalized in the laws of matter, the creative tendency of life is boundlessly continued in humans. In this regard freedom—that is, freedom from determinism and lawfulness—is the essence of humanity. And this freedom or creativity increases the more the past is incorporated in the present.

In order to wrest itself from matter, human consciousness also had to pay a price: it is dominated by intelligence, which has no eye for the living.

---

163. CE, 264.

164. In chapters 5 and 6 I address how Bergson reconceptualizes the modern concept of history.

Because of its practical function, the intellect provides us with not pure but useful knowledge of reality. Bergson describes this as follows:

> Harnessed, like yoked oxen, to a heavy task, we feel the play of our muscles and joints, the weight of the plow and the resistance of the soil. To act and to know that we are acting, to come into touch with reality and even to live it, but only in the measure in which it concerns the work that is being accomplished and the furrow that is being plowed, such is the function of human intelligence.[165]

Intelligence has enabled human beings to control their material environment, yet because intelligence is directed at matter, the intellect has also been formed after matter. In the course of evolution, "intellect and matter have progressively adapted themselves one to the other in order to attain at last a common form."[166] For this reason, the intellect only feels at home in "the given," that which has already been created, and disregards the creative aspect of reality. It is impossible for humans to have an intellectual understanding of the creative movement of life.

It is nevertheless still possible to gain contact with the living, namely when humans make use of intuition. Intuition is what is left in human beings from a primordial form of instinct. This intuition is, according to Bergson,

> a lamp almost extinguished, which only glimmers now and then, for a few moments at most. But it glimmers wherever a vital interest is at stake. On our personality, on our liberty, on the place we occupy in the whole of nature, on our origin and perhaps also on our destiny, it throws a light feeble and vacillating, but which none the less pierces the darkness of the night in which the intellect leaves us.[167]

Intuition moves in the opposite direction of the intellect. It unites us with what we are experiencing. As Eric Matthews writes, intuition "installs itself in that which is moving and adopts the very life of things."[168] We hereby coincide with what is unique in our experience.

---

165. CE, 191.
166. CE, 206.
167. CE, 267–268.
168. Bergson, cited in Eric Matthews, "Bergson's Concept of a Person," in *The New Bergson*, ed. John Mullarkey (Manchester: Manchester University Press, 1999), 121.

Intellect and intuition are each other's opposites, because they are both extensions of opposite tendencies: "Intuition and intellect represent two opposite directions of the work of consciousness: intuition goes in the very direction of life, intellect goes in the reverse direction, and thus finds itself naturally in accordance with the movement of matter."[169]

Bergson maintains that philosophers like Kant have often failed to take the evolutionary background of the intellect into account, because they tend to accept the intellect as a "given." They have therefore assumed that the intellect potentially encompasses all that can be known of reality. According to Bergson, however, the intellect has to be completed by intuition. The objective of *Creative Evolution* is, as Bergson points out in its introduction, to connect a theory of knowledge with a theory of life. Both are inseparable and "should join each other, and, by a circular process, push each other on unceasingly."[170] Bergson sees it as the task of philosophy to furnish a theory of life by appropriating the flickerings of intuition, maintaining them, extending them, and reconnecting them. Thus, an intuitive philosophy has to provide a continuation of the intellectual knowledge of science by "the study of becoming in general."[171]

As Jan Bor points out, the call for the development of intuition is, to Bergson, a way in which human evolution can be continued. This call should be understood not as a plea to return to an instinctive way of life, as Russell maintained, but as an attempt to raise instinct to the level of conscious and reflective thought. To Bergson, intuition as method is a way of "thinking in duration" that is complementary to intellectual knowledge. As philosophical method, intuition should accomplish, as Bor points out, a fusion of intellect and instinct that is tuned toward duration.[172]

4. CONCLUSION

In a critique of Bergsonian duration, Max Horkheimer argues that Bergson imagines himself to be "independent from time" because he adheres to a *metaphysics* of time. Horkheimer finds that Bergson does not take sufficient account of the historical context from which his own ideas arise. Bergson

---

169. CE, 267.

170. CE, xiii.

171. CE, 370.

172. Bor, *Bergson en de onmiddellijke ervaring*, 198.

fails, according to Horkheimer, to take into account that his metaphysics, like any metaphysical system, depends on specific historical conditions and exerts a social function. By implying that every epoch coincides with an "eternal creative power," Bergson merely provided an ideological justification for the ruling state of affairs.[173] Walter Benjamin has also contended that Bergson manages "to stay clear of that experience from which his own philosophy evolved or, rather, in reaction to which it arose," namely that of the "inhospitable, blinding age of big-scale industrialism."[174]

I have argued in this chapter, however, that Bergson's metaphysics does not imply an adherence to eternal metaphysical truths. Just as the universe is not a completed "system of reality," philosophical thought itself is also, according to Bergson, a becoming that should be radically non-systematic. There is, as Mullarkey points out, a "connection between content and expression"[175] in Bergsonism, because Bergson bases his metaphysics on experience, or,

---

173. Horkheimer: "The attempt to produce a philosophy of concrete time that is to comprehend reality not as something fixed in itself, only in time, extending to the 'fourth dimension of space,' but rather as itself development, transformation and change, while at the same time to abandon human history: this undertaking had to fail." Horkheimer, "On Bergson's metaphysics of time," 13.

174. Walter Benjamin, "On Some Motifs in Baudelaire," in *Charles Baudelaire: A Lyric Poet in the Era of High Modernism*, trans. Harry Zohn (London: Verso, 1997), 111. In this text—which is one of the few that relate Bergson to history—Benjamin discusses Bergson in the context of his exploration of modern experience. Benjamin states that *Matter and Memory* stands out among the philosophies of life from the nineteenth century that try to capture true experience. He praises Bergson for having constructed a theory that regards the structure of memory as decisive for the philosophical pattern of experience, yet criticizes him for having rejected any historical determination of memory. According to Benjamin, the "true experience" that Bergson is after in *Matter and Memory* has become impossible within the context of industrialized modernity. Instead, the "shock experience" has become the norm. Benjamin sees Bergson's philosophy of duration therefore as the expression of a nostalgic longing for an authentic experience, resulting from the destruction of the possibility of duration or *Erfahrung* under modern conditions. Claire Blencowe notes that Benjamin's analyses in *On Some Motifs* "can be understood as so many attempts to write the history of the transformation of the *durée* in the context of capitalist industrialization." See Claire Blencowe, "Destroying Duration: The Critical Situation of Bergsonism in Benjamin's Analysis of Modern Experience," *Theory, Culture & Society* 25 (2008): 140.

175. Mullarkey, *Bergson and Philosophy*, 4. Or, as Jankélévitch puts it, "Bergson's philosophy is one of the rare philosophies in which the investigation's theory blends with the investigation itself." Jankélévitch, *Henri Bergson*, 3.

in Bergsonian terms, the *intuition* of duration.[176] Intuition is not merely an instinct, inspiration, or feeling, but a proper philosophical method—according to Deleuze, even "one of the most fully developed methods in philosophy."[177] Philosophical intuition goes through several phases to establish a "thinking in terms of duration."[178]

Intuition is in the first instance a response to what Heidegger calls our "thrown" condition: the philosopher's (historically, socially, culturally, etc. determined) "lifeworld." It manifests itself as an immanent "power of negation" toward the dominant assumptions of an era.[179] James Gilbert-Walsh describes this as a "disclosive interruption" within a certain discursive context.[180]

Secondly, philosophical intuition takes account of the conditions under which these dominant ideas and assumptions have come into being. In this sense, intuition has similarities with what Ian Hacking understands by a "historical ontology" that addresses the historically shaped conditions or

---

176. In a letter from 1935, Bergson responds to Horkheimer's critique by pointing out that Horkheimer does not take into account that intuition is not merely a sympathy but amounts to a philosophical method. Some of Horkheimer's objections, argues Bergson, "do not take sufficient account of the method that I have tried to introduce into metaphysics and which consists of (1) dividing [*découper*] problems according to their *natural* lines; and (2) studying each problem *as if it was isolated*, with the idea that if, in each case, one finds oneself heading in the direction of the truth, the solutions will be joined together again, or pretty nearly so." Horkheimer, "On Bergson's metaphysics of time," 19.

177. Deleuze, *Bergsonism*, 13. To critics like Bertrand Russell who maintained that Bergsonism implied a "return to instinct," Bergson replies, "How could certain people have mistaken my meaning? To say nothing of the kind of person who would insist that my 'intuition' was instinct or feeling. Not one line of what I have written could lend itself to such an interpretation. And in everything I have written there is assurance to the contrary: *my intuition is reflection*." [italics added] CM, 69–70.

178. Jan Bor distinguishes these four phases. See Bor, *Bergson en de onmiddellijke ervaring*, 234.

179. In "Philosophical Intuition" (1911), Bergson describes this "immanent power of negation" as follows: "Faced with currently-accepted ideas, theses which seemed evident, affirmations which had up to that time passed as scientific, [intuition] whispers into the philosopher's ear the word: *Impossible!* Impossible, even though the facts and the reasons appeared to invite you to think it possible and real and certain. Impossible, because a certain experience, confused perhaps but decisive, speaks to you through my voice, because it is incompatible with the facts cited and the reasons given, and because hence these facts must have been badly observed, these reasonings false." CM, 89–90.

180. Gilbert-Walsh: "metaphysical intuition needs discourse, for it can take place as a disclosure only as the very point where this discourse interrupts itself, calling itself into question." James Gilbert-Walsh, "Revisiting the Concept of Time: Archaic Perplexity in Bergson and Heidegger," *Human Studies* 33 (2010): 187.

"conception of the world" within which certain epistemological "objects" or problems have come into existence.[181]

In his own historical ontologies, Bergson brings this approach into practice by shifting attention from finding *solutions* to the philosophical problems of his era (the mind-body problem, free will vs. determinism, the nature of evolution, etc.), to whether the statement of *the problem itself* is correct. A problem is *badly* stated, for instance, when we think in terms of more or less, which is to say, in "differences in degree," where in reality there are "differences in kind." This happens when we think about a qualitative phenomenon such as time in quantitative terms—when, in other words, we confuse time with space.[182] Bergson argues that "the great metaphysical problems are in general badly stated" and that speculative problems "frequently resolve themselves of their own accord when correctly stated."[183]

Thirdly, actually recovering the qualitative tendencies of duration requires an effort from us to reverse the ordinary direction of our thought. Our intelligence is inclined to frame our experiences by means of a set of *a priori*, ready-made concepts that are inflexible because they are fixed in language. Bergson argues that, instead, we have to base our concepts on intuitions.[184] Bergson hereto wants to develop, fourthly, "flexible, mobile,

---

181. As a form of "meta-epistemology," historical ontology investigates, according to Hacking, the historically shaped conditions or "conception of the world" within which certain epistemological "objects" have come into existence. These objects are no real-world "things" that can be "discovered" (like bacteria), but phenomena that are "created" (such as mental conditions like trauma or multiple personality disorder). These phenomena are performative in nature: they actively constitute our world according to the axes of knowledge, power, and morality, and hereby unlock new possibilities for choice and action. Historical ontologies allow us to understand how philosophical problems have become possible. Hacking says, "I still would like to act on the obscure conjecture that when it comes to philosophy, many of our perplexities arise from ways in which a space of possible ideas has been formed." Ian Hacking, *Historical Ontology* (Cambridge, MA: Harvard University Press, 2002), 26. There is a difference between Bergson's approach and Hacking's historical ontology. While Hacking explores "spaces of possible ideas" by connecting epistemology with *history*, Bergson relates these "spaces" to what he calls the *human state*, which is defined in terms of the evolutionary conditions of *life*. This does not mean that Bergson lacks a conception of history, but that human history has to be understood within the larger framework of the creative evolution of Life. See also chapter 6.

182. Deleuze, *Bergsonism*, 21.

183. CM, 77–78.

184. Bergson argues that an empiricism worthy of the name "cuts for the object a concept appropriate to the object alone, a concept one can barely say is still a concept, since it applies only to that one thing." CM, 147.

almost fluid representations" that should "mould" themselves to fleeting intuitions.[185] These fluid concepts are *themselves* in a state of becoming. They "embody" the movement of thought and are therefore, like their "object," *sub specie durationis*.

Philosophical intuition thus describes a circular movement that departs from a concrete historical situation, to which it subsequently returns in the form of an intervention by means of new concepts. The "truth" of intuition is not a "discovery" of some eternal truth that had always been there, but is always relative to a singular situation and to what is *new* in it. This also obtains for Bergson's own concepts. Notions like *durée* and *élan vital* are "fluid representations" bound up with the specific circumstances in which they were conceived—the modern regime of historicity and its crisis. In this sense, Bergson was certainly not "independent from time." Bergson's critique of the mechanistic worldview marks a historical breaking point, when the conception of time and space as homogeneous media could no longer account for an experience of time as a dynamic, creative, and transformative force. Bergson provides, as Richard Lehan points out, a highly original critique of the main assumptions of the Enlightenment and Darwinism with their models of "linear evolution" and "mechanical progress."[186]

---

185. CM, 104.

186. Lehan: "[Bergson] gave foundation to basic modernist tenets, and it was Bergson that cleared the modernist landscape of a materialistic underbrush that would have choked modernism off at the outset." Richard Lehan, "Bergson and the discourse of the Moderns," in *The Crisis in Modernism: Bergson and the Vitalist Controversy*, ed. Frederick Burwick and Paul Douglass (Cambridge: Cambridge University Press, 1992), 308.

CHAPTER 5

THE SURVIVAL OF THE PAST

> We want historians to confirm our belief that the present rests upon profound intentions and immutable necessities. But the true historical sense confirms our existence among countless lost events, without a landmark or point of reference.[1]
>
> —Michel Foucault, "Nietzsche, Genealogy, History," in *The Foucault Reader*

Henri Bergson rates as one of the most original and important twentieth-century thinkers about time. Jorge Luis Borges considered anything written on time after Bergson to be anachronistic.[2] It may therefore seem strange that the implications of Bergson's philosophy of duration for the philosophy of history have rarely been investigated. An important reason for this lacuna is, undoubtedly, that Bergson himself seems never to have had a particular interest in history. Maurice Merleau-Ponty remarks that it is "hard to understand why Bergson did not think about history from within as he had thought about life from within."[3] Other interpreters have even concluded that

---

1. Michel Foucault, "Nietzsche, Genealogy, History," trans. Donald F. Bouchard and Sherry Simon, in *The Foucault Reader*, ed. Paul Rabinow (New York: Pantheon Books, 1984), 89.
2. Mullarkey, *Bergson and Philosophy*, 1.
3. Merleau-Ponty continues: "Why did he not also set about investigating in history the *simple and undivided acts* which arrange fragmentary facts for each period or event? In maintaining that each period is all it can be, a complete event existing wholly in act, and that pre-Romanticism for example is a post-Romantic illusion, Bergson seems to reject this depth-history once and for all." Merleau-Ponty, "Bergson in the Making," 187.

duration is incompatible with a notion of history. Peter Osborne, for instance, recently argued that "the ontological monism underlying Bergson's account of temporality . . . cannot sustain any philosophical concept of history."[4]

The topic of history has not been entirely absent from Bergson's writings, however. Besides some references scattered throughout Bergson's oeuvre, history makes a dramatic and unexpected appearance in the conclusion to Bergson's last original book, *The Two Sources of Morality and Religion* (1932), which was published years after Bergson had traded in his academic career for international politics. It can therefore even be argued that, at least chronologically, Bergson's entire oeuvre steers toward the formulation of a theory of history.

In this chapter I will start exploring the theory of history that is implied by Bergson's philosophy of duration. I will argue that Bergson speaks so little and inconsistently about history because his thought implies a fundamental revision of the conventional meaning of the term *history*. As I have discussed in chapter 2, the emergence of the modern concept of history in the eighteenth century is entangled with the development of modern historical consciousness—or what François Hartog calls a *modern regime of historicity*. History as a discipline implies a qualitative difference between past and present. It is structured by the "arrow" of modern time, in that it presents history as a progress through time toward the future while the past is annihilated "behind us."

The notion of history implied by Bergsonian duration is fundamentally different from this modern concept of history. An entry to a Bergsonian perspective on history can be provided by reformulating the question posed by Merleau-Ponty and to ask "why *historians and philosophers of history* never thought about *life* from within." Bergson denies one of the fundamental premises of the "modern Constitution" (Latour) on which the modern concept of history is based, namely a strict division (and purification) of the natural and social world.

In *The Two Sources of Morality and Religion* in particular Bergson reunites the social and the natural world. He emphasizes that human culture and society have a "vital" basis and that the social is a manifestation of life. Human history has to be understood within the broader framework of the evolution of life. It only differs from natural evolution because human beings have taken their evolution into their own hands. Bergson's theory of history

---

4. Peter Osborne, "Marx and the Philosophy of Time," *Radical Philosophy* 147 (2008): 15.

is an attempt to go *beyond the human state*. Bergson may be considered as a representative *avant la lettre* of what has recently become known as the "posthuman turn" in philosophy and history.[5]

The majority of contemporary historiography is still based on an "absolute, homogeneous and empty time."[6] This means that it conceptualizes history not in terms of becoming but as given—a series of causally related historical events. The great contribution of Bergsonism to the theory of history is that it brings to the fore the underlying *creative* dimension of history, history as becoming or *duration*. Historical duration questions two ontological assumptions about the nature of reality that have shaped modern historiography. The first is that the past is essentially an absence or a nonentity and that it is the task of the historian to represent that which no longer exists. The second is that the historical past is an object of research that is *given*, an actualized and closed system or "whole."[7] Bergson opposes these assumptions by emphasizing, on the one hand, the *survival* of the past within duration, and on the other the *creative* nature of time, which turns history into what Deleuze calls an "open whole."

---

5. For this posthuman turn, see for instance the project by Ewa Domanska on "non-anthropocentric knowledges of the past." Ewa Domanska, "Retroactive Ancestral Constitution, New Animism and Alter-Native Modernities," *Storia della storiografia* 65 (2014): 61–75, and Manuel DeLanda, *A Thousand Years of Nonlinear History* (New York: Swerve Editions, 1997). David Christian's "big history" project is reestablishing a modern, multidisciplinary form of universal history that seeks to integrate different historically oriented disciplines, such as history, biology, geology, and cosmology. Also in *The History Manifesto* Jo Guldi and David Armitage make a plea for long-term historical narratives. Interesting in this respect are also the recent debates around the concept of the Anthropocene, which is the idea that we are currently living in an epoch in which "humankind has become a global geological force in its own right." Will Steffen, Jacques Grinevald, Paul Crutzen, and John McNeill, "The Anthropocene: conceptual and historical perspectives," *Philosophical Transactions of the Royal Society* 369 (2011): 842. Significant about the Anthropocene is that it "abolishes the break between nature and culture, between human history and the history of life and Earth." See Christophe Bonneuil and Jean-Baptiste Fressoz, *The Shock of the Anthropocene: The Earth, History and Us*, trans. David Fernbach (London: Verso, 2017), 19. According to historians Bonneuil and Fressoz, the forceful return of the history of the Earth into world history amounts to a "new human condition" and a need for "new environmental humanities to rethink our visions of the world and our ways of inhabiting the Earth together." (xii)

6. Lorenz and Bevernage, "Breaking up Time," 13.

7. The ontological assumptions with regard to the nature of the writing of history are noted in Jacques Bos, "Agency and Experience: Changing Views of the Subject in Gender History," *Jaarboek voor Vrouwengeschiedenis* 45 (2005): 25–48.

While the next chapter is primarily dedicated to a Bergsonian ontology of historical creation, this chapter will mainly focus on the first of these two assumptions, namely the status of the historical past. Section one relates the absence of history from Bergson's philosophy of time to how duration revises our conventional understanding of history. Section two highlights the way in which Bergson can help us to reconceptualize the ontological status of the historical past, through a discussion of Bergson's theory of memory that is based on a *survival* of the past. The third section explores some consequences for historical epistemology. A Bergsonian approach to history is compared with the contemporary notion of "the event" and a genealogical approach of history.

1. HISTORICAL DURATION

One reason for the marginalization of history in Bergson's writings may be that his works—rather than being contributions to sciences like psychology, biology, or physics—are primarily concerned with *problems*.[8] Even where history is addressed, in the Final Remarks of *The Two Sources of Morality and Religion*, it is in relation to a specific problem, namely that of war in the industrial age.

The reason for focusing on problems rather than disciplines is that a discipline demarcates its subject matter beforehand. It departs from a set of predetermined problems that prefigure their possible solutions. If the philosopher would treat speculative problems in this way, her work would resemble solving a jigsaw puzzle.[9] Instead, Bergson argues, it is important that we first ask ourselves whether a philosophical problem *itself* is correctly stated—for instance by asking whether the initial problem posed is not confusing time with space.

Bergson may have neglected history because he would not accept the ready-made terms in which "history" is framed by modern historiography. This does not mean, however, that, as Peter Osborne concludes, the philosophy of duration cannot sustain a philosophical concept of history. Bergsonism in

---

8. As Philippe Soulez argues, "What interests [Bergson] are *problems* rather than a subject matter or discipline." Philippe Soulez, "Bergson as Philosopher of War and Theorist of the Political," in *Bergson, Politics, and Religion*, ed. Alexandre Lefebvre and Melanie White (Durham, NC: Duke University Press, 2012), 109.

9. CM, 36. "One might just as well assign to the philosopher the role and the attitude of the schoolboy, who seeks the solution persuaded that if he had the boldness to risk a glance at the master's book, he would find it there, set down opposite the question."

fact does have implications for history that fundamentally revise the modern notion of history that still predominates in contemporary historiography.

In chapter 2 I discussed how modern history is entangled with the development of modern historical consciousness that results from an alteration in the European sense of time.[10] During what Reinhart Koselleck identifies as the *Sattelzeit* (1750–1850), an *acceleration* of time occurred. Time no longer followed the rhythms of nature but became a "dynamic and historical force in its own right."[11] The future came to be seen as open and radically new. Because the past no longer shed light on the future, history lost its traditional role of *magistra vitae*, teacher for life. The moderns see the past as a *foreign country*, placed at a distance from the present, that can only be understood in its own terms.[12] This turns the past into a potential "object" for scientific study, forming the basis for the development of history as a science during the nineteenth century.

History as a discipline generally uses the timeline to measure the distance between past and present. The assumption of empty and homogeneous time structures the modern understanding of history. Donald Wilcox has pointed to the affinities of modern historical research with Newtonian time. He argues that "the continuous and universal qualities of Newton's time and space have made it possible for historians—as well as the natural scientists—to view the basic components of reality not as processes or organic wholes but as a series of discrete events that can be placed on a single time line and at a single point in space."[13]

Wilcox argues that the BC/AD dating system (or, as many scholars now call it, the BCE/CE dating system) that is often used in history has all

---

10. See chapter 2. According to Jacques Bos, modern historical consciousness first manifests itself in the work of Renaissance historians Machiavelli and Guicciardini. In their writings "we can observe an early stage in the development of modern historical consciousness." As a consequence of the trauma of the *Calamità d'Italia*, a series of invasions of Italy by foreign powers, Machiavelli and Guicciardini experience a profound rupture with the past, which can therefore appear to them as an "object of study." Jacques Bos, "Renaissance Historiography: Framing a New Mode of Historical Experience," in *The Making of the Humanities*, vol. 1, *The Humanities in Early Modern Europe*, ed. Rens Bod, Jaap Maat, and Thijs Weststeijn (Amsterdam: Amsterdam University Press, 2010), 351–365.

11. Koselleck, *Futures Past*, 236.

12. L.P. Hartley, *The Go-Between* (London: Hamish Hamilton, 1953) opens with the lines "The past is a foreign country: they do things differently there."

13. Wilcox, *The Measure of Times Past*, 4. Wilcox: "modern historians operate under the assumption of an absolute and continuous time line, even if they are not always immediately aware of it, and this assumption colors their sense of what history is about."

the features of Newton's absolute, empty, and homogeneous time. It imposes a chronological order to history that attributes events with a precise "location" in time that can be expressed with a single number.[14] The timeline is therefore an essential tool for establishing historical facts and has contributed to the modern myth of historical objectivity. The numerical terms of the dating system provide history with a quantitative basis and form the point of departure for any interpretation of historical events. Historians, for example, can all agree on when the French Revolution happened, and can subsequently have different opinions about the meaning of this historical event.

The notion of an abstract and empty time and space is a modern invention that developed gradually between the thirteenth and eighteenth centuries.[15] In the Middle Ages time and space did not have homogeneous and universal properties. Premodern dating systems were, as Wilcox argues, not absolute and universal but tied to specific themes and events. There was no timeframe that "contained" a series of events, but instead a historical event created its own timeframe. For this reason, there existed a variety of relative dating systems. Modern scholars often see these relative timeframes as primitive and tend to regard them with condescension.[16]

A related feature of modern historical time is its suggestion of *neutrality*. As Elizabeth Ermarth points out, history claims a universal status for a single time—time as a universal medium that encompasses all historical events—which makes time homogeneous and unproblematic. The most important feature of this "convention of temporality" is the "omniscient narrator" through which "History" speaks. Ermarth writes, "Such 'Nobody' narrators literally constitute historical time by threading together into one system and one act of attention a whole series of moments and perspectives."[17]

But in spite of its suggestion of neutrality, modern historical time actually works *performatively*. It does not so much represent as actively *create* historical reality. The construction of a historical reality as object of scientific research can only take place on the condition that experiences that do not fit into the scheme of absolute, homogeneous, and empty time are excluded. The case of the Cenotaph provided us with an example of how this exclu-

---

14. Ibid., 8.

15. Lucian Hölscher, *Semantik der Leere: Grenzfragen der Geschichtswissenschaft* [A Semantics of the Empty: The Demarcation of the Historical Sciences] (Göttingen: Wallstein Verlag, 2009), 13–33.

16. Wilcox, *The Measure of Times Past*, 9–13.

17. Elizabeth Deeds Ermarth, *Sequel to History: Postmodernism and the Crisis of Representational Time* (Princeton, NJ: Princeton University Press, 1992), 27–28.

sion may work, and also showed how the eviction of the past from public life may result in a "return of the repressed." Through the Cenotaph the past came to intrude and haunt the post-war present of London and Great Britain (see chapter 1).

Other examples of haunting pasts are provided by Berber Bevernage, who has investigated three cases of transitional justice: the Argentinian *desaparecidos*, South African Apartheid, and the civil war in Sierra Leone. Bevernage argues that Newtonian time stresses the irreversibility of historical time. It establishes a distance between past and present by presenting the past as "irretrievably gone," an "endless linear continuum of passed historical presents."[18] Modern historians are therefore generally blind to cases where the past persists in the present, such as in historical traumas. Modern history tends to disregard past injustices because it has declared the past over and done with.

Because modern history is related to mechanistic "spatial" time and space, it is no wonder that the term rarely appears within Bergson's writings. As a fierce critic of the mechanistic model of reality, Bergson would reject modern historical time as an instrumental way of dealing with history. By refracting historical time through space, historical change is subjected to "precise measure and perfect mastery."[19] Although the modern notion of history *seems* to put time at the center of its concerns, it actually presents us with an abstraction that, according to Bergson, denies the *reality* of time, time as a creative force. This will distort our understanding of history in the same way that the spatial representation of movement distorts the race between Achilles and the tortoise.

In order to restore a perspective on the *reality* of time within history, on time as *duration*, we may have to follow Bergson's proposal and take our point of departure in *becoming* instead of being. A "thinking in terms of duration" will allow us to deconstruct the spatialized image of mechanistic time that fixates historical change. Such a notion of history appears in one of the rare passages in which Bergson refers to history:

> History does not repeat itself. The battle of Austerlitz was fought once, and it will never be fought again. It being impossible that the same historical conditions should ever be reproduced, the same historical fact cannot be repeated; and as a law expresses necessarily that to certain causes, always the same, there will

---

18. Bevernage, *History, Memory, and State-Sponsored Violence*, 95.
19. Sanford Kwinter, *Architectures of Time: Toward a Theory of the Event in Modernist Culture* (Cambridge, MA: MIT Press, 2001), 4.

correspond effects, also always the same, history, strictly speaking, has no bearing on laws, but on particular facts and on the no less particular circumstances in which they were brought to pass.[20]

By adhering to mechanistic time, modern history refracts historical change through space and fixates historical change. This suggests that history proceeds according to a logic of cause and effect. Historical duration, on the other hand, introduces a mode of *creative* time in history. It requires that we no longer base our understanding of history on the modern dichotomy of Nature vs. Culture. In *The Two Sources of Morality and Religion* Bergson emphasizes that the social and the natural are intertwined because the social is a manifestation of life. We need to acknowledge that humans are primarily *living* beings and that human history has a vital ground. History is a process made by human beings who have taken their evolution into their own hands.[21]

2. THE SURVIVAL OF THE PAST

The chronology of the timeline in history suggests that there exists a "distance" between past and present. Distance has been one of the fundamental principles in the development of history as a discipline. It already features in the background of Hegel's famous statement that "the owl of Minerva spreads its wings only with the falling of the dusk"[22]—meaning that only in retrospect, afterwards, can the historical meaning of an era be discerned.

Many modern historians see a distance in time as an indispensable prerequisite for historical interpretation. Frank Ankersmit maintains that "temporal distance between present and past or between different moments within the past forms the outset and point of departure for all historical writing."[23] Distance is what distinguishes the historian from the historical

---

20. ME, 78–79.

21. By negating the modern distinction between nature and culture, Bergson provides, according to Suzanne Guerlac, a *nonmodern* perspective on quintessentially modern problems. See her "Bergson, the Void, and the Politics of Life," 50.

22. "Die Eule der Minerva beginnt erst mit der einbrechenden Dämmerung ihren Flug." Georg Wilhelm Friedrich Hegel, *Sämtliche Werke VI: Grundlinien der Philosophie des Rechts* [Elements of the Philosophy of Right] (1821; repr., Hamburg: Felix Meiner Verlag, 2009) 19.

23. My translation. F.R. Ankersmit, *De navel van de geschiedenis: Over interpretatie, representatie en historische realiteit* [The Navel of History: on Interpretation, Representation and Historical Reality] (Groningen: Historische Uitgeverij, 1990), 110. In a recent article, Ankersmit proposes to replace the spatial metaphor of temporal distance with the notion of *function*. The notion of function does more justice to the fact that the historical text is

actors who "make" history. It allows the historian to take on the role of an "impartial bystander" who is not constrained by what goes on around him.[24] The famous Dutch historian Johan Huizinga for this reason rejected the writing of *contemporary* history, because "one doesn't see much with one's head in the clouds."[25]

Faced with historical phenomena or topics of research that defy historical chronology, such as that of memory studies, historians have often taken an activist stance. Topics like memory, presence, historical trauma, historical justice, or *lieux de mémoire* are dismissed by labeling them "unhistorical."[26] The exclusion of the past from the present is actively defended by historians. Gabrielle Spiegel argues, for instance, that the "time of history" should not be conflated with the "time of memory," which "refuses to keep the past in the past."[27] According to Spiegel there needs to be a clear distinction between past and present in history: "The very postulate of modern historiography is the disappearance of the past from the present."[28] Such "purification operations" intended to purify the present from all kinds of phenomena that cannot be understood in terms of "spatial" chronological time are characterized by Bevernage and Lorenz as "a kind of 'border patrol' of the relationship between past and present."[29]

The politics of time that is involved in the writing of history was already criticized by Walter Benjamin in his *Theses on the Philosophy of History*.[30] Benjamin argues that the nineteenth-century historicists' adherence to empty, homogeneous time allowed them to write history from the perspective

---

a *substitute* for the past discussed in it. F.R. Ankersmit, "The Transfiguration of Distance into Function," *History and Theory* 50 (2011): 136–149.

24. Lorenz and Bevernage point out that "the notion of an ever-increasing temporal 'distance' as automatically breaking up past and present has been of central importance for safeguarding this distinction between the 'involved' actor and the 'impartial' observer." Lorenz and Bevernage, "Breaking up Time," 10.

25. Jaap den Hollander, Herman Paul, and Rik Peters, "Introduction: the Metaphor of Historical Distance," *History and Theory* 50 (2011): 3.

26. Keith Jenkins's review of "presence" as discussed in chapter 1 might be considered as an example. Jenkins, "Inventing the new from the old."

27. Gabrielle Spiegel, "Memory and History: Liturgical Time and Historical Time," *History and Theory* 41 (2002): 149.

28. Spiegel, "Memory and History," 161.

29. Bevernage and Lorenz, *Breaking up Time*, 22. The authors refer to a metaphor by Joan W. Scott.

30. On the politics of time, see Peter Osborne, *The Politics of Time: Modernity and Avant-Garde* (London: Verso, 1995).

of the victors. Like Bergson, Benjamin considers the presentation of time as a homogeneous continuum an instrument for the domination of the past. It imposes a form on history that implies that the past is fixed and that it cannot be changed. This favors the victors of history, who have an interest in proclaiming that the past is over and done with. Benjamin shows how an ideology of historical progress could only be sustained by the assumption of empty and homogeneous time that excludes the victims of the same "progress."[31]

Bergson's philosophy of duration provides an interesting contribution to the contemporary debate about historical distance and the ontological status of the past. Instead of that which needs to be "eliminated" or "left behind" in order to go "forward," Bergson sees the past as a resource for autonomy and freedom. Duration as the "continuous creation of unforeseeable novelty" critically depends on a survival of the past. Duration thus provides an alternative to the modern regime of historicity, according to which the present necessarily excludes the past.

The "Existence" of the Past

One of the few contemporary interpreters who have related Bergson to history is Paul Ricoeur. In *Memory, History, Forgetting* (2004), Ricoeur investigates the role of *forgetting* in history. We can conceive of forgetting in two distinct ways. A common view is that forgetting consists of an "effacement of traces," which implies the radical *destruction* of the past. Ricoeur proposes an alternative view: forgetting occurs when we *lose sight of the past*. This implies that the past continues to exist, but in an unperceived form, removed from the vigilance of consciousness, and that there remains the possibility that the past can *return* in the present.[32] According to Ricoeur, the most important theoretician for this alternative conception of forgetting is Bergson.

---

31. Only an alternative model of historical time, which Benjamin called "now-time" (*Jetztzeit*), would allow us to read history "against the grain" and to redeem past injustices by doing justice to the victims of progress. Although Benjamin was critical of Bergsonism, his philosophy of history was also inspired by Bergson's theory of memory that was formulated in *Matter and Memory*. Benjamin found that *Matter and Memory* stands out among the philosophies of life of the nineteenth century and he historicizes the concept of experience that Bergson develops in this book. This, according to Andrew McGettigan, "almost secret engagement with Bergson" in Benjamin's philosophy of history reveals something of the potential that Bergsonism offers for reconceptualizing historical time. See Andrew McGettigan, "As Flowers Turn Toward the Sun: Walter Benjamin's Bergsonian Image of the Past," *Radical Philosophy* 158 (2009): 25–35.

32. Ricoeur, *Memory, History, Forgetting*, 440.

According to the trace theory, a memory is a trace or representation of the past in the present. The term "trace" can refer to three uses: a written and/or material trace (for instance a historiographical source), a psychological trace, or a neurological or corporeal trace.[33] Ricoeur maintains that the trace theory originates from Plato's view of memory. Plato tries to explain the paradox that memory is the "presence of an absent thing" by comparing it with the imprint in a block of wax. In the *Theaetetus*, Socrates tells Protagoras,

> Now I want you to suppose, for the sake of the argument, that we have in our souls a block of wax, larger in one person, smaller in another. . . . We make impressions upon this of everything we wish to remember among the things we have seen or heard or thought of ourselves.[34]

The wax metaphor has its modern equivalent in the representationalist (also called instructionist) view that memory can be reduced to neurological traces in the brain.[35] According to the representationalist view, the mind "stores" impressions from the environment and uses these for its cognitive operations. Memory is thus a neurophysiological process that functions like a camera: "It faithfully and neutrally records present experience as it flows into the past and then stores that experience in a neutral receptacle for later recall."[36]

Aristotle, however, pointed out that the wax metaphor does not account for the presence of an absence that is memory. How can a trace, which is fully *present*, simultaneously represent the *absent* past? As Ricoeur writes, "in the trace, there is no otherness, no absence. Everything is positivity and presence."[37] The trace theory is therefore unable to address the *historicity* of a memory, its historical feel that causes it to stand out distinct from the present.[38] As Aristotle already realized, this puts the *veridicality* of memory into question: "If the image [memory] is like an imprint or trace in us, why should the perception of this very thing be the memory of something else

---

33. Ibid., 15.

34. Plato, "Theaetetus," trans. M.J. Levett, rev. Myles Burnyeat, in *Plato: Complete Works*, ed. John M. Cooper (Indianapolis: Hackett Publishing Company, 1997), 212.

35. See for instance Dick Swaab, *We Are Our Brains: A Neurobiography of the Brain, from the Womb to Alzheimer's*, trans. Jane Hedley-Prole (New York: Spiegel and Grau, 2014).

36. Patrick McNamara, *Mind and Variability: Mental Darwinism, Memory, and Self* (Westport, Conn: Praeger, 1999), 20.

37. Ricoeur, *Memory, History, Forgetting*, 426.

38. Ibid., 433.

and not simply of itself?"[39] Bergson's radical answer to the enigma of the presence of absence in memory is, as we will see, that we know a memory from a perception because memory remains attached to the past by its deepest roots.[40]

Interestingly, the Aristotelian problem of the veridicality of memory seems to have its equivalent in postmodern philosophy of history in the debate about the status of the historical narrative. Narrativist philosophers of history argue that the only thing we have left from the past are the narrative representations by historians.[41] These narratives, they argue, do not reflect historical reality but are critically influenced by the ideological dispositions of the historian. Hayden White, for instance, notes with regard to a number of nineteenth-century historians (Michelet, Ranke, Tocqueville, and Burckhardt) and philosophers of history (Hegel, Marx, Nietzsche, Croce), "Their status as models of historical narration and conceptualization depends, ultimately, on the preconceptual and specifically poetic nature of their perspectives on history and its processes."[42]

But if the historical narrative is fully "present," what *does* it represent? White's answer is that we should admit that the discipline of history is primarily a literary practice and that the emplotment of a historical narrative is not essentially different from that in literary fiction.[43] Many historians have found this an unacceptable conclusion and there have been numerous attempts to dispute White's thesis. David Carr, for instance, argues that

---

39. Aristotle cited in McNamara, *Mind and Variability*, 22.

40. Bergson: "[if] it did not retain something of its original virtuality, if, being a present state, it were not also something which stands out distinct from the present, we should never know it for a memory." MM, 171. According to Ricoeur, this shows that Bergson's ontological thesis has a phenomenological basis. In Ricoeur's view, Bergson derives the survival of the past *by implication* from the phenomenon of recognition: "The experience of recognition, therefore, refers back to the memory of the first impression in a latent state." Ricoeur, *Memory, History, Forgetting*, 433–434.

41. See chapter 1. As Iggers notes, "The basic idea of postmodern theory of historiography is the denial that historical writing refers to an actual historical past." Iggers, *Historiography in the Twentieth Century*, 118.

42. White, *Metahistory*, 4.

43. In an essay on "The Historical Text as Literary Artifact" White famously writes that historical narratives are most manifestly "verbal fictions, the contents of which are as much *invented* as *found* and the forms of which have more in common with their counterparts in literature than they have with those in the sciences." Hayden White, *Tropics of Discourse: Essays in Cultural Criticism* (Baltimore: Johns Hopkins University Press, 1978), 82.

historical reality in itself has a narrative structure, which can be faithfully drawn up in a history text.[44]

Bergson provides a particularly original argument against the representationalist theory of memory. According to Bergson, the reality of *change* necessarily implies that the past has an ontological *existence*. According to our common-sense notion of past and present, the present becomes past (and part of memory) when it is *replaced* by a new present. But in order for the new present to come about, the old present would already have to "become past" at the same time as it is present. A present can therefore only "pass" because it is past *at the same time* as it is present. Deleuze writes: "There is here, as it were, a fundamental position of time and also the most profound paradox of memory: The past is 'contemporaneous' with the present that it *has been*."[45] The past is not constituted after the present, but past and present are two elements that *coexist*: "One is the present, which does not cease to pass, and the other is the past, which does not cease to be but through which all presents pass."[46] Deleuze sees the past as the "pure condition" without which the present would not pass. And because this pure past preserves itself in itself, it is the integral past, all of our past, which coexists with each present.

This argument implies that each present is twofold, consisting simultaneously of both memory and perception. According to Bergson, the phenomenon of the *déjà vu*, the feeling of having seen something before, sustains this. A *déjà vu* allows us to catch the formation of the past in the present due to a distortion of our "attention to life" that normally regulates consciousness. This shows us that memory does not *succeed* perception, but that the formation of perception is *contemporaneous with* the formation of memory:

> Step by step, as perception is created, the memory of it is created beside it, as the shadow falls beside the body. But, in the normal condition, there is no consciousness of it, just as we should be unconscious of our shadow were our eyes to throw light on it each time they turn in that direction.[47]

The coexistence of past and present once again shows that the spatial inclination of the mind distorts our grasp of temporal relations, because this can

---

44. Carr, *Time, Narrative, and History*.
45. Deleuze, *Bergsonism*, 58.
46. Ibid., 59.
47. ME, 157.

only be thought in a non-spatial sense. We must therefore resist the question of *where* memories are stored. In order to withstand the seduction of spatializing thought, Bergson replaces the question "where" with "how."[48] This forces us to start thinking in terms of duration, because it is in *duration* that the past preserves itself. Bergson illustrates the prolongation of the past into the present with the example of the pronunciation of a word:

> In order to pronounce [the word] we have to remember the first half of it while we are articulating the second. . . . But if that is the case for the first half of the word, it will be the same for the preceding word, which is an integral part of it as far as sound and meaning are concerned; it will be the same from the beginning of the sentence, and the preceding sentence, and the whole discourse that we could have made very long, indefinitely long had we wished. Now, our whole life, from the time of our first awakening to consciousness, is something like this indefinitely prolonged discourse.[49]

It is thus our attention to life that determines the difference between past and present, which allows for the possibility of an "actualization" of the past in the present.

Bergson's Theory of Memory

The non-spatial concept that Bergson introduces to characterize the pure past is "virtuality." The integral past that is preserved in pure memory consists of virtual images that seek actualization in the present. Virtual memories are similar to unperceived objects: "Beyond the walls of your room, which you perceive at this moment, there are the adjoining rooms, then the rest of the house, finally the street and the town in which you live."[50] In a similar way the past "exists" without us being conscious of it. This existence, stresses Ricoeur, we do not perceive but "remains at the level of presupposition and retrospection."[51] It *has to be the case*, because otherwise our explanations of a whole range of phenomena would run into insoluble contradictions.

---

48. According to Ricoeur, Bergson continuously confirms the conceptual chain "survival equals latency equals powerlessness equals unconsciousness equals existence." Ricoeur, *Memory, History, Forgetting*, 434–435.

49. CE, 58.

50. MM, 183.

51. Ricoeur, *Memory, History, Forgetting*, 434.

If the past indeed exists, what we have to account for is *forgetting* instead of remembrance. How is it possible that we remain unaware of the virtual memory-images in which we are steeped? The explanation lies in the structure of the brain, which regulates our attention to life by directing our gaze away from the past straight toward the future, in the direction we have to go. We are only aware of the past in the form of memories that "complete" our present experience. The brain is thus not a "storehouse of memories" as the wax metaphor suggests, but an *inhibitory device* that facilitates the *selection* of images.

The notion of "inhibition" already indicates that Bergson does not understand memory primarily as a *psychological* phenomenon tied to a subject. His analysis takes place at an *ontological* level, within the framework of an ontology of duration. The psychological subject is a manifestation of the supra-individual *becoming* of duration, and psychological memory is the result of an inhibition, made in service of life, of an ontological pure memory that encompasses all of the past. Concretely this means that we perceive only our direct surroundings because only these are of immediate interest for us as living and acting beings. Likewise we do not remember our entire history, because this serves no practical purpose to us.

The brain acts as a guide for the body, which is a "centre of action"[52] and therefore cannot give birth to representations. Bergson likens the relation between the brain and consciousness to a coat and the nail on which it hangs:

> Shall we say, then, that the shape of the nail gives us the shape of the coat, or in any way corresponds to it? No more are we entitled to conclude, because the physical fact is hung on to a cerebral state, that there is any parallelism between the two series psychical and physiological.[53]

Bergson distinguishes two fundamentally different forms of memory. First, there is habit recollection, which consists of motor mechanisms that are part of our present because they are preserved as corporeal, cerebral traces. This is memory by repetition, "lived and acted, rather than represented."[54] The second form is representational recollection, which is memory *par excellence* because it encompasses the whole of our past. Contrary to the former, representational recollection truly has its roots in the past. It is not immediate like a habit, but consists of a duration. Memory-images are actualized from

---

52. MM, 5.
53. MM, xi.
54. MM, 191.

pure memory and thus become part of our present. In this sense, representational recollection is "a corruption of pure memory."[55]

Bergson's theory of memory thus consists of three parts. There are, as Mullarkey summarizes,

> two types of recollection and one form of unrecollected pure memory.... This last memory ... is pure because of its unrecollected or virtual state, whereas any form of recollected or actual memory is one simplification or another of this virtuality.[56]

When a recollection comes to us in the form of an image, something of its "original virtuality" remains, which makes it stand out distinct from the present and which accounts for the enigmatic "presence of absence" that is memory. This is Bergson's original solution to the problem of the veridicality of memory that was posed by Aristotle.

How does the process of remembrance proceed, according to Bergson? Initially, remembrance is triggered by some external or internal "cue"—for instance a current perception—that causes us to release our attachment to the world. We now place ourselves at once, in a leap, in the past in general, and subsequently in what Bergson calls "a certain region of the past."[57] These regions, as Deleuze points out, do not contain particular elements of the past, but each represents the whole of our past in a more or less contracted state. Deleuze calls these "ontological regions of the past 'in general,'"[58] represented in Bergson's memory-cone by subsections A'B' and A"B".

S: enduring present/acting body/bodily memory/memory-images

AB: pure memory/the past

SAB: *L'esprit*

PLANE P: representation of the material world/aggregate of images

Although the cone figure seems rather speculative, neuroscientist Patrick McNamara argues that Bergson's model actually corresponds with the practical workings of the mind. McNamara adopts an agnostic position with regard

---

55. Deleuze, cited in Mullarkey, *Bergson and Philosophy*, 51.
56. Ibid.
57. Deleuze, *Bergsonism*, 61.
58. Ibid., 61.

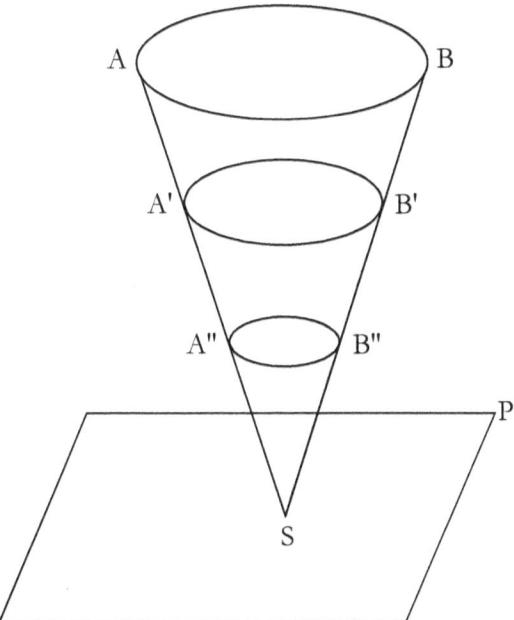

Figure 5.1. Drawn reproduction of Bergson's memory-cone that appears in *Matter and Memory*, 211. Author's own reproduction.

to the ontological nature of the past and focuses on Bergson's evolutionary-inspired notion of memory. According to McNamara, the leap into the past should be understood as a relaxation of the inhibitory function of the brain. This initiates a "proliferation phase" in which "multiple moments of duration" are generated "that represent past perceptions as possible states of affairs or possible worlds."[59] In the proliferation phase, the search for the appropriate memories is contextualized. In response to a cue an initial set of memory-images or representations analogous to the cue are evoked, followed by a secondary set that is causally related to the first.

In the initial proliferation phase a huge array of images becomes available to the rememberer, from which the relevant memory-images are then selected in a "selection or actualization phase." In this selection phase memory proceeds from the past toward the present. According to Bergson this involves two aspects, a *translation-contraction* and a *rotation* by which the present is addressed:

---

59. McNamara, *Mind and Variability*, 37.

> memory, laden with the whole of the past, responds to the appeal of the present state by two simultaneous movements, one of translation, by which it moves in its entirety to meet experience, thus contracting more or less, though without dividing, with a view to action; the other of rotation upon itself, by which it turns towards the situation of the moment, presenting to it that side of itself which may prove to be the most useful.[60]

Although contraction consists in "an inhibition of a multitude of irrelevant images," it is experienced in consciousness as an *expansion*, because more and more memory-images are now becoming available. McNamara writes, "After inhibition and suppression do their work, we are left with a narrow range of images or moments of duration, and these are experienced as veridical memories of a real past state of affairs."[61]

We do not mistake perceptions for memories because memory-images are obtained by inhibiting portions of past memory. Thus a memory-image is lifted from sequential time, as "a figure extracted from ground," and becomes part of a duration, while a present perception is part of spatialized sequential time. Bergson's theory of memory is unique in the sense that the selection criterion for memory-images is the extent in which they increase our autonomy. Memory, which is to say our past, allows us to escape from the rhythm of necessity of present reality and choose our actions freely.[62]

According to McNamara, Bergson's "selectionist theory of mind" is nowadays by no means obsolete. In his *Mind and Variability: Mental Darwinism, Memory, and Self* (1999), McNamara argues that Bergson, together with William James, provides a blueprint for *mental Darwinism*, an approach to the mind that maintains that Darwinistic principles of natural selection are highly appropriate for explaining the workings of memory. Bergson's selectionism allows us to question the instructionism that is predominant in contemporary cognitive sciences.[63] Bergson's model corresponds with the three essential aspects of a selectionist system: (1) a pre-existing variation on which evolution works; (2) confrontation of a biological system with an

---

60. MM, 220.

61. McNamara, *Mind and Variability*, 41.

62. Ibid., 36. McNamara: "Memory's usefulness lies in the fact that it allows us to escape the influence of the present environment and thus confers on us a certain measure of autonomy."

63. According to the instructionist model, the mind is similar to a camera. It stores impressions from the external world for later use. This model resembles Plato's wax metaphor.

environment and, as a consequence, the *inhibition* of certain elements of this system; (3) "differential amplification" of those components of the system that survive the confrontation with the environment.[64] In his book, McNamara gives a wide range of empirical evidence from neuropsychology that favors selectionism over instructionism.

According to Bergson the distinction between past and present is based not so much on a contemplative "distance" as on a more pragmatic "attention to life," which has to be understood in terms of action. The present is "that which acts" while the past is "that which no longer acts."[65] The past is incorporated in the present to the extent that it participates in present action, while the past that lies outside the scope of the present is a past the existence of which we could consider "dead" or latent or virtual, inactive and powerless.

In his essay "The Perception of Change," Bergson relates history to the aspects of the past that *no longer* belong to the present:

> our present falls back into the past when we cease to attribute to it an immediate interest. What holds good for the present of individuals holds also for the present of nations: an event belongs to the past, and enters into history when it is no longer of any direct interest to the politics of the day and can be neglected without the affairs of the country being affected by it.[66]

An antiquarian approach to history, one that studies the past for the sake of the past, may focus exclusively on this "dead" past. To Bergson, however, the past is more significant than this. It is an important resource for freedom, one that allows for the *transformation* of the present and the *invention* of the future. According to a Bergsonian logic, historiography would have to take into account how the past is tied to the present and manifests itself in our actions. This will be discussed in more detail in the next chapter.

---

64. McNamara, *Mind and Variability*, 2–3. If monkeys would have the characteristic to be fearful of large predators, an *instructionist* model would explain this from a transferral of data from the environment of the monkeys—the monkeys learn the danger of approaching large animals, store this information and pass down this quality to their offspring. The *selectionist* approach simply maintains that only those monkeys that were fearful of large animals have been able to survive.

65. Guerlac, *Thinking in Time*, 120.

66. CM, 127.

3. DURATION AND HISTORICAL EPISTEMOLOGY

Memory has often been contrasted with history. As Frank Ankersmit notes, "Until recently, 'memory' referred to how we remember our personal past as individuals, whereas the notion of history was traditionally reserved for our collective past."[67] Yet since the 1980s memory has also gained importance as a category of historical research, to the extent that some theorists even speak of a "memory boom."[68] These memory studies were accompanied by a critique of historiography. In contrast to traditional historiography, which was considered artificial and manipulative, the study of memory was seen as a more authentic and truthful way of dealing with the past. Memory theorists pointed out that historical narratives are influenced by the ideological dispositions of historians and had often served as nationalistic instruments of emerging nation-states.[69]

Many historians, on the other hand, defended the boundaries of their discipline by arguing that memory is an even more dangerous subject of manipulation than history. Memory and history, according to them, should not be conflated. Jacques Le Goff, for instance, sees memory as the "raw material" of history: "Whether mental, oral, or written, it is the living source from which historians draw."[70] Memory refers to the "messy" temporality of historical actors in which past and present are conflated, while the *representation* of history crucially depends on a clear distinction between past and present, or *res gestae* and *historia rerum gestarum*. Le Goff states: "To privilege memory excessively is to sink into the unconquerable flow of time."[71] Only because of this distinction can the historian take on the role of "impartial observer."

Historians often dismiss attempts to reconceptualize historical time by arguing that this breaks with the disciplinary conventions of the "modern enterprise of historiography."[72] On this basis, R.G. Collingwood denied the

---

67. Ankersmit, *Historical Representation*, 154. Ankersmit continues: "'Memory' stands for all that was repressed, ignored, or suppressed in the human past and therefore by its very nature could never attain to the public sphere of what is collectively known and recognized—that which has always been the proper domain of 'history' in the traditional sense."

68. Lorenz, "Blurred Lines," 51.

69. For an account of this, see Benedict Anderson's *Imagined Communities* (London: Verso, 1985).

70. Jacques Le Goff, *History and Memory*, trans. Steven Rendall and Elizabeth Claman (New York: Columbia University Press, 1992), xi.

71. Ibid., xii.

72. Spiegel, "Memory and History," 149.

relevance of Bergsonism to history. According to Collingwood, Bergson's philosophy of duration—a "mental process of direct experience"—has little relevance for history because it does not refer to a *historical* process: "[duration] falls short of being a genuinely historical process because the past which is preserved in the present is not a known past, it is only a past whose reverberations in the present are immediately experienced."[73] Collingwood saw duration as an experiential and memorial time and hence as fundamentally different from the time of history. Collingwood's critique raises questions such as How does a psychological and subjective phenomenon like memory relate to the historical process? Is a conflation of memory and history even possible? And if so, how does the "survival of the past" in memory apply to history?

Considered from the perspective of Bergsonism, it can be argued that these questions arise from a "badly stated problem." They are based on the assumption that memory and history are opposed to one another. But in terms of duration, memorial and historical time should not be seen as fundamentally different. Pure memory should be understood not as primarily a subjective, psychological phenomenon, as Collingwood seems to do, but as an *ontological* notion. Bergson's theory of memory is part of an ontology of time as duration. This means that the survival of the past does not depend on a notion of the subject or individual psyche, but rests in the final instance on the nature of *duration*. As Bergson puts it:

> the preservation of the past in the present is nothing else than the indivisibility of change. . . . It is enough to be convinced once and for all that reality is change, that change is indivisible, and that in an indivisible change the past is one with the present.[74]

The study of memory has simply provided Bergson with a case that allowed him to thematize the survival of the past as an aspect of duration. It is also *through* duration that Bergson's theory of memory can be related to history.

---

73. R.G. Collingwood, *The Idea of History* (1946; repr., Oxford: Oxford University Press, 1973), 188. According to Collingwood, a historical process is a rational process, while duration is the opposite: "[Duration] is not a succession of thoughts, it is a mere succession of immediate feelings and sensations . . . in experiencing them we are not knowing anything that is independent of the experience." Bergson's conception of time is, according to Collingwood, antithetical to the essence of historiography, which is "reflection, mediation, thought," because duration cannot be "known" or put into words and can only be noticed through its *reverberations*.

74. CM, 129–130.

Because the preservation of the past applies to all durational processes, it also applies to the historical process to the extent that it is a duration. As Elizabeth Grosz summarizes this point, "it is we who are in time, rather than time that is in us; it is time which inhabits us, subsists or inheres within and beyond us as the milieu of the living and as the order and historicity of the universe itself."[75]

In chapter 6 we will see that the preservation of the past in duration is so important to Bergson because it is the only way in which the nature of "creative change" can be comprehended. The great paradox of duration is that change depends on the actualization of the past in the present. The more the past is actualized, the more creation, innovation, and change is brought about. A "Bergsonian modernism" hereby offers a compelling alternative to what we might call a "modern-capitalist" idea of change that is based on an *elimination* of the past. A durational model of creative change might be of significance in the face of a series of global problems that seem to indicate the limitations of processes of modernization based on "creative destruction" (Marx, Schumpeter, Berman). Before discussing historical creation in the following chapter, however, I will conclude this chapter by returning to the issue of historical chronology discussed in section one of this chapter and by highlighting some implications of a philosophy of duration for historical epistemology.

Rethinking "the Event"

To think of history in terms of duration has epistemological implications. It forces us to rethink a number of important notions from the theory of history, such as the role of causality in history, the relation between the possible and the real, the historical past as "object" of study, and the problem of representation and historical truth. Bergson argues that it is problematic to know the "causes" of events in history because historical duration is not a mechanistic process that proceeds according to a logic of cause and effect. As a product of duration, a historical event contains an element of "irreducible novelty." Its occurrence therefore cannot be explained in terms of the preceding circumstances out of which it emerged.

By conceptualizing the course of history as a timeline that diachronically orders historical facts, modern historical time suggests otherwise. It implies that history is given, a *fait accompli*, and as such is an "object of study." Bergson argues that thereby the *creative* aspect of history is eliminated, namely history as a process that brings about *genuine novelty*:

---

75. Grosz, *Time Travels*, 3.

Precisely because it is always trying to reconstitute, and to reconstitute with what is given, the intellect lets what is new in each moment of a history escape. It does not admit the unforeseeable. It rejects all creation.[76]

To Bergson it makes no sense to investigate the historical "causes" of events like World War I or the French Revolution, because this would imply that these events would already have taken place, when in fact they are genuine creations.

Modern homogeneous time dictates that historical events can be explained by their historical antecedents. To Bergson, such an approach of history is anachronistic and lacks explanatory power, because any event can be explained by an arbitrary choice of antecedent events.[77] We thereby assume that the possibility of things precedes their existence. But this denies duration, the extent to which history is an emergence of unforeseeable novelty. It suggests that "the possible would have been there from all time, a phantom awaiting its hour; it would therefore have become reality by the addition of something, by some transfusion of blood or life."[78]

If this were the case, history would already have been created beforehand. Bergson argues instead that the relation between the possible and the real is exactly reversed. There is not less but *more* in the possible than in the real. The possible is the combined effect of a reality once it has appeared with something added, namely a "condition which throws it back in time." Bergson states,

> As reality is created as something unforeseeable and new, its image is reflected behind it into the indefinite past; thus it finds that it has from all time been possible, but it is at this precise moment that it begins to have been always possible, and that is why I said that its possibility, which does not precede its reality, will have preceded it once the reality has appeared.[79]

An unforeseeable and "new" historical reality thus becomes "retroactively possible." This means that the historical past is not fixed, in the sense of an object placed on a timeline that can be studied on its own terms. In

---

76. CE, 163.
77. CM, 110.
78. CM, 82.
79. Ibid.

duration, the past is constantly being reshaped by the present: "Backwards over the course of time a constant remodelling of the past by the present, of the cause by the effect, is being carried out."[80]

This makes a notion of objective historical truth which is, as Wilhelm von Humboldt put it, "like the clouds which take shape for the eye only at a distance," problematic.[81] The historian cannot understand the historical past on its own terms. Presenting "what actually happened" is impossible, because the historical meaning of an era will only become clear in light of an indeterminate and unforeseeable future.[82] In duration there is a "retrograde movement of the truth." Drawing on a cloud-metaphor similar to von Humboldt's, Bergson explains this phenomenon with the example of early romanticism:

> If there had not been a Rousseau, a Chateaubriand, a Vigny, a Victor Hugo, not only should we never have perceived, but also there would never really have existed, any romanticism in the earlier classical writers, for this romanticism of theirs only materialises by lifting out of their work a certain aspect, and this slice (*découpure*), with its particular form, no more existed in classical literature before romanticism appeared on the scene than there exists, in the cloud floating by, the amusing design that an artist perceives in shaping to his fancy the amorphous mass. Romanticism worked retroactively on classicism as the artist's design worked on the cloud. Retroactively it created its own prefiguration in the past and an explanation of itself by its predecessors.[83]

Explaining historical events from their antecedents is like supposing that we are the materialization of the image that we see of ourselves in the mirror.[84] However, our image in the mirror is of course not displayed if we ourselves do not first position ourselves in front of it. This shows us that it is not the past that contains a historical event as virtual possibility, but that there is first the historical event which is truly new, that subsequently rearranges

---

80. CM, 84–85.

81. According to Wilhelm von Humboldt (1767–1835), historiography is the narration of "what has happened": "The historian's task is to present what actually happened. The more purely and completely he achieves this, the more perfectly has he solved his problem." Wilhelm von Humboldt, "On the Historian's task," *History and Theory* 6 (1967): 57–58.

82. CM, 13–14.

83. CM, 12.

84. CM, 82–83.

the past and in a sense *produces* its own causes. Bergson does not just state that, like Hegel's owl of Minerva, only afterwards is the meaning of an era unveiled, nor that every epoch holds its own unique *interpretation* of "the" past as some fixed entity in time. He goes further than this. Within duration, the past is constantly reworked. With a new reality truly comes the creation of a truth about the past, which means that the historical past is not given but actually *changes* within duration. The pure past that survives in its entirety is not a past that is set in stone, fixed forever "as it actually happened," but is itself subject to change through our actions.[85]

This Bergsonian ontology has conspicuous similarities with what has become known as "the event." In recent years, this concept has become enormously popular among philosophers and historians to account for occurrences that radically interrupt our sense of continuity. By labeling, for instance, the Arab Spring, the financial crisis of 2008, or 9/11 as "events," theorists emphasize the discontinuous nature of these happenings and prevent them from being dissolved in the continuum of history. In a recent work, Slavoj Žižek defines the event in its purest and most minimal as "something shocking, out of joint, that appears to happen all of a sudden and interrupts the usual flow of things; something that emerges seemingly out of nowhere, without discernible causes, an appearance without solid being as its foundation."[86]

Like Bergson, Žižek describes the event as a "retroactive illusion" and as "an effect that seems to exceed its causes." In a Bergsonian fashion, Žižek even maintains that the event brings about its *own* causes: "[The event] is a manifestation of a circular structure in which the eventual effect retroactively determines its causes or reasons."[87] Žižek illustrates this with the event of falling in love. We do not love someone for specific reasons—his smile, the way she looks—but we find these things attractive *because* we already love the person. Žižek considers it a great merit of events that they undermine any stable order, precisely *by* reconfiguring the past. A true event does not stand of itself but brings about a change in the frame of reference from which we understand and relate to the world: it is a radical change of reality itself.

There are interesting parallels to be drawn between the event as conceptualization of the "radically new" and a Bergsonian ontology of historical

---

85. Žižek clarifies this dynamic with a comparison to the Protestant belief in predestination: predestination does not mean that our fate is forever set in stone in the form of a text that has existed forever in a Godly Mind. Instead, the text that predestines us pertains to the virtual pure past and can be reworked retroactively through our deeds.

86. Slavoj Žižek, *Event: A Philosophical Journey Through a Concept* (London: Penguin Books, 2014), 2.

87. Ibid.

creation. On the one hand, we might consider the event from a Bergsonian viewpoint as a somewhat artificial explanation for historical discontinuity. The event seems to gain its explanatory power from the presupposition of a historical continuity that is being interrupted by the radically new and unexpected. A Bergsonian historical ontology problematizes exactly this assumption by maintaining that a creation of the new belongs to the texture of the historical process. To Bergson, "each instant" is a "fresh endowment" and "the new is ever upspringing."[88] Or in the words of Vladimir Jankélévitch: "Bergson's continuity is discontinuity to infinity."[89] On the other hand, the concept is very useful for determining the historical significance of historical creativity within an ontology of duration. The significance of the event is that it allows us to articulate historical duration.

Genealogy

Once the new is produced we tend to regard it as "an effect determined by its causes," while actually the causes are part of the effect. This makes a notion of historical representation that is based on a clear distinction between *res gestae* and *historia rerum gestarum* problematic. As Grosz summarizes,

> Differentiation renders history as the discursive representation of the past for the interests of the future problematic. This is not to make the study of the past impossible or unedifying. It is simply to complicate the ways in which history may be harnessed to understand change in terms of what is known, already contained, and understood.[90]

In duration, there is not "a" historical reality that can be objectively represented. The distinction between the historian as "impartial observer" of history and a historical reality that is "made" by historical actors is an abstraction from duration facilitated by the timeline. Historical reality is more like a mirror in which the present is being reflected, because the historical past is being transformed in light of the present.

This raises the question of which tools are still available to the historian that can do justice to the creative nature of the historical process. We have

---

88. See chapter 6.

89. Vladimir Jankélévitch, "What is the value of Bergson's thought? Interview with Françoise Reiss (1959)," in *Henri Bergson*, trans. Nils F. Schott (Durham, NC: Duke University Press, 2015), 252.

90. Grosz, *Time Travels*, 111.

already discussed the notion of the event. Another example of a historical technique that I would like to briefly discuss at the end of this chapter is the genealogical method. In "Nietzsche, Genealogy, History," Foucault explores Nietzsche's genealogical approach to history as a way of resisting the tendency of historians to incorporate the singularity of the event into the continuum of history. While a historical tradition aims at dissolving a singular event into an ideal continuity, Foucault maintains that genealogy deals with the unique characteristics of events. Although Foucault's and Nietzsche's genealogies are quite different, as Gary Gutting points out, Foucault's summary of Nietzsche's view of genealogy helps us to highlight the main principles of genealogy.[91]

Genealogy is a "history of the present," because it wants to understand the emergence, in all its contingency, of who and what we have become.[92] In doing so, it serves to get rid of our ingrained prejudice that the present rests upon "profound intentions and immutable necessities."[93] Genealogy, instead, "disturbs what was previously considered immobile; it fragments what was thought unified; it shows the heterogeneity of what was imagined consistent with itself."[94] Foucault himself, of course, would direct his genealogical investigations at the rules, practices, or institutions that are claiming an authority over us.[95] Significantly, Foucault maintains that the objective of genealogy is the construction of a "counter-memory" toward the present that may bring about "a transformation of history into a totally different form of time."[96]

In order to accomplish its task, genealogy does not want to go back in time in order to restore an unbroken continuity, but instead it cultivates the "details and accidents that accompany every beginning."[97] It traces the "emergence" of things by maintaining passing events in their "proper dispersion." Foucault writes, "it is to identify the accidents, the minute deviations—or conversely, the complete reversals—the errors, the false appraisals, and the faulty calculations that gave birth to those things that continue to exist and have value for us; it is to discover that truth or being does not lie at the root of what we know and what we are, but the exteriority of accidents."[98]

---

91. Gary Gutting, *Foucault: A Very Short Introduction* (Oxford: Oxford University Press, 2005), 34.

92. Ibid., 35.

93. Foucault, "Nietzsche, Genealogy, History," 89.

94. Ibid., 82.

95. Gutting, *Foucault*, 35.

96. Foucault, "Nietzsche, Genealogy, History," 93.

97. Ibid., 80.

98. Ibid., 81.

The genealogical examination of the emergence of things is opposed to history in a more traditional sense. Foucault defines three uses of history that are available to the genealogist for constructing a counter-memory toward the present. The first is a *parodic* use of history, in which the genealogist offers a proliferation of alternative and more individualized identities as opposed to the traditional historical tendency to identify with "solid" identities of the past. The second is a *dissociative* use of history that provides an antidote for the suprahistorical perspective of traditional historiography, which reduces the diversity of time to a "completed development," a "totality fully closed upon itself." According to Foucault, the genealogist must introduce discontinuity into our very being by cultivating a "kind of dissociating view" that is "capable of shattering the unity of man's being through which it was thought that he could extend his sovereignty to the events of his past."[99]

The third genealogical use of history is therefore *sacrificial* toward the subject of knowledge. Historians should no longer efface their own individuality, but must also recognize that they themselves are grounded in a particular time and place. Genealogists affirm that historical knowledge is ultimately perspectival. The myth of a neutral historical consciousness that is devoid of passions and committed solely to truth has to be exposed for what it really is, namely, a will to knowledge: "instinct, passion, the inquisitor's devotion, cruel subtlety, and malice."[100]

I do not want to suggest that genealogy is a Bergsonian historical methodology, or that Foucault is a secret Bergsonian.[101] Nonetheless, the genealogical approach does illustrate how we may do justice to the "heterogeneous continuity" of historical duration. Both Foucault and Bergson reject teleological explanations of history, which are characteristic of a modern regime of historicity. In Bergson's case, this once more becomes clear when he discusses "humanity's movement towards democracy":

> the trend of that movement was at that time no more marked than any other, or rather it did not yet exist, since it was created by the movement itself,—that is, by the forward march of the men who have progressively conceived and realized democracy. The premonitory signs are therefore, in our eyes, signs only because we

---

99. Ibid., 87.

100. Ibid., 95.

101. Interesting parallels can certainly be drawn between Bergson's method of intuition and Foucault's genealogical approach. Mikko Tukhanen draws this comparison and writes, "Bergson's thinking appears both incompatible with the dry precision of the genealogical approach and reminiscent of the oddness of some of Foucault's writings on ascetics." Mikko Tukhanen, "Ontology and Involution," *Diacritics* 35 (2005): 33.

now know the course, because the course has been completed. . . .
In other words then, the historical origins of the present in its
most important aspect, cannot be completely elucidated, for they
would only be restored in their completeness if it had been possible for the past to be expressed by its contemporaries in terms
of an indeterminate and therefore unforeseeable future.[102]

Bergson rejects the way a future state of affairs (in this case democracy) is taken as the inevitable outcome of the historical process. Such an anachronistic reading of history denies the contingent nature of history. In *The Two Sources of Morality and Religion* Bergson argues that democracy is the result of a series of creative acts in history.

A Bergsonian reconceptualization of historical time accentuates the present over the past-in-itself and connects, in this sense, with a presentistic regime of historicity. However, this is not a conventional presentism. In duration, the past is not external to the present and the present is not a "now-point." Bergson distances himself from a form of presentism based on spatial time, where "everything is in a present which seems constantly to be starting afresh." In duration the past is immanent to the present, which makes the present "thick" and "elastic":

> which we can stretch indefinitely backward by pushing the screen which masks us from ourselves farther and farther away; let us grasp afresh the external world as it really is, not superficially, in the present, but in depth, with the immediate past crowding upon it and imprinting upon it its impetus; let us in a word become accustomed to see all things sub specie durationis: immediately in our galvanized perception what is taut becomes relaxed, what is dormant awakens, what is dead comes to life again.[103]

4. CONCLUSION

The thick and durational present may be relevant now that we are faced with a crisis of the modern regime of historicity, in which we find ourselves in a *présent perpétuel*. Late modernity is characterized by a fragmentation of temporality and historicity. In chapter 2 we related this to an *acceleration of*

---

102. CM, 13–14. This example can be read as critique of the modern regime of historicity, in which the future is taken as a point of reference that organizes past and present.
103. CM, 106.

time. Late modernity is, according to Rosa, nothing but modern society accelerated and desynchronized beyond the point of possible reintegration. On both an individual and a social and political level, the fragmentation of historicity and the desynchronization of society have affected the agency of the late-modern subject. A paradoxical "standstill of history" seems to have come about due to an "inability to control social change" and, as a consequence, an "overwhelming sense of directionless change." For this reason, the formation of a new, *presentistic* regime of history faces the challenge, as François Hartog puts it, to "restore some form of communication" between past, present and future.

Bergson indeed (re)connects the present with a notion of past and future. But this relation is not contemplative. The past is not relevant insofar as it lies "behind" us. This would support an exclusively antiquarian approach to the past. Instead, the relation between past and present is understood in terms of action. The past is a "vehicle for change." In this sense, the philosophy of duration can strengthen our sense of agency, it can give us the feeling that we are no longer "cogs in a machine," as Charlie Chaplin depicted in Modern Times. Faced with the "moving originality of things" we can become aware of our capacity for creative action. In the conclusion to "The Possible and the Real," Bergson argues that a reflection on duration is a preparation for what he calls the "art of living":

> But above all we shall have greater strength, for we shall feel we are participating, creators of ourselves, in the great work of creation which is the origin of all things and which goes on before our eyes. By getting hold of ourselves, our faculty for acting will become intensified.[104]

Bergsonism provides us with an alternative model for creative change rooted in history.

---

104. CM, 124.

CHAPTER 6

HISTORICAL CREATION

> For the health of a single individual, a people, and a culture the unhistorical and the historical are equally essential.[1]
>
> —Nietzsche, *On the Use and Abuse of History for Life*

Historians often have difficulty accounting for historical change. Within historiographical texts, historical events are frequently attributed meaning by relating them to prior "causes" in time. This runs the risk of anachronism, because it suggests that an event is contained in what came before and that history could not have unfolded in any other way. As a narrative tool, a causal-mechanistic model of explanation echoes the modern regime of historicity. A future state of affairs—an event that needs to be explained historically—is taken as the narrative point of departure that orders the historical past. Bergson offers an original approach to the problem of continuity and discontinuity in history: we can account for both continuity and discontinuity by thinking of history in terms of duration. Duration is a *heterogeneous continuity*—past and present form an indivisible continuity and therefore each moment in duration contains an element of irreducible novelty.

Connecting duration to history is, as I have pointed out, not self-evident. Bergson himself did not thematize history until the last chapter of his last book, *The Two Sources of Morality and Religion*, which will be the subject of the next chapter. I will nevertheless contend that the ontology of duration can be understood as profoundly historical. This becomes clear once we compare Bergsonism to the ontological presuppositions regarding

---

1. Nietzsche, *On the Use and Abuse of History for Life*, 1.

the nature of history in nineteenth-century German historicism. Bergson's philosophy of life has often been conceived as anti-historicist, because it goes "beyond the human state." Yet there are also interesting parallels to be drawn between Bergsonism and historicism. As we will see, Bergson shares some of the ontological principles of historicism, such as a similar notion of change, an emphasis on individuality, and a holistic conception of reality.

I will argue that Bergsonism has nevertheless not been identified as a form of historicism, because of its *nonmodern* nature. While the historicists separate nature from history, Bergson integrates these domains. For Bergson, it is not only human history that is the domain of freedom and creation, but life as a whole. This leads to a qualitatively different view of historical change and introduces a mode of creative time in the theory of history. Ultimately, Bergsonism may offer an antidote to the historicist tendency to dissolve historical discontinuity in the "continuum of history."

In this chapter I intend to develop a Bergsonian ontology of history. Section one explores the question of whether duration is a continuity or a discontinuity. I will argue that duration is both, namely a "heterogeneous continuity," because duration is a "virtual whole." Section two claims that, as virtual whole, the ontology of duration may be understood as a form of historicism, albeit of a particular kind. Bergsonism differs from, and goes beyond, historicism in its nonmodern approach, which sheds light on the *creative nature of history*. I will consider this to be the most important contribution of Bergsonism to the theory of history. Section three compares a Bergsonian historical ontology to Hegel's philosophy of history. While Hegel adopts the modern regime of historicity and turns history into a "closed whole," Bergson's nonmodern ontology implies that history is an "open whole."

1. DURATION AS HETEROGENEOUS CONTINUITY

In her successful book *Stil de tijd* [Silence the Time] from 2009, the Dutch philosopher Joke Hermsen makes a plea for what she calls a "slow future."[2] Hermsen argues that in the last 150 years the experience of time in our daily lives has fundamentally changed. Drawing on Bergson's distinction between social time and individual duration, Hermsen maintains that modern societies have been increasingly regulated by the universal time of the clock. Under the influence of capitalist modes of production and innovation and a neoliberal ideology, time has accelerated beyond control, to the extent that we

---

2. Joke Hermsen, *Stil de tijd: Een pleidooi voor een langzame toekomst* [Silence the Time. A Plea for a Slow Future] (Amsterdam: De Arbeiderspers, 2009).

can no longer keep up with it. The time of the clock has alienated us from ourselves by turning us into cogs in a machine, for example as depicted by Charlie Chaplin in his film *Modern Times* (1936).

According to Hermsen, Bergson can help us to reclaim time. In a chapter on Bergson, she makes an argument for "silencing the time" by radically breaking away from fast-paced everyday life. Only by withdrawing from social life (in her case by retreating to the French countryside, leaving her agenda at home) are we able to regain an intuitive contact with ourselves—that is, with time as duration, the flow of time that runs deep within us. Only by allowing ourselves to do nothing and become bored will we be able to reflect, create, and be free. Hermsen's interpretation of duration emphasizes that duration is essentially *discontinuous*. While we all partake in one public, social time, duration is highly individual, a private time that we encounter deep within ourselves.

The enormous success of *Stil de tijd* in the Netherlands (more than 35,000 copies of the book were sold) shows that Hermsen's plea for silencing the time struck a chord with her Dutch audience. But her embrace of a Bergsonian lifestyle of isolation, duration, and creativity also provoked criticism. In *Ritme: Op zoek naar een terugkerende tijd* [Rhythm: In Search of a Repeating Time] (2011), Marli Huijer questions whether withdrawing from social life will in fact increase our creativity.[3] Huijer mentions the example of the best-selling author who decides to quit his job to dedicate himself entirely to becoming a full-time writer. Every day the author sits behind his desk ready to write, but nothing happens. Or the scholar, who takes a sabbatical to finish his book but drowns in the sea of time that suddenly becomes available to him. According to Huijer, silencing the time will not bring us back in contact with a true inner time of creativity, but is actually profoundly empty, precisely *because* it makes us forget the people around us. Huijer argues that we should not withdraw from social time, but engage in it by finding the right rhythm. Rhythm is, according to Huijer, "discipline and freedom united in one."[4]

Inspired by the critique that Gaston Bachelard formulated on Bergson in his *La dialectique de la durée* (1927), Huijer doubts whether Hermsen's highly personal "durational" time should be opposed to the "social" time of the clock. She argues that Bergsonian duration is already a social time from the outset, because it is a flow in which all of us partake:

---

3. Marli Huijer, *Ritme: Op zoek naar een terugkerende tijd* [Rhythm: In Search of a Repeating Time] (Zoetermeer: Uitgeverij Klement, 2011).

4. My translation. Ibid., 9.

> But, thinking with Hermsen, is that highly personal time not precisely the common time? After all, we all partake in the "real" time that runs within us? This would make the inner time into something superhuman, something metaphysical or religious. It would be a current of which we would have to believe that we are all absorbed in it and that carries or surrounds us all.[5]

According to Huijer, in other words, Bergsonian duration is not a discontinuity but a *continuity*—a metaphysical "supertime" in which all of us partake. This supertime underlies all particular durations.

Huijer rejects this notion of a single, continuous flow of time. Following Bachelard, she argues that time is in fact a discontinuity. Every single human life, for instance, has its own duration and there is no continuity between one life and the next. To illustrate the discontinuous nature of time, Huijer recalls the summer vacations she spent as a child with her family in Ouddorp. When she returns to the village many years later, she realizes that the family members who used to live there are now gone:

> I could of course pretend that my parents live on in my memory, as if the time with them is not permanently over. But I know that the memories I have of my parents are misleading . . . I experience a break between the time during which my father lived and the time thereafter. He does not live on in the present, his existence ended more than a quarter of a century ago and the memory of him diminishes and becomes fuzzier as time progresses.[6]

Huijer wants to use these childhood memories to illustrate the fact that there are *many* durations instead of one homogeneous flow of time, and that time consists of a "temporal multiplicity of appearances." Huijer sees duration as self-contradictory, because it combines a "survival of the past" with the "creation of the new."[7] The new can only be understood if we accept that time is not a continuous duration but a *discontinuity*. The continuous flow of time in duration is merely a construction *a posteriori* by means of which we establish order in our lives.

Hermsen and Huijer offer two contradictory interpretations of Bergson's conception of duration. According to Hermsen, duration is a discontinuity,

---

5. My translation. Ibid., 38.
6. My translation. Ibid., 39.
7. Ibid., 40–41. Huijer's argument echoes Bachelard's critique of Bergsonism expressed in *La dialectique de la durée* (1927).

a plurality of individual times, while Huijer sees Bergsonian duration as a continuity, a metaphysical supertime that leaves no room for discontinuity. I would like to add a third position to this discussion. I will argue that duration is both a continuity *and* a discontinuity. This becomes clear once we start to see duration for what it is: namely, a *virtual whole*.

As a virtual whole, duration is a *heterogeneous* continuity. Within a homogeneous medium, the new can only be understood as a rupture with what came before. As a heterogeneous continuity, however, duration is *both* an indivisible continuity (of past and present states) *and* a process of qualitative, heterogeneous change. Continuity is bound up with discontinuity, because the creation of "unforeseen novelty" depends on the preservation of the past. Only by thinking of time as duration can we understand what discontinuity means.[8]

2. BERGSON'S NONMODERN HISTORICISM

The role of the virtual in Bergsonism has gained importance through the work of Deleuze.[9] The virtual allows us to think duration as a single time,

---

8. See Ansell-Pearson, *Philosophy and the Adventure of the Virtual*, 74. Ansell-Pearson notes that duration unites *both* continuity and discontinuity: "it is only by thinking of time as duration that the features of rupture and discontinuity can be rendered intelligible."

9. Alain Badiou has argued that although Deleuze tries to think difference and becoming without immutable ground, the concept of the virtual seems to introduce such a "ground" through the backdoor. Badiou maintains that a philosophy of the virtual, though meant as a philosophy of immanence, is still a form of transcendentalism because the virtual serves as kind of philosophical foundation or "reservoir" from which actual expressions emanate. See Alain Badiou, *Deleuze: The Clamor of Being*, trans. Louise Burchill (Minneapolis: University of Minnesota Press, 2000). Whether Badiou's controversial reading of Deleuze strikes any ground or not, we may question whether Deleuze's actualization of Bergson that prioritizes the virtual over the actual remains faithful to Bergson's concept of duration. John Mullarkey has noted that there is a tendency among Deleuzean interpreters of Bergson to favour the virtual over the actual; to consider the virtual, difference, and multiplicity as "good," while the actual, continuity, and identity as "bad." Mullarkey points out that such interpretations are mainly based on one text from Bergson's oeuvre, namely the third chapter of *Matter and Memory*. The rest of Bergson's writings display not virtualism but *actualism*. Bergsonism, according to Mullarkey, amounts to a process metaphysics and does not ontologically depend on a ground that is not its own, such as virtuality. He considers Bergson's notion of becoming as even more radical than Deleuze depicts it, because it radically departs from a notion of duration as "fundamental change." This seems to coincide with Bergson's thesis that "There are changes, but there are underneath the change no things which change: change has no need of a support." CM, 122. Mullarkey stresses that the Bergsonian virtual should not be conceived as an ontological

without having to adopt a concept of time as a metaphysical "stream" in which individual temporalities partake. Instead, the virtual refers to the *immanent* nature of duration as a whole. As Bergson states in *Creative Evolution*, "duration is immanent to the whole of the universe. The universe *endures*."[10] The holistic nature of duration is fundamentally different from the atomistic principles of mechanistic theories of time. Atomism treats time as a succession of independent temporal instants. This premise seems to inform the theories of Huijer and Hermsen. From this perspective, we can think of time only as a continuity *or* a discontinuity. A holistic theory of time, on the other hand, gives priority to time as a whole. Duration as a whole is more than a collection of moments. By isolating temporal instants within duration as a whole, we end up with a concept of time that is an abstraction from real duration.

Through an examination of duration as a virtual whole, I will argue that duration is in fact profoundly historical. I will establish this by a comparison with German historicism. Friedrich Meinecke characterized historicism as the greatest intellectual revolution in the Western world of the last two hundred years. It instigated, he argued, an entirely new worldview based on a new form of historical consciousness.[11]

Historicism came into being during the eighteenth and especially the nineteenth century within a very particular historical context marked by the emergence of the modern nation-states. This is reflected in historicism's para-

---

"past in general" from which new presents "emerge." This does not mean that there is not something which we see as the past that guarantees the novelty of the changing present and the reality of "our past." Yet, according to Mullarkey, we will not know it any better by labelling it as "the virtual," which, furthermore, suggests that the virtual past is knowable through art or science. John Mullarkey, "Forget the Virtual: Bergson, Actualism, and the Refraction of Reality," *Continental Philosophy Review* 37 (2004): 470. Mullarkey's interpretation puts into question attempts by philosophers of history such as Jay Lampert or Craig Lundy to develop a "virtual history" in order to escape "the traditional and dominant conceptions of history as representational, casual-linear and teleological." Craig Lundy, "Bergson, History, and Ontology" (paper presented at the conference The Future of the Theory and Philosophy of History, Ghent, Belgium, July 10–13, 2013). Although I agree with Mullarkey that the virtual as "object of research" is a reification of duration and that the virtual is a theoretical construct, I would nevertheless argue that the virtual does allow us to understand the holistic nature of duration—duration as both one (a virtual whole) and many (a plurality of becomings).

10. CE, 11.

11. F.R. Ankersmit, "Historicism: An Attempt at Synthesis," *History and Theory* 34 (1995): 143. On Meinecke's historicism, see R.A. Krol, *Het geweten van Duitsland: Friedrich Meinecke als pleitbezorger van het Duitse historisme* [Germany's Conscience: Friedrich Meinecke as Advocate of German Historicism] (PhD diss., University of Groningen, 2013).

doxical character. On the one hand, historicism established history during the nineteenth century as a rigorous science. Historicism was, as Frank Ankersmit has argued, the result of a de-rhetorization of the historical writing from the Enlightenment.[12] Historical science came to be practiced by specialists at the universities, and historians now had to live up to a scientific ethos of impartiality and objectivity. The objective of history as a science was, according to Leopold von Ranke, merely to show "what had actually happened."

Yet on the other hand, historicism was also profoundly ideological in character. Historicism comprised a total philosophy of life, because it combined a conception of the human and cultural sciences with a conception of the social and political order.[13] The "impartial" approach of disciplinary history revealed a world full of meaning and value and particularly provided an ideological justification for the social and political institutions of the state.[14] This gave professional historians during the nineteenth century an important cultural and political role. As Georg Iggers notes, "Historians went into the archives to find evidence that would support their nationalistic and class preconceptions and thus give them the aura of scientific authority."[15]

In this section I will focus on the ontological presuppositions of historicism regarding the nature of history. I am well aware that this is a limited approach to the historicist tradition that does not do justice to its complexity and manifold character. I hereby hope, however, to show that a number of important ontological principles of the historicist worldview return in Bergsonism. I will furthermore argue that Bergson goes *beyond* historicism, because he does not restrict the meaning of "history" to the study of the *human* world—as the modern connotation of the term prescribes—but applies it to the whole of the universe.

Historicism

Historicism has been defined in many different ways, some of which even contradict each other.[16] In order to bypass the debate on how to define

---

12. Ankersmit, "Historicism," 143.

13. Iggers, *Historiography in the Twentieth Century*, 29.

14. Iggers, *The German Conception of History*, 7. The historicists indeed viewed the state as an end in itself, as the "product of historical forces."

15. Iggers, *Historiography in the Twentieth Century*, 28.

16. As Maurice Mandelbaum states, "The thinkers who are invariably classified as clear examples of historicism are representative of a wide variety of philosophic positions, and they spring from diverse intellectual ancestries. For example, Herder, Hegel, Comte,

historicism, I have chosen to adopt here a recent, very broad and inclusive definition of historicism by Frederick Beiser, which is *prescriptive* rather than descriptive.[17] What makes historicism a coherent intellectual tradition is, according to Beiser, its agenda or goal, namely to legitimize history as a science.[18]

While science during the Enlightenment was mainly directed at the universal laws that govern the natural world, the historicists attempted to create a science of the human world, which would take the particularity of social and cultural reality into account. In general, the historicists maintained that science should not only be about universal laws but should also take the particularity of things into account. This particularity of a thing is determined by its specific history. For this reason, history, according to the historicists, deserves a scientific status similar to that obtained by the natural sciences in the seventeenth and eighteenth centuries.[19]

Despite their aversion to metaphysics, the historicists did adhere to a number of ontological presuppositions about the nature of history. The most important was that—like Bergson—they placed "change" at the center of their worldview. According to Mandelbaum, indeed, "historicism is the belief that an adequate understanding of the nature of any phenomenon and an adequate assessment of its value are to be gained through considering it in terms of the place it occupied and the role which it played within a process of development."[20] The historicists assume that the world is in a state of incessant flux and that "everything in the human world changes with history."[21] Consequently, the historicists reject permanent forms and eternal essences.

Marx, and Spencer are all generally considered to provide classic examples of historicism, yet their philosophic systems are obviously antagonistic in many fundamental respects." Maurice Mandelbaum, *History, Man, and Reason: A Study in Nineteenth-Century Thought* (Baltimore: The Johns Hopkins Press, 1971), 42.

17. A "descriptive" definition, according to Beiser, tries to determine the meaning of a word, while a "prescriptive" definition refers to what it "ought to" mean and how it "should be" used. The prescriptive definition of historicism allows Beiser to understand "the origins and foundations of Meinecke's intellectual revolution." Frederick C. Beiser, *The German Historicist Tradition* (Oxford: Oxford University Press, 2011), 2.

18. Ibid., 6–8. The following historicists are seen by Beiser as the most important contributors to the philosophical discussion about the status of history as a science: Chladenius, Möser, Herder, von Humboldt, von Savigny, von Ranke, Lazarus, Droysen, Windelband, Rickert, Lask, Dilthey, Simmel, and Weber.

19. Ibid., 4.

20. Mandelbaum, *History, Man, and Reason*, 42.

21. Beiser, *The German Historicist Tradition*, 2–3.

By maintaining that the essence of social and cultural phenomena lies in their history, the historicists historicized the timeless, ahistorical conception of the social and political world of the Enlightenment's philosophy of natural law, which considered human nature to be universal and ahistorical.[22] The historicists see an organic continuity between past and present. Accordingly, history is the only guide for understanding the human world.[23] This is a completely new attitude toward the past, because the past is seen not as lost forever but as part of a living present. The past "remains present with us here and now, for it is the past that has made us who we are."[24] We find this historicist premise also at the heart of Bergson's concept of identity, which is based on a notion of the survival of the past. In *Creative Evolution* for instance, Bergson writes, "What are we, in fact, what is our *character*, if not the condensation of the history that we have lived from our birth—nay, even before our birth, since we bring with us prenatal dispositions?"[25]

Besides an emphasis on (historical) change, there are two other important ontological principles that are associated with historicism, namely a focus on "individuality" and a "holistic" conception of history. These principles also return in Bergson's philosophy of duration. While historical writing in the Enlightenment tended to focus on general trends and universal laws, the historicists see the individual as the principal object of historical research. As Jacques Bos says, "Historicist authors are primarily concerned with the description of individual events, which they consider to be the results of intentional actions of individual persons."[26] Because history is constituted by individual acts, human agency is of crucial importance to historicists.

Yet these actions do not stand by themselves, but take place in the context of larger organic wholes. This highlights the second ontological principle of historicism, namely its holism. The historicists reject the Enlightenment's atomism and related mechanism, which conceives of wholes as no more than the sum of their parts. To the historicists, the whole is an indivisible unity that is "prior to its parts and the very condition of their existence and identity."[27]

---

22. See Jacques Bos, "Nineteenth-century Historicism and Its Predecessors: Historical Experience, Historical Ontology and Historical Method," in *The Making of the Humanities*, ed. Rens Bod, Jaap Maat, and Thijs Weststeijn, vol. 2, *From Early Modern to Modern Disciplines* (Amsterdam: Amsterdam University Press, 2012), 131, and Ankersmit, "Historicism," 145.

23. Iggers, *The German Conception of History*, 5–33.

24. Beiser, *The German Historicist Tradition*, 17.

25. CE, 5.

26. Bos, "Agency and Experience," 29.

27. Beiser, *The German Historicist Tradition*, 12.

Beiser points out that historicism's individuality and holism are closely related: wholes are individuals, while individuals are wholes.[28] Individuality does not exclusively refer to individual people but can also concern collectives, such as nations or states.[29] Johann Gottfried Herder, for instance, transposed the characteristics of persons to nations. Nations should, according to him, be seen not merely as a collection of individuals but as organisms with their own spirit and lifespan.[30]

It is often assumed that, because of its holism, historicism is "infested with metaphysics."[31] Beiser argues that this is a misunderstanding. He points to the influence on historicism of nominalism, a philosophical tradition that goes back to the fourteenth-century philosopher William of Ockham. Nominalists maintain that only the particular is real and that universals are merely constructs of mental activity. This explains the emphasis on individuality within the historicist tradition: only the individual is real, which makes history the most "real" of all the sciences.[32] At first sight, however, historicism's holism seems to contradict nominalism. If only the particular is real, how can there also be wholes? Beiser emphasizes that holism does not necessarily imply a commitment to abstract entities or universals. It is not necessary for the holist to claim that the whole "exists" apart from the parts. The whole can also exist *in and through the parts* and have "only a *logical* or *explanatory* priority over them."[33]

Bergson's Nonmodernity

This paradoxical "nominalist holism" is, according to Beiser, a fundamental trait of the historicist tradition and it can also help us to understand the status of duration. As a virtual whole, duration should not be seen as a transcendent and metaphysical "stream of time" that "carries" all humans, as Huijer maintains. Instead, the virtual nature of duration as a whole refers to a "mode of time" that is immanent to the universe. In chapter 4 it became clear that this mode of time consists of two virtual tendencies or movements: a "downward" homogeneous tendency toward material repetition, and an

---

28. Ibid., 5.
29. Bos, "Nineteenth century historicism," 132.
30. Iggers, *The German Conception of History*, 35.
31. Beiser, *The German Historicist Tradition*, 6.
32. Ibid., 5.
33. Ibid., 6.

"ascending" heterogeneous tendency of life and creation. Bergson himself describes these as follows:

> in the universe itself two opposite movements are to be distinguished . . . 'descent' and 'ascent.' The first only unwinds a roll ready prepared. In principle, it might be accomplished almost instantaneously, like releasing a spring. But the ascending movement, which corresponds to an inner work of ripening or creating, endures essentially, and imposes its rhythm on the first, which is inseparable from it.[34]

These virtual tendencies are, as Mullarkey points out, the condition of possibility for any organic form, in the sense that every organism is a "forced accommodation" of the two tendencies. The virtual status of the whole is similar to that within historicism, where the whole has a "logical or explanatory priority" over the parts. Duration as a virtual whole also has a purely theoretical-ideal status.[35] Duration exists as a virtual whole only in the process of its actualization. As Ansell-Pearson notes:

> the whole, *qua* a virtual whole, *only exists in terms of its divisions and differentiations*. It is only in artificial terms that the whole, as virtual, can be thought in abstraction from its actual divisions and movements (by turning time into space).[36]

The virtual can explain how Bergson can combine a commitment to one single (virtual) mode of time with a radical, irreducible pluralism of different temporalities that represent different degrees or rhythms of duration.

Of the two virtual tendencies, the "ascending" tendency of life and creation is, so I want to claim, a historical tendency *par excellence*. This places history at the center of Bergson's ontology of duration. The ascending tendency is creative because it incorporates the past into the present. Bergson also associates this virtual movement, in accordance with the first of the two ontological principles of historicism, with a tendency toward individualization. In *Creative Evolution*, for instance, Bergson maintains that "life manifests a search for individuality."[37] This tendency is opposed by the

---

34. CE, 11.
35. Mullarkey, "Forget the Virtual," 81–83.
36. Ansell-Pearson, *Philosophy and the Adventure of the Virtual*, 95.
37. CE, 15.

"material" tendency toward repetition: "it may be said of individuality that, while the tendency to individuate is everywhere present in the organized world, it is everywhere opposed by the tendency towards reproduction."[38] Individuality is therefore never perfect in the organized world.

Despite the fact that Bergson associates creation with individualization, like the historicists Bergson does not let go of his holistic premise. Each individual living organism has to be regarded as a whole. Its organization should not be compared with a single material object but with "the whole of the material universe":

> Like the universe as a whole, like each conscious being taken separately, the organism which lives is a thing that endures. Its past, in its entirety, is prolonged into its present, and abides there, actual and acting. How otherwise could we understand that it passes through distinct and well-marked phases, that it changes its age—in short, that it has a history?[39]

This holistic individualism also applies to the evolution of life in general, which is characterized by "individual wholes" that "differentiate" and thereby produce new "individual wholes":

> The reproduction of unicellular organisms consists in just this—the living being divides into two halves, of which each is a complete individual. True, in the more complex animals, nature localizes in the almost independent sexual cells the power of producing the whole anew.[40]

If it is indeed true that some of the most important ontological premises of the German historicist tradition of the nineteenth century are reproduced in Bergsonism, the question then arises of why Bergson has never been associated with historicism, and why a Bergsonian theory of history, which, as we have seen, is implied by the ontology of duration, has been largely overlooked by both philosophers of history and interpreters of Bergson?

For an answer to this question we must return to what Beiser identified as the original mission of historicism, namely to legitimize history as a science. Georg Iggers points out that "the core of the historicist outlook

---

38. CE, 13.
39. CE, 15.
40. CE, 14.

lies in the assumption that there is *a fundamental difference* between the phenomena of nature and those of history, which requires an approach in the social and cultural sciences fundamentally different from those of the natural sciences"[41] (emphasis added). This ambition reproduces, in other words, what we have identified as the "modern Constitution" (Latour), which entails a strict division and purification of the domains of nature and culture and which prescribes that the scientific representation of nature should not be confused with the political representation of human beings. While nature is associated by the historicists with the eternally recurrent, history is about unique and inimitable human acts.

Within an ontology of duration, however, nature and history are intertwined. The two virtual tendencies that Bergson distinguishes—one repetitive and the other creative—are not separate but interrelated. Bergson hereby undermines the modern Constitution that is reproduced within the historicist tradition and allows us to revise the modern significance of the term "history." When Bergson refers to history he refers to the "history of life," to evolution. This accomplishes the task that Bergson has set for himself, which is to go "beyond the human state" and to connect a theory of knowledge with a theory of life.

A Bergsonian objection to the modern Constitution is that human history is isolated from the history of life as a whole. In this, a perspective on duration, or in other words, on the *creative* aspect of history, is being obscured. We can understand this elimination of duration better if we take a closer look at the way in which Bergson evaluates science—after all, the historicists wanted to legitimize history as a science. Mechanistic sciences from the eighteenth and nineteenth centuries, according to Bergson, eliminate duration by isolating or "cutting out" systems from the Whole of duration. These "closed systems" are not entirely artificial. Matter indeed consists—as we have discussed in chapter 4—in a tendency to constitute isolable systems that can be treated geometrically. Yet Bergson stresses that this is only a tendency and that the isolation of these material systems is never complete: "The systems marked off by science endure only because they are bound inseparably with the rest of the universe."[42] Science does not take the connection of material systems to the whole of the universe into account; it isolates and closes systems for the convenience of study. With this it eliminates duration and thereby the creative "historical" movement in which these isolated systems partake.

---

41. Iggers, *The German Conception of History*, 4–5.
42. CE, 11.

A metaphor may clarify this:

> Though our reasoning on isolated systems may imply that their history, past, present, and future, might be instantaneously unfurled like a fan, this history, in point of fact, unfolds itself gradually, as if it occupied a duration like our own. If I want to mix a glass of sugar and water, I must, willy nilly, wait until the sugar melts. This little fact is big with meaning. For here the time I have to wait is not that mathematical time which would apply equally well to the entire history of the material world, even if that history were spread out instantaneously in space. It coincides with my impatience, that is to say, with a certain portion of my own duration, which I cannot protract or contract as I like. It is no longer something thought, it is something lived. It is no longer a relation, it is an absolute. What else can this mean than that the glass of water, the sugar, and the process of the sugar's melting in the water are abstractions, and that the Whole within which they have been cut out by my senses and understanding progresses, it may be in the manner of a consciousness?[43]

We have to reconnect these closed systems to the Whole: "there is no reason, therefore, why a duration, and so a form of existence like our own, should not be attributed to the systems that science isolates, provided such systems are reintegrated into the Whole."[44]

In order to gain, in accordance with Bergson's proposal, a perspective on the creative nature of history—on historical duration—history should no longer be approached as a closed system that is radically separated from life as a whole—or, in other words, from evolution. We would have to go "beyond the human state." While historicism entails "the belief in the fundamental historicity of man and culture,"[45] Bergson extends this historicity to "life" and its evolution. Bergson maintains that the history of man can only be understood within the framework of life as a whole: "The evolution of the living being, like that of the embryo, implies a continual recording of duration, a persistence of the past in the present, and so an appearance, at least, of organic memory."[46]

---

43. CE, 9–10.

44. CE, 11.

45. Bos, "Nineteenth-Century Historicism," 131.

46. CE, 19.

This turns Bergsonism into what we could call a "nonmodern form of historicism." This Bergsonian historicism seeks not to *legitimize* history as a science, but to *extend* its scope. The fruit of extending the scope of history is a notion of historical creativity. It has been a common complaint about historicism that it cannot cope with historical discontinuity. Historicists are directed at creating historical continuity through their narratives—on telling, as Benjamin put it, the sequence of events "like the beads of a rosary." In this way history is being turned into a "closed whole" that obscures a perspective on the creative aspect of the historical process. History is being written from the perspective of the victors of history. However, thinking in terms of duration can help us to break open the continuum of history.

In order to explore history as an "open whole," we will now shift attention from historical epistemology to the philosophy of history. Historicism is characterized by a concern for methodology and epistemology, which makes it a philosophical tradition. It should not, however, be confused with *philosophy of history*. This latter tradition is concerned not with epistemology but with metaphysical issues, such as the meaning, laws, and ends of history in itself.[47]

3. A COMPARISON WITH HEGEL

The implications of a Bergsonian historical ontology become clear when we juxtapose Bergsonism with Hegel's philosophy of history. There are a number of remarkable similarities between the two thinkers. Both, for example, adhere to a holistic concept of history, although while Hegel has a teleological concept of history, historical duration is an emergence of "unforeseen novelty."

The difference between both philosophers can be traced back to how they relate to modernity. Contrasting Bergson's conception of "the whole" with that of Hegel will highlight what I see as Bergson's most important contribution to the philosophy of history, namely a perspective on the *creative nature* of history.

Hegel's Philosophy of History

Hegel's philosophy of history is a typical product of the modern regime of historicity. It shares with the historicists the notion that the essence of human activity lies in its history. Hegel is nonetheless also an heir of the Enlightenment, because he places Reason at the center of his philosophy.

---

47. Beiser, *The German Historicist Tradition*, 8.

Hegel maintains that the history of the world is a rational process.[48] This follows from his absolute idealism, the notion that reality is ultimately not matter but *Mind* or *Spirit*. The essence of Spirit is Reason. Spirit is "absolute" and "universal," meaning that reality does not consist of a collection of independent, individual minds but that there is one ultimate reality, which is universal reason, in which the minds of individual people partake.[49] Spirit is, however, not aware of its universal nature because it is alienated from itself. It takes what is really a part of itself as something alien and hostile.[50]

Because of its alienated state, Spirit is divided against itself. It works in two areas. First there is the objective domain or Objective Spirit. This refers to things in objective reality that function according to rational principles. Nature, for instance, embodies Reason because "it is unchangeably subordinate to universal laws."[51] The second area is Subjective Spirit, which is the Spirit of knowing subjects who are equally rational because they have the capacity to acquire knowledge about the rational principles that structure objective reality. As rational beings we have, for instance, the ability to discover the laws of nature.

History is of crucial importance to Hegel's absolute idealism, because the historical process describes the continuing identification of the Subjective and Objective Spirit. History is a process in which the Universal Spirit gradually overcomes its state of alienation by gaining self-awareness. This process is teleological because history has a final goal, namely the self-awareness of Spirit. History will enter its last stage when the Universal or Absolute Spirit is realized and the Subjective and Objective Spirit are in harmony—when Spirit recognizes itself for what it is. The consequence of this argument is that Spirit realizes itself in the work of Hegel, which represents the final stage of World-History.

There is progress in history, because Spirit's growing self-awareness coincides with the advancement of freedom.[52] Hegel maintains that "the

---

48. G.W.F. Hegel, *The Philosophy of History* (1837), trans. J. Sibree (1857; repr., Kitchener: Batoche Books, 2001), 22. According to Hegel history is "the rational necessary course of the World-Spirit."

49. "My mind, your mind, and the minds of every other conscious being are particular, limited manifestations of this universal mind." Peter Singer, *Marx: A Very Short Introduction* (1980; repr., Oxford: Oxford University Press, 1996), 17.

50. Ibid., 18.

51. Hegel, *The Philosophy of History*, 25.

52. Frederick C. Beiser, *Hegel* (New York: Routledge, 2005), 266.

essence of Spirit is freedom."[53] The realization of freedom is hence the purpose of history. The identification of freedom with Reason or Spirit means that Hegel's concept of freedom is different from our liberal concept of "negative freedom."[54] For Hegel, freedom is not defined as the freedom from interference by others. According to Hegel we are free when we choose and act in accordance with the universal principles of Reason—when we are not influenced by our surroundings or accidental circumstances in which we happen to find ourselves. Freedom lies for Hegel in universal rational principles. In order to realize freedom, the obstacles in objective reality that prevent freedom from realizing itself have to be removed. This process takes time and involves the course of World-History. As Singer explains:

> Mind [i.e., Spirit] cannot be free in an alienated state, for in such a state it appears to encounter opposition and barriers to its own complete development. Since Mind is really infinite and all-encompassing, opposition and barriers are only appearances, the result of Mind not recognizing itself for what it is, but taking what is really a part of itself as something alien and hostile to itself. These apparently alien forces limit the freedom of Mind, for if Mind does not know its own infinite powers it cannot exercise these powers to organize the world in accordance with its plans.[55]

Freedom is thus realized when Reason has obtained knowledge of itself, or when the Absolute Spirit is realized. The actions of people will now no longer enter into conflict with their surroundings. This corresponds, according to Hegel, with the establishment of an organic community that is rationally organized and in which individual interests and communal interests coincide. I can, in other words, accomplish my freedom by serving the objective form of the universal, which, according to Hegel, is the state.[56] The progress of Reason through history therefore also equals the development of the state. Hegel's definition of freedom is, again, different from the liberal, individualistic concept of freedom, because Hegel sees people as part of an organic whole—the state—which means that people only act freely when they act in accordance with the interests of the state. Because freedom and Reason

---

53. Hegel, *The Philosophy of History*, 31.
54. Peter Singer, *Hegel: A Very Short Introduction* (1983; repr. Oxford: Oxford University Press, 2001), 34.
55. Singer, *Marx*, 18.
56. Hegel, *The Philosophy of History*, 31.

imply one another, the rationally organized state will ultimately guarantee individual freedom.

The emphasis on an organic community already reveals the holistic nature of Hegel's philosophy of history. Like Bergson, Hegel rejects mechanistic explanations of history. Historical events cannot be properly understood in terms of "external necessity" that explains events from prior "causes" in time.[57] Instead, history unfolds in accordance with an "internal necessity," an underlying purpose which is derived from the goal of history as a whole, which is "the rational necessary course of the World-Spirit."[58] This is Hegel's teleological explanation of history.

The purpose of History as a whole is to Hegel "first only in order of explanation, not order of existence."[59] It reveals itself in the course of World-History. Hegel therefore does not completely exclude mechanical explanations of history. As Beiser states,

> Mechanical explanation is perfectly valid of all parts within a whole; but it is inadequate from the standpoint of the whole itself. . . . The workings of mechanical causality are simply the means or instruments by which the purposes of history are realized.[60]

It is the concrete activities of men that "actualize" the purpose of history. Hegel calls this the "cunning of reason": reason sets the passions of men to work for itself. In their free actions, individuals unwittingly fulfill the purpose of history. An example is what Hegel calls "World-Historical Individuals."[61] These are "great historical men," such as Caesar, Alexander, or Napoleon, who embody the World-Spirit in their epoch. As practical and political men they had no consciousness of the general Idea that they were unfolding in pursuing their own aims. They were driven by an "unconscious impulse" that "occasioned the accomplishment of that for which the time was ripe."[62]

---

57. As Bergson states in *Creative Evolution*, "the present moment of a living body does not find its explanation in the moment immediately before, . . . *all* the past of the organism must be added to that moment, its heredity—in fact, the whole of a very long history." CE, 20.

58. Hegel, *The Philosophy of History*, 24.

59. Beiser, *Hegel*, 264.

60. Ibid., 265.

61. Hegel, *The Philosophy of History*, 44.

62. Ibid.

The fate of these great men is often not good. They are murdered or die prematurely. Once they have played their part in World-History "they fall off like empty hulls from the kernel."[63]

Bergson's Nonmodern Ontology

Hegel can be seen as a typical representative of the modern regime of historicity. Dan Edelstein describes a regime of historicity as "an almost existential condition," a way in which we reach an understanding of events through the narrative organization of past, present, and future.[64] The *modern* regime of historicity involves a narrative that takes the future as point of departure. In modern narratives of history it is the future that organizes past and present. An example is Hegel's narrative treatment of the French Revolution. Eelco Runia points out in *The Pathology of Battle* that instead of finding the historical causes for the Revolution—which would have been the most obvious thing to do—Hegel turns the tables and uses the French Revolution to explain history: "Hegel's genial discovery was that he explained the French Revolution by considering it as a given—he had the courage to choose a perspective from which it changes from *explanandum* into *explanans*."[65] Hegel reinterpreted history as a whole from the fact that it could have produced an event such as the Revolution. According to Runia, the triangle French Revolution–Napoleon–Hegel marks not so much the "end of history"—as Hegel himself suggests—as the end of Hegel's *emplotment* of the past. The meaning that Hegel in his Universal History attributes to the past should be sought in the way in which Hegel ordered the succession of historical events in a narrative, by means of the "metaphor of reason."

The primacy of Reason in history also reveals the influence of the modern Constitution on Hegel's ideas about history—the division and purification of the domains of nature and culture. In *The Philosophy of History* Hegel distinguishes "World" from "Spirit." World is the domain of "physical and psychical Nature"[66] and represents unfreedom. As Hegel writes in *The Philosophy of Nature*: "Nature exhibits no freedom in its existence, but only

---

63. Ibid., 45.
64. Edelstein, *The Enlightenment*, 16.
65. My translation. E.H. Runia, *De Pathologie van de Veldslag: Geschiedenis en geschiedschrijving in Tolstoj's Oorlog en Vrede* [The Pathology of Battle: History and Historiography in Tolstoj's War and Peace] (Amsterdam: Meulenhoff Boekerij, 1995), 166.
66. Hegel, *The Philosophy of History*, 30.

necessity and contingency."⁶⁷ The domain of History, on the other hand, is the domain of Spirit and freedom.⁶⁸

As we have seen, Bergsonism allows us to question this modern Constitution. Drawing on the insights of the life-sciences in the nineteenth century, Bergson claims that the social is entangled with "life as a whole," which is something that is overlooked and prohibited by the modern Constitution. The moderns neglect the biological origins of human society. While Hegel presents the social and the natural in accordance with the Enlightenment tradition as two isolated domains placed side by side, Bergson would topple this scheme on its side in arguing that "the vital" *underlies* the social.

Hegel:

Nature/Life | Social/History

Bergson:

Social/History
—↑— ↑— ↑— ↑—
Nature/Life

In this way, Bergson allows us to reverse the "emancipation of historical time from the rhythm of nature" (Koselleck) that lies at the foundation of the modern concept of history. Historical time should be considered in light of the time of life, or, in other words, duration. While Hegel, in accordance with the Enlightenment, sees humans as rational beings, Bergson sees humans first and foremost as *living* beings. This means that decisive aspects of human life are the product of evolution, which also goes for history. History originates in life.

Reason itself is also, according to Bergson, derived for evolutionary purposes from a wider, general consciousness, in order to facilitate human action on its material surroundings: "The history of the evolution of life . . . shows us in the faculty of understanding an appendage of the faculty of acting, a more and more precise, more and more complex and supple adaptation of the consciousness of living beings to the conditions of existence that are made for them."⁶⁹ Human intelligence is accordingly formed after material

---

67. G.W.F. Hegel, *The Philosophy of Nature* (Whitefish, MT: Kessinger Publishing, 2004), 1.
68. Hegel, *The Philosophy of History*, 30.
69. CE, ix.

relations.⁷⁰ Our intellect "feels at home among solids, where our action finds its fulcrum and our industry its tools . . . our intellect triumphs in geometry, wherein is revealed the kinship of logical thought with unorganized matter, and where the intellect has only to follow its natural movement."⁷¹ Yet while the inert naturally enters into the frames of the intellect, the living is adapted to these frames only artificially.⁷² Because Reason is at home among "repetitive" material relations, it remains blind to "creative" vital processes such as biological or historical duration.⁷³

Hegel maintains that there are good arguments for assuming that history is governed by Reason. The empirical evidence points in this direction. If we take a close look at the course that world history has taken, we can see rational principles at work. This is expressed in Hegel's famous statement that

> To him who looks upon the world rationally, the world in its turn presents a rational aspect. The relation is mutual.⁷⁴

Reality functions according to rational principles, because we humans, as rational beings, are capable of understanding these principles. For Hegel this is proof that history is governed by Reason.

We may now formulate a Bergsonian critique of this Hegelian thesis. Through Bergson we can admit that Reason may recognize itself in history. But what Reason finds in history is what it had already placed there from the outset. If we look at the historical process from the perspective of Reason, the rational aspect of history is reflected back to us. By identifying the historical process with Reason, history is turned into a closed system. Human history is isolated from the whole of duration (or, Life in general) from which it emanates, similar to the way in which science "cuts out" closed material systems from the whole of the universe for the convenience of study. This

---

70. CE, 186.

71. CE, ix.

72. CE, 197–198.

73. "Now, when the intellect undertakes the study of life, it necessarily treats the living like the inert, applying the same forms to this new object, carrying over into this new field the same habits that have succeeded so well in the old; and it is right to do so, for only on such terms does the living offer to our action the same hold as inert matter. But the truth we thus arrive at becomes altogether relative to our faculty of action. It is no more than a *symbolic* verity . . . The duty of philosophy should be to intervene here actively, to examine the living without any reservation as to practical utility, by freeing itself from forms and habits that are strictly intellectual." CE, 195–196.

74. Hegel, *The Philosophy of History*, 24–25.

creates the illusion that the historical process is predictable and answers to laws. The "rational" side of history merely corresponds to one of the two virtual tendencies of duration, namely the "material" tendency toward repetition and homogeneity. The creative aspect of history remains out of sight. This is the second virtual tendency of duration, which I identified as the truly historical, creative tendency that corresponds to the movement of life.

Reason locks us up in that which is given or already created. Bergson consequently does not associate freedom with Reason. To the contrary: in order to be free and create the new, we must *break free* from the frames of Reason. This is only possible by taking action:

> If we had never seen a man swim, we might say that swimming is an impossible thing, inasmuch as, to learn to swim, we must begin by holding ourselves up in the water and, consequently, already know how to swim. Reasoning, in fact, always nails us down to the solid ground. But if, quite simply, I throw myself into the water without fear, I may keep myself up well enough at first by merely struggling, and gradually adapt myself to the new environment: I shall thus have learnt to swim. So, in theory, there is a kind of absurdity in trying to know otherwise than by intelligence; but if the risk be frankly accepted, action will perhaps cut the knot that reasoning has tied and will not unloose.[75]

Once the leap toward a "new" reality is made, Reason will immediately accommodate this within the frames of the already known, as it is the natural function of the intellect to "bind like to like."[76] Now swimming suddenly does not seem that unreasonable at all, as it is merely an extension of the act of walking. The creative act that actually leads to swimming is hereby hidden from view. This is also what happens when historians dissolve historical discontinuity in the continuum of history.

In order to truly act freely and create, though, we must once more plunge into pure duration. This involves an actualization of the past:

> We must, by a strong recoil of our personality on itself, gather up our past which is slipping away, in order to thrust it, compact and undivided, into a present which it will create by entering. Rare indeed are the moments when we are self-possessed to this extent: it is then that our actions are truly free.[77]

---

75. CE, 192.

76. CE, 200.

77. CE, 200.

A Bergsonian nonmodern ontology implies that, in order to gain a perspective on the creative nature of history, we must reintegrate the domains of nature and history.

Dialectics and Duration

Hegel maintains that the logic according to which historical contradictions are overcome toward a unity is dialectical. Dialectics is a "logic of the negative." Every incomplete conception of reality suffers from inherent contradictions because it excludes something, which is its negation. Every thesis, in other words, logically gives rise to its antithesis. This antithesis can contribute to the formation of a new, more inclusive concept that better approximates the nature of reality (i.e., Universal Reason) because it is more inclusive and overcomes the original contradiction. This is the synthesis of thesis and antithesis. To conclude this chapter, I will briefly highlight Hegel's dialectics and contrast it with Bergsonian intuition.

In the *Science of Logic*, Hegel applies the dialectical method to the category of Being. Investigating the notion of Being, Hegel concludes that pure Being lacks determination. It is "pure indeterminateness and emptiness."[78] Yet the absence of all determination is in fact nothing. In this way, the inherent contradiction within the notion of pure Being, the "indeterminate immediate," is that it turns into its antithesis, which is pure Nothingness. Nothing is the absence of determination and therefore the same as pure Being. But though inseparable, Being and Nothingness are simultaneously also absolutely distinct. They are opposites. The truth of Being and Nothingness—their synthesis—is Becoming, a movement in which the one vanishes into the other, "in which both are distinguished, but by a difference which has equally immediately resolved itself."[79]

To Hegel, dialectics is not a purely formal logical structure. A consequence of Hegel's absolute idealism is that dialectical concepts existing on the level of ideas manifest themselves in World-History. There is no objective reality independent from Reason, according to Hegel, and hence no distinction between content and form.[80] This means that material history is shaped after the development of the concepts of Reason.

In *The Philosophy of History*, Hegel describes World-History as the dialectical movement toward the realization of freedom. In order to illustrate this, Hegel describes world history from the early civilizations of China, India, and Persia to ancient Greece and Rome. From there it goes on to the

---

78. G.W.F. Hegel, *Science of Logic* (Whitefish, MT: Kessinger Publishing, 2001), 35.
79. Ibid., 36.
80. Singer, *Hegel*, 233–234.

"Germanic Period," which encompasses the Reformation, the Enlightenment, and the French Revolution, and which culminates in Hegel's own time. The Oriental World is the phase of the Absolute Spirit. In these civilizations only one person, the ruler, is free. All others are subject to the will of the despot and lack any concept of individual conscience. True history begins with the idea of individual freedom. The principle of freedom animated the Greek World. Greek society was founded on the community, in which a concept of individual conscience did not exist. Yet the principle of freedom requires independent critical thought. Freedom could consequently not be achieved within Greek society. This becomes clear in the conviction of Socrates, whose independent thought threatened the communal existence of ancient Greece.[81]

The principle of independent thought develops under Christianity, especially during the Reformation with its acceptance of the right of individual conscience. This is the negation of the first stage, its antithesis. The absolute freedom of the individual, however, proves too abstract to serve as the basis for a society. Absolute freedom results in the terror of the French Revolution. A synthesis has to be established between customary harmony and absolute freedom, which is the organic community of German society of Hegel's time, which because of its rational organization preserves individual freedom.[82] With Hegel, history has come to an ending.

How would Bergson evaluate Hegel's dialectical model? According to Bergson, dialectics misconceives duration. It is an abstraction from the original creative movement of history. Dialectics illustrates how Reason operates. The intellect works retrospectively on what is already created and reduces movement and change to the already known. Dialectical concepts hence offer an external view on duration. Because of this, dialectics is too abstract and too general.[83] It thinks in terms of abstract oppositions and therefore grasps reality in terms of differences in degree, thereby disregarding differences in kind. Instead of the external difference of dialectics, duration is an immanent, *internal difference* that, as Deleuze points out, "does not go and must not go to the point of contradiction, to alterity, to the negative, because these three notions are in fact less profound than it or are merely external views of this internal difference."[84]

Abstract dialectical concepts, according to Bergson, can never recompose the real. No matter by how much we multiply our external points of view of

---

81. Ibid., 62–77.

82. Ibid., 241.

83. Gilles Deleuze, "Bergson's Conception of Difference," in *The New Bergson*, ed. John Mullarkey, trans. Melissa McMahon (Manchester: Manchester University Press, 1999), 46.

84. Ibid., 49.

the race between Achilles and the tortoise, we will never be able to reconstruct their original movements. Dialectics suffers from arbitrariness because "there is scarcely any concrete reality upon which one cannot take two opposing views at the same time and which is consequently not subsumed under the two antagonistic concepts."[85] Bergson therefore sees dialectical concepts and reasoning in general as merely a compensation for the limited scope of our perceptual apparatus.[86] He even maintains that it was the "insufficiency of our faculties of perception" that gave birth to philosophy.

The Bergsonian method of intuition can be considered a reversal of the dialectical approach. Through intuition we do not pass from concepts to things, but we go from things to concepts. This provides an antidote to a purely conceptual philosophy: "Since any attempt at purely conceptual philosophy calls forth antagonistic efforts, and since, in the field of pure dialectics there is no system to which one cannot oppose another, should we remain in that field or, (without, of course, ceasing to exercise our faculties of conception and reasoning), ought we not rather return to perception, getting it to expand and extend?"[87] Only in this way can we do justice to duration.

Difference has to be understood on a more fundamental level than dialectics can provide. In chapter 7 I will further explore Bergson's alternative to dialectics. It will become clear that Bergson himself eventually also recognized that his philosophy of life contained a historical dimension.

4. CONCLUSION

In this chapter I have highlighted what I see as Bergson's second and most important contribution to the theory of history, which is a unique perspective on history as a "continuous creation of unforeseen novelty."

We have seen that duration surprisingly shares its most important ontological principles with historicism. Although they disagree about its nature, both Bergson and the historicists place *change* at the center of their worldview. They assume that the world is in a state of incessant flux and that the human world changes with history. There are two other important ontological principles of historicism, namely a focus on *individuality* and a *holistic* concept of history. Historicism's "nominalist holism" (Beiser) entails

---

85. CM, 148–149.

86. In CM Bergson states that "Conceiving is a make-shift when perception is not granted us, and reasoning is done in order to fill up the gaps of perception or to extend its scope." CM, 155.

87. CM, 110.

that "the whole" is not some metaphysical entity with an existence apart from its parts, but that the whole exists *in and through* the parts.

Duration combines individuality and holism in a similar way. Duration is not a metaphysical "stream of time" in which individual temporalities partake, but a "virtual whole" (Deleuze). As such, duration has a theoretical-ideal status and exists only in its actualizations. This allows Bergson to combine a commitment to both one single (virtual) mode of time and a radical pluralism of different temporalities, or "rhythms of duration."

A crucial difference between Bergsonism and historicism is that the historicists maintained that the social and historical sciences require a fundamentally different approach from the natural sciences, because there is a fundamental difference between the phenomena of nature and those of history. According to Bergson's ontology of duration, however, nature and culture are intertwined. Isolating human history from the history of life as a whole turns history into a closed system. To regain a sense of the creative nature of history, the history of man would have to be reintegrated within the framework of life as a whole. What I call a Bergsonian "nonmodern historicism" seeks not, like the historicists, to *legitimate* history as a science, but to *extend* the scope of history as a science "beyond the human state."

Bergsonism can be compared to the philosophy of history of Hegel. Although both Bergson and Hegel adhere to a holistic concept of history, the crucial difference between both thinkers is how they relate to the modern regime of historicity. Hegel bases his philosophy of history on a distinction between "World" (nature/life) and "Spirit" (history). We might say that Bergson places this scheme on its side by arguing that the vital (nature/life) underlies the social (history). This reveals that history originates in life.

By identifying the historical process with Reason, Hegel turns history into a "closed system." This creates the illusion that the historical process is predictable and answers to laws. The "rational" side of history, however, merely corresponds with one of the two virtual tendencies of duration, namely the "material" tendency toward repetition and homogeneity. The creative aspect of history remains out of sight. This is the second virtual tendency of duration, which I have identified as a truly historical, creative tendency that corresponds with the movement of life. This confirms once more that a perspective on historical duration requires a broader, nonmodern conception of history.

This chapter has made clear that Bergson's relation to modernity is ambiguous. Bergson connects with the maelstrom of perpetual change that characterizes the modern condition. The Bergsonian concept of change, however, is not an expression of the modern regime of historicity. Bergson's concept of history is not teleological but *creative*, and historical duration is an emergence of unforeseen novelty. A Bergsonian regime gives critical importance to the past as a vehicle for change. An "enduring" change requires that we find new ways of (re-)connecting with the past, within an environment in which this connection is no longer obvious. Having focused on the ontological implications of Bergson's philosophy of duration, we will now seek confirmation of this historical reading of Bergsonism in Bergson's own work.

CHAPTER 7

THE DREAM OF PROGRESS

> The concept of man's historical progress cannot be sundered from the concept of its progression through a homogeneous, empty time. A critique of the concept of such a progression must underlie any criticism of the concept of progress itself.[1]
>
> —Walter Benjamin, "Theses on the Philosophy of History," in *Illuminations*

> Mankind lies groaning, half crushed beneath the weight of its own progress. Men do not sufficiently realize that their future is in their own hands.[2]
>
> —Henri Bergson, *The Two Sources of Morality and Religion*

The Two Sources of Morality and Religion was published years after Bergson had traded in his academic career for politics. During the Great War, Bergson was sent on various diplomatic missions to the United States. Here he met with Woodrow Wilson, whom he tried to convince to enter the war on the European continent.[3] After the war, Bergson became involved in the establishment of the League of Nations. As president of the International Committee on Intellectual Cooperation (CIC), Bergson helped to advance

---

1. Walter Benjamin, "Theses on the Philosophy of History," in *Illuminations*, ed. Hannah Arendt, trans. Harry Zohn (New York: Schocken Books, 1968), 261.
2. TS, 317.
3. For a detailed account of Bergon's diplomatic missions, see Philippe Soulez, *Bergson politique* (Paris: Presses Universitaires de France, 1989).

the objective of the League of Nations to create an international community that should prevent future wars.

Because of Bergson's involvement in politics the surprise was great when in 1932 *The Two Sources* appeared, twenty-five years after the publication of *Creative Evolution*.[4] Although *The Two Sources* is far less known than *Matter and Memory* or *Creative Evolution*, it is one of Bergson's greatest books and also his most historical work. Its contents closely connect with the ideals of the League of Nations. The text explores the vital "sources" of morality and religion in order to construct an evolutionary social theory, which revolves around a notion of the closed and open society—concepts that became tremendously influential after they were adopted a decade later by Karl Popper in his famous *The Open Society and its Enemies* (1945).

I will argue that *The Two Sources* is a historical work on at least two levels. First, the book is not some casual theorizing about the nature of morality and religion, but seeks to intervene in a particular historical situation. *The Two Sources* acquires its urgency from the years of the Interbellum, when the Great War had shattered the optimistic belief in progress of the Belle Époque and a new war already loomed on the horizon. Bergson identifies these years as a decisive moment in history. Achieving progress for mankind seemed more necessary than ever before—especially under the threat of new weapons of mass destruction such as the atomic bomb, the invention of which Bergson predicts[5]—but how to achieve this was no longer clear. The "problem of war" that the League of Nations tried to solve also motivated Bergson to write *The Two Sources*.

The Two Sources of Morality and Religion is also, secondly, a historical work on the level of its philosophical argumentation. In order to explore the possibility of progress, Bergson tries to understand the dynamics of history. To Bergson, the idea of historical progress is a product of a "retrospective illusion" which conceives of progress in quantitative terms. The narrative of the Enlightenment, for instance, assumes that an open society can be established by extending the loyalty we feel toward our community to the nation, and

---

4. On one fine day, Jacques Maritain noted, "without any publicity, without any press release, without anyone, even among the author's closest friends, having been informed, the work that had been anticipated for twenty-five years appeared in bookstores." Jacques Maritain, cited in Alexandre Lefebvre, *Human Rights as a Way of Life: On Bergson's Political Philosophy* (Stanford: Stanford University Press, 2013), xiii.

5. TS, 287. "At the pace at which science is moving, that day is not far off when one of the two adversaries, through some secret process which he was holding in reserve, will have the means of annihilating his opponent. The vanquished may vanish off the face of the earth."

finally to humanity as a whole.[6] In this process, the primitive war instinct is gradually erased from human civilization. Bergson argues, however, that this neglects the biological origins of our society. It is an illusion to assume that the civilization process will abolish the tendency to war. The war instinct is indeed "the first to appear when we scratch below the surface of civilization in search of nature."[7]

In this chapter, I will examine the theory of history that Bergson articulates in *The Two Sources*. I will do this by arguing that Bergson rethinks the modern idea of historical progress. Bergson's theory of history has often been ignored by his interpreters. By showing how Bergson develops the historical implications of his philosophy of life, I will confirm my thesis that Bergson deserves to be taken seriously as a historical theorist.

Section one relates *The Two Sources* to a number of theorists who have reflected on the idea of progress and its origins in the Enlightenment. I argue that *The Two Sources* can be read as a critique of the modern ontology that underlies the "story" of the Enlightenment. Section two shows that Bergson redefines progress by reconceptualizing the closed and open society. Bergson argues that humans are not primarily rational beings but *living* beings. Human history is a particular form of evolution and therefore determined by life's two virtual tendencies—one toward "closure" and conservation, the other toward "openness" and creation.[8] These provide *two* sources of morality and religion, and are tendencies that differ in kind but not in degree.

Section three proceeds with a discussion of the theory of history that Bergson lays out in the Final Remarks of *The Two Sources*. Bergson identifies the years of the Interbellum here as a historical moment of crisis that is produced by industrial modernity and that threatens the future of humanity. Progress is not the inevitable outcome of a pre-determined historical process, but should be achieved "in the present." I will conclude that Bergson's articulation of a theory of history adds a historical dimension to Bergson's philosophy of life that had remained implicit in his previous works.

---

6. According to Suzanne Guerlac, Bergson thinks here primarily of Émile Durkheim, who distinguishes in his *Moral Education* three different phases in human social and moral evolution: the family, the fatherland or political community, and humanity. The progress of civilization has to run through these three stages. Guerlac states, "The implication is clear: European nations (and they alone) are spiritual states on their way to realizing, to one degree or another, the ideal of humanity." Guerlac, "Bergson, the Void, and the Politics of Life," 41. For an evaluation of Bergson's critique of Durkheim, see Lefebvre, *Human Rights as a Way of Life*, 32–48.

7. TS, 284.

8. See chapter 4.

1. PROGRESS AND THE ENLIGHTENMENT

Immanuel Kant was one of the first to reflect on the nature of Enlightenment. In "An answer to the question: 'What is Enlightenment?'" (1784), published in the *Berlinische Monatschrift*, Kant proclaims that "Enlightenment is man's emergence from his self-incurred immaturity." By immaturity, Kant refers to the inability to use one's own understanding. I am immature if I do not make any effort at all to think for myself: "If I have a book to have understanding in place of me, a spiritual adviser to have a conscience for me, a doctor to judge my diet for me, and so on."[9] The motto of the Enlightenment is therefore *sapere aude!*—have courage to use your own understanding. The Enlightenment represents that moment in history when man starts to rely on his own reason instead of on some external religious authority.

Kant's reflection is still very influential for the way in which we conceive of the Enlightenment. Maybe the most significant feature of Kant's account is, according to Michel Foucault, that it displays a new form of historical awareness. Foucault identifies Kant's essay as the first time that a philosopher connects his philosophical project to his place in history: "It is in the reflection on 'today' as difference in history and as motive for a particular philosophical task that the novelty of this [Kant's] text appears to me to lie."[10] By reflecting on the Enlightenment as "historical event," Kant provided a justification for his critical-philosophical project. In an "age of reason" it is of vital importance to define the conditions under which the use of reason is legitimate. This, Foucault argues, is precisely what Kant tries to establish in his three *Critiques*. The *Critiques* can in this sense be seen as "handbooks of reason" for an age of Enlightenment.[11]

Kant's essay about the nature of Enlightenment can therefore be considered an affirmation of the *story* of the Enlightenment that had taken shape during the eighteenth century. Historian Dan Edelstein sees the Enlightenment primarily as a *narrative invention by contemporaries* that revolved around the notion of a "philosophical spirit" and that accounted for the scientific and technological innovations of the seventeenth and eighteenth centuries.[12]

---

9. Immanuel Kant, *An Answer to the Question: What is Enlightenment?* trans. H.B. Nisbet (1991; repr., London: Penguin Books, 2009), 1.

10. Michel Foucault, "What is Enlightenment?" in *Essential Works of Foucault 1: Ethics, Subjectivity and Truth*, ed. Paul Rabinow, trans. Catherine Porter (New York: The New Press, 1997), 309.

11. Ibid., 308.

12. Edelstein, *The Enlightenment*, 28.

This narrative displayed a new, modern form of historical consciousness that Edelstein traces to the "quarrel of the ancients and the moderns"—a debate among French poets, critics, and philosophers that occurred from the mid-seventeenth until the early eighteenth century over the status of Antiquity in relation to modern scientific achievements. The participants in the quarrel were aware of a "vast historical evolution" that separated an "ancient" past from a "modern" present. While both ancients and moderns were processing a defamiliarization of the past, they differed over how this historical progress should be understood.[13]

The Enlightenment narrative that emerged during the quarrel saw the scientific revolution as a product of an age characterized by a "philosophical spirit" (*esprit philosophique*), turning a discourse on science into one about *society*. The idea of "society" that emerged for the first time at the end of the seventeenth century designated a world of human interaction independent from the state.[14] As a worldly notion, it replaced religious accounts of history and could serve as a yardstick of progress.

An important feature of the philosophical spirit was its flexibility. It had no fixed content and could be attached to a variety of works, initiatives, and practices. Edelstein therefore argues that the Enlightenment narrative is best understood in terms of a new regime of historicity, which he defines, after Hartog, as the narrative configuration of past, present, and future. The philosophical spirit was "always something that defined the present moment."[15] It expressed the sense of living in a new time that was directed toward an even more glorious future. The structure of this modern regime of historicity returns, for instance, in Kant's account of the Enlightenment. Kant argues that in his own time only a few had succeeded in freeing themselves from immaturity by cultivating their own minds. He sees the enlightenment of the entire public as a task for the *future*, but is in no doubt that this enlightenment of the public will, however, inevitably take place.

---

13. Larry Norman, *The Shock of the Ancient: Literature and History in Early Modern France* (Chicago: The University of Chicago Press, 2011), 11–14. Norman rejects the "total binary opposition" of Ancients and Moderns. The Moderns adopted a notion of linear historical progress that included the arts, while the Ancients also celebrated scientific progress, but they could simultaneously defend the superiority of Ancient culture in other aspects, such as morality, literature, or art. The quarrel would have a great influence on later historical thinkers such as Montesquieu, Hume, and Voltaire, and eventually even German historicism (33).

14. Edelstein, *The Enlightenment*, 29–32.

15. Ibid., 72–73.

All that is needed is the freedom to make public use of one's reason in all matters.[16]

Reinhart Koselleck has drawn attention to the political significance of the Enlightenment narrative, maintaining that its importance went beyond the intellectual upper class that frequented the salons and coffee houses of Paris. He has argued that while the narrative of the Enlightenment was a product of the political stability provided by the eighteenth-century Absolutist State, it eventually came to undermine this very stability by bringing about the French Revolution.

Important in this respect was the strict distinction that the Absolutist State established between a public domain of politics and a private domain of morality. This successfully brought an end to the destructive religious wars that had devastated Europe for centuries. Yet while the public realm of politics remained under strict control of the absolute monarch, the private realm allowed for an inner moral freedom that facilitated the emergence of a philosophy of history. As this philosophical sense of history was unrestricted by "real" and concrete historical conditions, it remained a stranger to political reality. As a consequence, it developed a utopian belief in historical progress.[17]

Koselleck maintains that below the surface of the apparent stability of the eighteenth-century Absolutist State, out of sight for contemporaries, the seeds of the French Revolution were planted. The Enlightenment critique would eventually direct itself against the same Absolutist principles that had made its emergence possible in the first place. Absolutism came to be seen as an obstacle to the realization of the utopian future. Hence the philosophy of history invaded the public sphere and put the state on trial. Critique then turned into crisis: "Absolutism necessitated the genesis of the Enlightenment, and the Enlightenment conditioned the genesis of the French Revolution."[18]

Koselleck considered the eighteenth century as the "antechamber" to the twentieth century. His *Critique and Crisis* was published in 1959, at the height of the Cold War, when two superpowers, each with their own utopian project, laid claim to "a single global world." Koselleck wanted to draw attention to the dangers of the tendency of philosophies of history to create a utopian planning of the future. He saw a "link between the origins of the

---

16. Kant, "An Answer to the Question: What is Enlightenment?" 3.
17. Reinhart Koselleck, *Critique and Crisis: Enlightenment and the Pathogenesis of Modern Society* (Cambridge, MA: MIT Press, 1988), 6–11.
18. Ibid., 8.

modern philosophy of history and the start of the crisis which, initially in Europe, has been determining political events ever since 1789."[19]

The political dangers of philosophies of history were also addressed by Karl Popper in his famous *The Open Society and its Enemies* (1945), which has been interpreted as a response to Kant's *sapere aude!*[20] In *The Open Society*, Popper argues that what he calls "historicism" presents a great threat to free and open, liberal-democratic societies. By the term historicism, Popper refers not so much to the nineteenth-century German historians who wanted to establish history as a science as to speculative philosophies of history that pretend to know the laws of history and that make long-term historical prophecies.[21] Two important opponents in *The Open Society* are Hegel and Marx. According to Popper, scientific prediction has to be distinguished from historical prophecy. We cannot predict our future in the same way as we may predict, for instance, a solar eclipse.[22] Popper maintains that philosophies of history are dangerous, because they may provide a basis for totalitarianism. "Utopian social engineering" paves the way for a politics in which the end justifies the means. It prompts the extermination of all elements that can be considered as "obstacles" to historical progress. In this sense, Popper's diagnosis has an affinity with Koselleck's *Critique and Crisis*.

Popper's concept of the open society is still very influential. It appears regularly in debates about freedom and democracy. The open society has, for instance, served as inspiration for the Open Society Foundations of billionaire investor and philanthropist George Soros.[23] Popper uses the open and closed society as ideal types. The closed society refers to a tribal community that is defined by a belief in magical forces. The open society, on the other hand, reflects the ideals of the Enlightenment. It is organized in accordance with the principles of freedom and equality and directed at setting free the

---

19. Ibid., 6.

20. Ian Jarvie and Sandra Pralong, "Introduction," in *Popper's Open Society After Fifty Years: The Continuing Relevance of Karl Popper*, ed. Ian Jarvie and Sandra Pralong (London: Routledge, 1999), 3.

21. Karl Popper, *The Open Society and Its Enemies: New One-Volume Edition* (1945; repr., Princeton: Princeton University Press, 2013), xliii.

22. F.R. Ankersmit, *Denken over geschiedenis: Een overzicht van moderne geschiedfilosofische opvattingen* [Thinking about History: an Overview of Modern Perspectives on the Philosophy of History], 2nd ed. (Groningen: Wolters-Noordhoff, 1986), 53.

23. In order "to help countries make the transition from communism." The Open Society Foundations, accessed July 19, 2014, http://www.opensocietyfoundations.org.

"critical powers of man."[24] In an open society, people take a critical stance toward magical taboos. Popper identifies this critical attitude with a rational and scientific approach.[25]

Although Popper is often thought to be the inventor of the closed and open society, this is actually not the case. Popper derives his ideal types from Bergson's *The Two Sources of Morality and Religion*.[26] Bergson struggles in *The Two Sources* with a problem similar to Popper's, which is the problem of war and how to evade it. While *The Open Society* bears the stamp of World War II, the horrors of World War I reverberate in *The Two Sources*. Yet *The Two Sources* is more critical of the project of the Enlightenment than *The Open Society*. According to Bergson, the closed and open society should not be adopted as a model for historical development. As we will see, Bergson maintains that it is dangerous to assume a linear historical progression from the closed to the open society, because it presents us with an unrealistic image of the nature of human society and the menace of war.

The Enlightenment's idea of progress suggests that war will be eradicated from civilization once the universal principles of justice are adopted. These are principles that every rational being should necessarily accept. Opposed to an open society stands the closed society, which is one that does not include all human beings and that is based on the principle that, as Frédéric Worms

---

24. Popper, *The Open Society*, xli.

25. Ian Jarvie, "Popper's Ideal Types: Open and Close, Abstract and Ideal Societies," in *Popper's Open Society*, ed. Jarvie and Pralong, 73.

26. Although Bergson, according to Popper, has "a fundamentally different approach to nearly every problem of philosophy," he also admits to "a certain similarity" with Bergson's uses of these terms. The main difference with Bergson, Popper explains in an extensive note, is that Popper's distinction is rationalist, while Bergson has a religious distinction in mind. Popper sees Bergson's "religion of creative evolution" as "irrationalist" and "Hegelian," and thereby as ultimately an adversary to the open society. Popper continues: "This explains why [Bergson] can look upon his open society as the product of a mystical intuition, while I suggest (in chapters 10 and 24) that mysticism may be interpreted as an expression of the longing for the lost unity of the closed society, and therefore as a reaction against the rationalism of the open society." Popper also criticizes what he perceives as both Hegel's and Bergson's dependence on "great men" or leaders. With regard to *Creative Evolution*, Popper remarks that "the Hegelian character of this work is not sufficiently recognized; and, indeed, Bergon's lucidity and reasoned presentation of his thought sometimes make it difficult to realize how much his philosophy depends on Hegel." In chapter 6 I have addressed the similarities and differences between the philosophies of history of Hegel and Bergson. Popper, *The Open Society*, 512–513.

puts it, "where society stops so too does its morality."²⁷ It is the exclusionary nature of the closed society that creates the conditions for war. According to an idea of linear historical progress, war can be prevented if we succeed in extending the circle of the closed society from our family to the local community, then to the nation-state, and finally to humanity as a whole.

An example of such a model of development is the European Union. European integration was started after World War II in order to overcome nationalism, which was seen as the main cause of the great cataclysms of the twentieth century. The objective of European integration is to extend the boundaries of the nation-state in order to reach a higher form of social organization at a European level. By including "the other" into one's own community, one will prevent nationalistic strife, or so goes the theory.

From a Bergsonian viewpoint, the problem with such models of historical progress is that they once more oppose Nature and Culture. In chapter 6 I associated this opposition with the metaphor of the "modern Constitution." Latour defines the modern Constitution as a strict division and purification of the domains of Nature and Culture.²⁸ He argues that modernity not only entails the birth of man, of Culture, but consequently also of non-humans, of things, objects, and beasts, of Nature, and the beginning of a "crossed-out God" that is "relegated to the sidelines."²⁹ Within the domains of Nature and Culture a purifying operation takes place. Elements of Nature are evicted from the domain of human Culture, while Culture develops in opposition to the repetitiveness of Nature.³⁰ In order for the Constitution to work, the scientific representation of things cannot be confused with the political representation of humans.³¹ In chapter 2 we saw that the modern concept of history is based on the modern Constitution, because modern historical time originates in "emancipation from the rhythms of nature" (Koselleck).

---

27. Frédéric Worms, "The Closed and the Open in The Two Sources of Morality and Religion: A Distinction That Changes Everything," in *Bergson, Politics, and Religion*, ed. Alexandre Lefebvre and Melanie White (Durham, NC: Duke University Press, 2012), 30.

28. See for a comparison of Bergson and Latour: Guerlac, "Bergson, the Void," 50–52.

29. Bruno Latour, *We Have Never Been Modern*, 13.

30. Early-modern philosophers such as Hobbes, Locke, and Rousseau, for example, describe civilization as a movement away from a natural state. To Hobbes, human society begins when humanity lifts itself out of its state of nature, which is a "war of all against all." The social-political world is, according to Hobbes, established by the exclusion of Nature. Only by transcending its natural state of being may humanity cherish the hope of abolishing war.

31. Harbers, "Van mensen en dingen," 7.

Bergson criticizes this metaphysics because it eliminates a creative, vital mode of time that also permeates history. In its place, Bergson adopts a non-modern ontology according to which Nature and Culture are entangled.[32] Bergson argues that the modern idea of progress fails to take the biological origins of human society into account. Already in *Creative Evolution*, Bergson maintains that what we have designated as the modern Constitution obscures the fact that human beings are not primarily *rational* but *living* beings. In order to deal with the problems of modern society, it is of crucial importance that we recognize that the vital underlies the social and that evolution determines key aspects of human life. Human society is evolution's answer to vital needs. History as a creative process cannot be properly understood if we neglect its connection to biology.

War will remain a problem within modern, cosmopolitical societies because we can never entirely escape our biological constitution. The problem of war is now even greater, because war is fought with modern, industrial means. If anything, this is what World War I had made abundantly clear. If we neglect the fact that war is still a problem for us, our destruction is imminent. *The Two Sources* is an attempt to revise the terms in which the problem of war is stated, in order to circumvent the war instinct. For this purpose we must first understand the evolutionary origins of human society.

2. THE OPEN AND CLOSED SOCIETY

Bergson criticizes modern social and historical theories that do not ask how human society has come about. Such theories "would like to have it believed that 'human society' is already an accomplished fact."[33] This obscures the biological origins of society. Understanding society as "given" creates a retrospective illusion of historical progress.[34] We see this for instance in Hegel, who took the Prussian state in which he lived as the culmination of a historical narrative about the progress of freedom. World-History is the

---

32. Guerlac: "When Bergson writes: 'the social is, fundamentally, a function of the vital [est au fond du vital]' he performs the distinctly unmodern gesture of collapsing culture into nature by subjecting the notion of society to a biological interpretation." Guerlac, "Bergson, the Void," 46.

33. TS, 32.

34. "We are fond of defining the progress of justice as a forward movement towards liberty and equality. The definition is unimpeachable, but what are we to derive from it? It applies to the past; it can seldom guide our choice for the future." TS, 79.

inevitable development from a "primitive" oriental world, in which only one person, the ruler, is free, to nineteenth-century Germany where freedom for the whole of humanity is being realized. Any form of historical creativity is eliminated.

Taking society as given leads to a distorted view of its moral foundations. Bergson argues that this becomes clear in Kant's moral philosophy. In the *Critique of Practical Reason*, Kant answers the question "How should I act?" with an appeal to Reason. To Kant, human beings are rational beings, and through the use of reason humans may cherish the hope of transcending nature. Kant asserts that to determine the universal principles of justice, we must not let reason be contaminated by our passions. Reason produces practical and objective laws that are "valid for the will of every rational being."[35] Practical reason is different from instrumental reason in that it has no specific objective or content. The practical law contains the "same determining basis of the will in all cases and for all rational beings."[36] Practical laws are similar to natural laws but do not so much *determine* our actions as *demand* from us that we act in accordance with them. A rational being ought to follow the "categorical imperative"—an "objective necessitation of the action . . . which signifies that if reason entirely determined the will then the action would unfailingly occur in accordance with this rule."[37] Kant's categorical imperative is universal because it is rational: it applies to every rational being and embraces the whole of humanity.

Bergson argues that Kant fails to understand the nature of moral obligation because he takes human society for granted.[38] We cannot deduce moral obligation from reason: "the essence of obligation is a different thing from a requirement of reason."[39] Understandably for an eighteenth-century philosopher, Kant neglects the evolutionary origins of human society. Yet Bergson argues that the nature of morality can only be understood by asking what function morality performs within society. According to Bergson, moral obligation is a force that "ensures the cohesion of the group by bending all individual wills to the same end."[40] In this way, morality introduces an attitude of discipline

---

35. Immanuel Kant, *Critique of Practical Reason*, trans. Werner S. Pluhar (Indianapolis: Hackett Publishing Company, Inc., 2002), 29.

36. Ibid., 38.

37. Ibid., 30–31.

38. TS, 91.

39. TS, 24.

40. TS, 266.

that allows us to protect ourselves from outside enemies. Bergson argues that "it is primarily as against all other men that we love the men with whom we live."[41] Contrary to what the rationalists want us to believe, therefore, moral obligation is not universal but primarily applies to one's own group.

Moral obligation does not come down from above, that is, from an "idea" of the good that forces itself upon us. As if, states Bergson, "an idea could ever categorically demand its own realization!"[42] Moral obligation comes up from below, as a pressure that forms the basis of society. The categorical imperative is merely an abstraction from moral obligation that is experienced as a living force. It introduces a logical consistency "into a line of conduct subordinated by its very nature to the claims of society."[43] Thus, ultimately, reason also has a social function. It provides an *a posteriori* justification for social rules and thereby reinforces social obligation.[44]

Bergson realizes that his argument for the particularity of moral obligation goes against the *communis opinio* in society, which would like us to believe that its moral principles are universal and apply to the whole of humanity: "Oh, I know what society says (it has, I repeat, its reasons for saying so); but to know what it thinks and what it wants, we must not listen too much to what it says, we must look at what it does."[45] Bergson points out that in

---

41. TS, 32–33.

42. TS, 96.

43. TS, 23.

44. Bergson illustrates this function of reason with the following analogy: "An ant, accomplishing her heavy task as if she never thought of herself, as if she lived only for the ant-hill, is very likely in a somnambulistic state; she is yielding to an irresistible necessity. Imagine her suddenly becoming intelligent. She would reason about what she had done, wonder why she had done it, would say it was very foolish not to take things easy and have a good time. 'I have had enough of sacrifice, now is the time for a little self-indulgence.' And behold the natural order completely upset. But nature is on the watch. She provided the ant with the social instinct; she has just added to it, perhaps in response to a transitory need of instinct, a gleam of intelligence. However slightly intelligence has thrown instinct out of gear, it must incontinently set things to rights and undo what it has done. An act of reasoning will therefore prove that it is all to the interest of the ant to work for the ant-hill, and in this way the obligation will apparently find a basis. But the truth is that such a basis would be very unsafe, and that obligation already existed in all its force; intelligence has merely hindered its own hindrance. Our ant-hill philosopher would be none the less disinclined to admit this; he would doubtless persist in attributing a positive and not a negative activity to intelligence. And that is just what moral philosophers have done." TS, 93–94.

45. TS, 31.

times of war, when we need the high-flown Enlightenment ideals the most, these very ideals are the first that go out the window:

> Murder and pillage and perfidity, cheating and lying become not only lawful, they are actually praiseworthy. The warring nations can say, with Macbeth's witches: 'Fair is foul, and foul is fair.'[46]

Moral obligation is felt only toward the members of one's own community, not to humanity as a whole. Not only that, but the implication of Bergson's argument is that moral obligation is even constituted *because of* the existence of "the other" that may pose a threat:

> the two opposing maxims, *Homo homini deus* and *Homo homini lupus*, are easily reconcilable. When we formulate the first, we are thinking of some fellow-countryman. The other applies to foreigners.[47]

This undermines the optimism of the Enlightenment that the "ideal of humanity" may be realized by extending the love for one's family to the nation-state, and subsequently to humanity as a whole. We love the group to which we belong *because of* our hate toward "the other." Bergson's conclusion is therefore that there is a *qualitative* difference, not a difference in *degree*, between the closed and open society—between love for the community in which we live and a love of mankind.[48]

To be able to correctly state the problem of war, this qualitative difference has to be properly understood. To overcome the ingrained way in which we conceptualize the closed and the open society, Bergson proceeds by separating both tendencies in order to study them in isolation. In this section we will follow Bergson's example. Both tendencies will be reunited in the third section of this chapter, which allows us to outline Bergson's theory of history.

Closed Society

The narrative of the Enlightenment associates progress with an improvement of the human condition through the use of reason. To Popper, for instance,

---

46. TS, 31.
47. TS, 286.
48. TS, 32.

a closed society is submitted to magical forces and superstitions, while the open society is based on reason and science and takes a critical stance toward magical beliefs and religious dogmas. At the beginning of the twenty-first century, the world seems far removed from the realization of the ideals of the Enlightenment. Paradoxically, modernization and globalization have not disposed with religion, but go hand-in-hand with a worldwide religious resurgence. Newspapers are littered with articles on sectarian violence and killings in the name of religion. It appears that, despite enormous technological and scientific advances, people continue to find meaning and consolation in the most irrational systems of belief.

From the perspective of the Enlightenment's project of modernity it is difficult to account for this "paradox of modernity." Claiming that the Enlightenment is still an "unfinished project" seems too easy a way out. In *The Two Sources*, Bergson tries to find a better explanation. He poses the question of why "*Homo sapiens*, the only creature endowed with reason, is also the only creature to pin its existence to things unreasonable." How can we explain that the triumph of human reason goes together with the most absurd religious beliefs that are "humiliating for human intelligence"?[49]

Bergson claims that it is not in spite of, but *because* of humans being endowed with reason that they adhere to religious ideas and myths. The paradox of modernity is solved once we recognize the vital basis of reason. Religious beliefs are a product of what Bergson pinpoints as our "myth-making faculty." This faculty provides an evolutionary counterweight against the dissolving power of intelligence. While ants and bees retain social cohesion through instinct, this is different for intelligent beings. Reflection enables humans to invent and society to progress, but may also endanger social discipline:

> What if the individual diverts his reflexion from the object for which it was designed . . . and focuses it on himself, on the constraint imposed on him by social life, on the sacrifices he makes for the community? . . . Endowed with intelligence, roused to thought, he will turn to himself and think only of leading a pleasant life.[50]

If intelligence would be left to itself, it would "counsel egoism first" and stop working in service of society, for which it was originally designed. In

---

49. TS, 102.
50. TS, 121.

Figure 7.1. Front page of *Le Matin*, August 4, 1914. Bibliothèque nationale de France, accessed September 30, 2018, https://gallica.bnf.fr.

order to compensate for the "dissolvent power of intelligence" nature has endowed intelligent beings with a myth-making faculty.[51]

Natural or "static" religion assures that we keep doing our duty in spite of the terrible realities that intelligent beings have to face, such as their own death. Bergson gives a telling example of the workings of the myth-making faculty from his own experience. He recalls the outbreak of the First World War, and how, reading about the declaration of war in *Le Matin*, he suddenly felt an invisible presence, as if all of the past since the Franco-Prussian War of 1871 had prepared for this moment, which had now suddenly become a reality:

> It was as though some creature of legend, having escaped from the book in which its story was told, had quietly taken possession of the room.... It had bided its time; and now unceremoniously it took its seat like one of the family. It was to intervene just at this moment, in this place, that it had been vaguely interlinked with my life-story. To the staging of this scene, the room with its

---

51. TS, 119–122.

> furniture, the paper upon the table, myself standing in front of it, the event pervading every nook and cranny, forty-three years of vague foreboding had all been leading up. . . . who would have thought that so terrible an eventuality could make its entrance into reality with so little disturbance?[52]

Static religion strengthens the social function of morality. By associating the members of a group intimately with each other in rites and ceremonies, static religion contributes to social cohesion and helps to defend the group against the danger of other groups. Both static religion and moral obligation make up what Bergson calls the "very substance of closed society."[53] This is a society

> whose members hold together, caring nothing for the rest of humanity, on the alert for attack or defence, bound, in fact, to a perpetual readiness for battle. Such is society fresh from the hands of nature. Man was made for this society, as the ant was made for the ant-heap.[54]

Paradoxically it is *because of* the existence of "the other"—another nation, religious group, or enemy—that there exists a "we." Although it may claim otherwise, society in its natural form is based on *exclusion*. Moral values are not universal by nature. Love for one's neighbor goes naturally together with hatred toward foreigners.[55]

This makes a war instinct a natural feature of human society. As soon as a population starts to grow, it will enter into conflict with other communities over the ownerships of scarce natural resources (territory, raw materials, access to markets, luxury goods, etc.). Bergson says, "So strong, indeed, is the war instinct, that it is the first to appear when we scratch below the surface of civilization in search of nature."[56] The war instinct also explains the enthusiasm of a people at the outbreak of a war, something which happened at the beginning of World War I. This responds to the sense that we

---

52. TS, 160.
53. TS, 267.
54. TS, 266.
55. TS, 286.
56. TS, 284.

are made for a life of "risk and adventure," as though peace is only a pause between two wars.[57]

Open Society

A new paradox has now emerged in place of the paradox of modernity: while closed morality was designed to assure the survival of the species, it has also created a necessity of progress, of transcending the species.[58] Bergson's analysis of the closed society, however, has rendered the ideal of progress highly problematic. The consequence of the structure of the closed society is that mankind seems to be locked in a self-perpetuating cycle of war. Breaking this cycle would require that we cancel out the distinction between "us" and "them." Instead of a love for merely one's own community, our love would have to embrace the whole of mankind. Yet this seems a logical impossibility, as moral obligation is by nature based on exclusion, namely on "the necessity for a community to protect itself against others."[59]

Nevertheless, Bergson does not discard the possibility of progress. What we may draw from the paradox of the closed society is that there is a difference in kind, not in degree, between the closed and open society:

> Never shall we pass from the closed society to the open society, from the city to humanity, by any mere broadening out. The two things are not of the same essence.[60]

We cannot realize the ideal of humanity by simply broadening out our sympathies for the family to our country, and finally to humanity as a whole. Such a model is based on a purely intellectualist conception.[61] Bergson emphasizes that there is a *qualitative* difference between the family or one's country and humanity as a whole:

---

57. TS, 285.

58. Alexandre Lefebvre and Melanie White, "Introduction: Bergson, Politics, and Religion," in *Bergson, Politics, and Religion*, ed. Lefebvre and White (Durham, NC: Duke University Press, 2012), 9.

59. TS, 32–33.

60. TS, 267.

61. TS, 32.

> The first [two] imply a choice, therefore an exclusion; they may act as incentives to strife, they do not exclude hatred. The latter is all love.[62]

Even the noblest people who are willing to sacrifice themselves for others sense this qualitative difference as they will experience a "sudden chill" at the notion that they are working "for mankind."[63]

This does not mean that all hope is lost. Despite this qualitative difference, progress has been a reality in human history. Bergson argues that "in all times there have arisen exceptional men"[64] that incarnated a complete or open morality. While closed morality is impersonal and coincides with *social* obligation, open morality is incarnated by privileged *individuals*. Certain individuals may have the ability to break away from the pressures of society. Bergson identifies these privileged individuals as mystics. Throughout *The Two Sources* he refers to the sages of Greece, the prophets of Israel, the Aharants of Buddhism, and the Christian saints, and also to historical figures like Socrates, Joan of Arc, St. Francis, and Jesus Christ. These privileged individuals broke free from social norms. They did not remain within the limits of the group, but "were borne on a great surge of love towards humanity in general."[65] Their ecstasies, visions, and raptures allowed them to escape for a moment "the law which demands that the species and the individual should condition one another."[66]

That open morality is embodied by individuals does not mean that open morality is purely individual*istic*. To the contrary, privileged persons have an important social function. They set an example for us to follow. While closed morality is like a pressure that assures social cohesion, open morality "has the effect of an appeal."[67] If we encounter a problem in our personal lives, for instance, we may imagine what such an admired person would expect from us. It is now not *fear* that motivates us—the fear that constitutes a closed morality—but an attraction that is inspired by an attitude of *love*. The love of mystics even goes beyond humanity and "may extend to animals, to plants,

---

62. TS, 39.
63. TS, 36.
64. TS, 34.
65. TS, 95.
66. TS, 228–230.
67. TS, 34.

to all nature."⁶⁸ While closed morality depends on exclusion and does not rule out hatred, open morality is all love.

It may have become clear that, according to Bergson, our moral principles can be traced back to emotional dispositions. Here lies an important difference with Kant's approach to morality. According to Kant, universal or—as Bergson would call it—open morality, is established by pure reason, that is, reason free from interference by the passions. As Kant writes in his *Critique of Practical Reason*, "In a practical law reason determines the will directly, not by means of an intervening feeling of pleasure or displeasure, . . . only that reason can be practical as pure reason makes it possible for it to be *legislative*."⁶⁹ To Bergson, however, a morality without the passions has no practical value. It is the passions that ultimately motivate our moral actions. This is not to say that Bergson trades in rational deliberation for a politics of emotion. Bergson's point is, as Lefebvre and White tell us, that reason and emotion should not be conceived as opposites. We must treat emotions like fear and love as a "concrete and practical political force."⁷⁰ Morality and politics can never take place exclusively within the boundaries of reason. As Bergson states, "It is the emotion which drives the intelligence forward in spite of obstacles."⁷¹

There are thus "two sources of morality and religion," which explains the title of Bergson's last book. There is a tendency toward the closed and a tendency toward the open, and these differ in kind. These sources have to be understood within the framework of the ontology of duration. "Social pressure" and "impetus of love" are two complementary manifestations of life. They coincide with the two virtual tendencies that constitute duration as

---

68. TS, 38.
69. Kant, *Critique of Practical Reason*, 37–38.
70. Lefebvre and White, "Introduction," 9.
71. TS, 46. Bergson clarifies: "Which amounts to saying that, in attributing to emotion a large share in the genesis of the moral disposition, we are not by any means enunciating a 'moral philosophy of sentiment.' For we are dealing with an emotion capable of crystallizing into representations and even into an ethical doctrine. From this particular doctrine we could never have elicited the moral disposition any more than from any other; no amount of speculation will create an obligation or anything like it: the theory may be all very fine, I shall always be able to say that I will not accept it; and even as I do accept it, I shall claim to be free and do as I please. But if the atmosphere of emotion is there, if I have breathed it in, if it has entered my being, I shall act in accordance with it, uplifted by it; not from constraint or necessity, but by virtue of an inclination which I should not want to resist." (47–48)

a whole.[72] Fear amounts to a social pressure and is the manifestation of the closed tendency toward preservation, while love is a creative emotion, the essence of the creative effort.[73] Closed morality is supposed to be immutable, while open morality is "the very essence of mobility," a "forward thrust."[74] Its movement is that of the *élan vital*, which is "communicated in its entirety to exceptional men who in their turn would fain impart it to all humanity and by a living contradiction change into creative effort that created thing which is a species, and turn into movement what was, by definition, a stop."[75] Mystics are the manifestation of a love that is the essence of the creative effort.[76]

The effort of creative evolution that these individuals represent is like the appearance of a new species composed of a single individual. We might say that it is with these privileged individuals that history is made.[77] By taking evolution into its own hands through the creative efforts of privileged individuals, humanity has been able to transcend the restrictions that were imposed on it by nature. Bergson points out that open morality, indeed, "had no place in nature's plan."[78] Nature might have foreseen a certain limited expansion of social life through intelligence, but certainly not one that endangered the original structure, which is closed society. By extending social solidarity into the "brotherhood of man," man has been able to outwit nature by circumventing the innate war-spirit in human beings. While the structure of society for which man was made required both a strong group solidarity and a virtual hostility between groups, the leaders of humanity have been able to "break down the gates of the city" by placing themselves in the current of the creative vital impetus.

Bergson can now draw up the figure of the open society, which is constituted by an open morality and dynamic religion:

> The open society is the society which is deemed in principle to embrace all humanity. A dream dreamt, now and again, by chosen

---

72. For the ontology of duration, see chapter 6.

73. TS, 95–97.

74. TS, 58.

75. TS, 235.

76. TS, 95.

77. TS, 234–235. Mystics follow the creative impetus, and help "to complete the creation of the human species and make of humanity what it would have straight away become, had it been able to assume its final shape without the assistance of man himself."

78. TS, 56.

souls, it embodies on every occasion something of itself in creations, each of which, through a more or less far-reaching transformation of man, conquers difficulties hitherto unconquerable.[79]

Bergson's emphasis on individuality once again confirms his affinity with historicism and its ontology of individuality. Mystical individuals determine our historical evolution. Bergson's account of the historical role of privileged individuals may also remind us of Hegel's "World-Historical Individuals" that embody the World-spirit in their time. Another parallel that can be drawn is with Nietzsche, although Nietzsche, contrary to Bergson, was deeply suspicious of mystics and mystical experiences.[80]

Although Bergson did not recognize the direct influence of Nietzsche (though some references in *Creative Evolution* do suggest that Bergson was familiar with Nietzsche's work), his account of "privileged individuals" that constitute a "new species" and make history has similarities with Nietzsche's idea of the Superman or overman. The arrival of the overman is prophesized by Zarathustra in *Thus Spoke Zarathustra*. When Zarathustra first speaks to the people gathered on the marketplace, he says: "*I teach you the overman*. Human being is something that must be overcome."[81] Like Bergson's mystics, the overman is also a higher evolutionary species, a new phase in the evolution from ape to man. The overman is, as Elizabeth Grosz formulates it, "the highest possibility of man's evolution beyond man".[82]

To Nietzsche, the overman is "the meaning of the earth." He is an answer to the "death of God," the moment when human beings realize that God and religion are their own inventions and that God is merely a name for the creative power of man. Similar to Bergson's mystical individuals, the overman embodies the divine creative power that exists in man. In the face of the death of God, the overman, who has no religion, salvages the sanctifying powers for man's earthly existence.[83]

---

79. TS, 267.

80. Keith Ansell-Pearson and Jim Urpeth, "Bergson and Nietzsche on Religion: Critique, Immanence, and Affirmation," in *Bergson, Politics, and Religion*, ed. Lefebvre and White (Durham and London: Duke University Press, 2012), 255. The authors nevertheless point to a fundamental similarity between both thinkers: "both Bergson and Nietzsche urge us to attend to those aspects of nature in which the creative becoming of life is apparent." (260)

81. Friedrich Nietzsche, *Thus Spoke Zarathustra*, ed. Adrian Del Caro and Robert Pippin, trans. Adrian Del Caro (Cambridge: Cambridge University Press, 2006), 5.

82. Grosz, *The Nick of Time*, 148.

83. Rüdiger Safranski, *Nietzsche: A Philosophical Biography*, trans. Shelley Frisch (London: Granta Books, 2002), 272.

To the overman, the death of God requires an affirmation of the possibility of self-overcoming, which does not mean a self-overcoming toward a better version of ourselves or the realization of some other ideal of progress, but that we must "become who we are," that the "being" of human nature is "becoming." Only the overman has the strength to bear and affirm "the eternal return of the same." He has no hope for a life "beyond," but unconditionally accepts the world as it is, to the point where he wills that everything should be repeated, exactly as it has been, in eternal cycles.[84] Grosz: "The overman is the one who can say: I would will it all again, in every last detail."[85]

The similarities between Nietzsche and Bergson go beyond the overman. Grosz points out that both Nietzsche and Bergson have derived a similar conception of life from Darwin. She draws a comparison between the ontologies of time of Nietzsche and Bergson. Both recognize the creative and vital force of time. Grosz argues that Nietzsche's view of life as the "will to power" is equivalent to Bergson's *élan vital*. Nietzsche and Bergson have indeed been identified as the first to understand life in terms of will.[86] It was mainly under the influence of Nietzsche and Bergson that, around the time of World War I, many cultural commentators adopted "Life" as an elastic and all-inclusive term, "a plethora of forms, a wealth of invention, and an ocean of possibilities so incalculable and adventurous that no 'beyond' would be required, since it would be amply represented in the here and now."[87]

3. A PENDULUM ENDOWED WITH MEMORY

Bergson's analysis of the closed and open society culminates in the Final Remarks of *The Two Sources of Morality and Religion* in a cultural critique that takes on the form of a theory of history. This theory of history allows Bergson to restate the problem of war in qualitative terms.

Bergson's cultural critique shares some of the characteristics of other "diagnoses of the time" that were formulated during the Interbellum and that processed the blow that World War I had dealt to the belief in histori-

---

84. Michael Tanner, *Nietzsche* (Oxford and New York: Oxford University Press, 1996), 50.
85. Grosz, *The Nick of Time*, 152.
86. Arnaud François and Roxanne Lapidus, "Life and Will in Nietzsche and Bergson," *SubStance* 36 (2007): 100. The authors note that "Admittedly, we find a similar doctrine already in Schopenhauer. But when Schopenhauer speaks of will-to-life, he considers will as a thing in itself, and life as a phenomenon."
87. Safranski, *Nietzsche: A Philosophical Biography*, 319.

cal progress. A series of pamphlets and polemics addressed the decadence of Western civilization and the negative cultural effects of modern technology, whereby empirical observations and normative statements often blended.[88] Two influential cultural critics in the 1920s and 1930s were Oswald Spengler and José Ortega y Gasset.

Spengler formulated an influential and much-debated critique of Western civilization. In his *The Decline of the West* (1918–1922), Spengler replaces a view of history as a linear progress with a "morphology" portraying world history in terms of a plurality of cultural developments. According to Spengler, a culture has a life-course that is similar to that of an individual human being. He compares the stages that a culture goes through with the seasons in a year.[89] Western culture, Spengler argues, has entered its winter phase. It has exhausted its inner possibilities and has become a "civilization," which is the fulfilment of a culture.[90] Symptomatic for the winter phase of the West are an emphasis on technological development, which is nothing more than an inorganic repetition of accomplishments from the past, and a process of urbanization that has produced a new kind of mass man.[91] Like Bergson, Spengler opposed a spatial and mechanistic natural world to an organic world of life, history, and temporal development.[92]

The rule of the mass man was also noted by the Spanish philosopher José Ortega y Gasset. In *The Revolt of the Masses* (1930), Ortega argues that the masses had obtained a "complete social power."[93] The mass embodies the mediocrity of the average man. It "crushes beneath it everything that is different, everything that is excellent, individual, qualified and select."[94] Like Spengler, Ortega maintains that the mass man is a typical product of modern European civilization, where liberal democracy has affirmed the political

---

88. René Boomkens, *Erfenissen van de Verlichting: Basisboek cultuurfilosofie* [Inheritances of the Enlightenment: Basic Book of Cultural Philosophy] (Amsterdam: Boom, 2011), 93.

89. Northrop Frye, "'The Decline of the West' by Oswald Spengler," *Daedalus* 103 (Winter 1974): 2.

90. Oswald Spengler, *The Decline of the West, Part 1: Form and Actuality*, trans. Charles Francis Atkinson (New York: Knopf, 1926), 31.

91. Frye, "'The Decline of the West' by Oswald Spengler," 2–3.

92. Ibid., 1–2.

93. Ortega maintained that "the reality of history lies in biological power, in pure vitality, in what there is in man of cosmic energy, not identical with, but related to, the energy which agitates the sea, fecundates the beast, causes the tree to flower and the star to shine." José Ortega y Gasset, *The Revolt of the Masses*, trans. anonymous (1932; repr., New York: W.W. Norton, 1993), 35.

94. Ibid., 18.

power of the majority and technological innovations have brought about a mass culture. Mass men display what we would today call a "consumer mentality": "they do not see, behind the benefits of civilization, marvels of invention and construction which can only be maintained by great effort and foresight, they imagine that their role is limited to demanding these benefits peremptorily, as if they were natural rights."[95] The rule of the mass leaves no room for the minority, for noble men who lead a life of effort, active instead of reactive, and who strive to excel themselves.

Both Spengler and Ortega have their own versions of the "privileged individual" or overman. Ortega maintains that only the spiritual power of an intellectual aristocracy can help Europe to overcome its state of decadence, while according to Spengler a strong man could save Western civilization from self-destruction. Although Spengler detested the Nazis, Adolf Hitler, himself convinced that he was the man of destiny, for this reason visited Spengler in 1933.[96]

Bergson addresses some of the same themes and preoccupations of critics such as Spengler and Ortega, but a distinguishing characteristic of Bergson's cultural diagnosis is that it springs from his ontology of duration. In the Final Remarks of *The Two Sources*, Bergson argues that history is made through the creative efforts of individuals, by which humanity takes evolution into its own hands. These creative efforts turn biological evolution into a "historical" evolution. The ideal of humanity will not be realized by merely broadening out the circle of the closed society. The closed and the open correspond with the virtual tendencies of life toward conservation and creation, which differ in kind and not in degree. In order to circumvent the cycle of war, which is a "natural" part of the human condition, a "historical" evolution by which man "overcomes" itself as a species is of crucial importance.

In the following I will outline Bergson's theory of history by focusing on the dynamics of the closed and the open. This reveals a historical dimension to Bergson's philosophy of life that remained unaccounted for in his previous works.

Two Historical Laws

We have seen that, for Bergson, creation lies not in *solving* problems but primarily in *stating* a problem correctly, before finding solutions. Biological evolution is determined by problems that are immanent to the evolution-

---

95. Ibid., 60.

96. Philipp Blom, *Fracture: Life and Culture in the West, 1918–1938* (London: Atlantic Books, 2015), 47.

ary process.[97] When the *élan vital*—life's tendency to change—encounters an obstacle in the form of an external, material condition, it circumvents this obstacle by breaking up into opposite but complementary tendencies or lines of evolution.[98] Bergson calls this the "law of dichotomy."[99] It is because of the resistance that life meets from inert matter that life breaks into individuals and species (see also chapter 4).[100]

The law of dichotomy has, for instance, caused intelligence and instinct to split up into different lines of evolution.[101] Intelligence and instinct are opposite but complementary ways of acting upon the material world.[102] Instinct acts on matter directly by means of organic instruments. Intelligence deals with matter indirectly by making use of artificial instruments. Because these tendencies could not be intensified within one and the same species, the *élan vital* dissociated into evolutionary lines toward animal life and human life.[103]

Characteristic for *historical* evolution is humanity having the ability to make its *own* history by constructing and solving its *own* problems.[104] Deleuze even maintains that becoming conscious of this activity is like the conquest of freedom.[105] This freedom means that human development is no longer determined by problems that contingently arise from its natural environment. Bergson makes use of this freedom in *The Two Sources*, which is dedicated to the construction of the problem of war. In accordance with his method, Bergson is not primarily interested in a solution to the problem of war. First, the problem itself has to be correctly stated. This is all the more necessary, since the problem of war has not been understood correctly by modern thinkers.

Bergson exposes the framing of the problem of war in terms of historical progress as a false problem. Between the closed and open society there is a difference not in degree but in kind. To correctly state the problem of war we have to understand how history evolves. Historical evolution unfolds

---

97. Ansell-Pearson, *Philosophy and the Adventure of the Virtual*, 80.

98. "Life is essentially determined in the act of avoiding obstacles, stating and solving a problem. The construction of the organism is both the stating of a problem and a solution." Deleuze, *Bergsonism*, 16.

99. TS, 294.

100. CE, 98.

101. TS, 294–295.

102. CE, 135.

103. CE, 143.

104. According to Deleuze, instinct is the faculty of finding solutions, while the intellect is the faculty of stating problems in general. See also chapter 4.

105. Deleuze, *Bergsonism*, 16.

within the larger framework of the evolution of life.[106] Bergson says that he does not believe in unescapable historic laws, but that there are biological laws and that "human societies, in so far as they are partly willed by nature, pertain to biology on this particular point."[107] There are nevertheless some characteristics that distinguish historical evolution from biological evolution.

History is the domain of *human* evolution. This constitutes a crucial difference from biological evolution. While in biological evolution the tendencies produced by the law of dichotomy assume a material form that prevents them from reuniting—for instance the "plant-form" and "animal-form" as two different but complementary ways of conserving energy from the sun—historical evolution takes place within one and the same species, individual, or society. In history there is no definitive splitting up of tendencies, but an oscillation that allows now one, and subsequently the other, tendency to prevail. If a tendency has the upper hand, the counter-tendency clings to it, waiting for a chance to take over the initiative. Bergson compares this to opposing political parties, in which the party in power has a chance to realize its program, while the other party has to wait until the pendulum of history swings its way. Once this happens it may take over the initiative and realize its political goals.

Bergson identifies two historical laws that determine this "dynamical dialectic," as we might call it. These are the law of dichotomy, already mentioned above, and the "law of twofold frenzy." Although Bergson speaks of historical laws, he also stresses that these laws are by no means *necessary*. In fact, they should be seen as "regularities" that are deduced from the way in which history has evolved.[108] In a strict sense, laws do not apply to history, because history is the "field of liberty" and "action on the move creates its own route, creates to a very great extent the conditions under which it is to be fulfilled, and thus baffles all calculation."[109] Bergson establishes these "laws," in other words, for a very specific purpose, which is to restate the problem of war.

---

106. Bergson: "We do not believe in the fatality of history. . . . There is thus no unescapable historic law. But there are biological laws; and the human societies, in so far as they are partly willed by nature, pertain to biology on this particular point. If the evolution of the organized world takes place according to certain laws, I mean by virtue of certain forces, it is impossible that the psychological evolution of individual and social man should entirely renounce these habits of life." TS, 293.

107. TS, 293.

108. TS, 296. "Now we must not make exaggerated use of the word 'law' in a field which is that of liberty, but we may use this convenient term when we are confronted with important facts which show sufficient regularity."

109. TS, 296.

According to the law of dichotomy, the *élan vital* splits up into two divergent but complementary tendencies that assume a material form when confronted with a problem. As we have seen, this law dictates that evolutionary creation works through differentiation. The second law, the law of twofold frenzy, is specific for history and means that each tendency, once materialized, is pursued as far as possible. A tendency will often stop only "at the very brink of disaster." This is the moment when the counter-tendency may step in, which also goes as far as it can but in the opposite direction. Thus a dynamic appears in which "one frenzy brings on the counter-frenzy."[110]

The two historical laws assure a "maximum of creation, in quantity and quality."[111] If the tendencies had "journeyed together" they would have moderated one another. Bergson maintains that "the mere fact of taking up all the room imparts to each of [the tendencies] such an impetus that it bolts ahead as the barriers collapse one by one."[112] The struggle of tendencies is hence only the superficial aspect of an underlying advance, a "single original tendency." This is the *élan vital*, the creative mode of time that pervades life in general and history in particular. A conventional, "non-dynamical" dialectic tends to fixate this movement by translating the interaction of frenzies into a logic of opposition, of thesis and antithesis. Duration is hereby misconceived, argues Deleuze: in the domain of history "the 'dialecticians' have substituted a simple opposition in place of a differentiation."[113]

This model of historical evolution actualizes Bergson's ontology of duration. The essence of the historical process is creative change. This is of course not the same as historical *progress*. Yet historical creativity does lay out the conditions under which historical progress is possible. Bergson maintains that the progress of humanity may assume a certain regularity if history takes its "natural" course—if, in other words, historical development conforms to the two historical laws of evolution.[114]

These laws state that progress may come about through oscillation. Historical progress can be achieved when a tendency that behaves frantically does not discard the achievements of its opposite movement, but includes them in its frenzy. In a parliamentary system, for instance, a party that was part of the opposition and that takes over the power will profit, if it is

---

110. TS, 303.

111. TS, 297.

112. TS, 296.

113. Deleuze, "Bergson's Conception of Difference," 49.

114. Bergson: "And it is precisely when it imitates nature, when it yields to the original impulsion, that the progress of humanity assumes a certain regularity and conforms—though very imperfectly, be it said—to such laws as those we have stated." TS, 297.

intelligent, from the experience of the previous ruling party. It should modify the content of its ideas and the significance of its principles in accordance with this experience. In this way progress becomes possible—not in spite of, but *because of* the swing of the pendulum of history. History's pendulum then becomes "endowed with memory." Rather than the oscillations of a pendulum, the movement of history more resembles the shape of a spiral. The spiral expresses how progress is achieved through the periodical alternations of divergent tendencies.

Industrial Modernity and the Problem of War

This "dynamical dialectic" seems abstract, but it becomes tangible once Bergson applies it to the problem of war. The problem of war is to Bergson the most important challenge in his lifetime, especially because warfare has become enmeshed with industrial modernity.

In order to correctly state the contemporary problem of war, Bergson traces the origins of the industrial effort. He argues that up until the late Middle Ages, life was dominated by an ascetic ideal: "Rich and poor did without superfluities which we consider as necessities."[115] One of the main causes of war was a combination of scarcity and overpopulation, which forced people to struggle over the available resources. These circumstances produced a desire for easier material conditions that could break the perpetual cycle of war.

During the fifteenth and sixteenth centuries an industrial frenzy took over from the ascetic frenzy of the Middle Ages. The spirit of invention which accompanied this has been very successful in removing the main causes of war, because it has been able to satisfy real human needs. The industrial frenzy produced a sense of progress and faith in human reason, to which the narrative of the Enlightenment testified. Indeed, "for a long time it was taken for granted that industrialism and mechanization would bring happiness to mankind."[116] Yet Bergson notes that this is no longer the case. A concern for comfort and luxury has increasingly turned into the main preoccupation of humanity. With the industrial effort came an ideal of material progress, which prescribes that we should crave pleasure and are "supposed to" move up the scale from comfort to luxuries: "when we have made sure of our comfort we want to cap it with pleasures, then comes love of luxury on top of all."[117]

---

115. TS, 298.

116. TS, 291.

117. TS, 303.

The spirit of invention is now guided by artificial needs. It is directed at creating "comfort and luxury for the few" instead of "liberation for all." Rather than satisfying basic human needs such as solving the problem of starvation, industry produces "with no other thought than that of selling."[118] Bergson reproaches mechanization with "having fostered luxury, with having favoured the towns to the detriment of the countryside, lastly with having widened the gap and revolutionized the relations between employer and employed, between capital and labour."[119]

The industrial frenzy—originally an answer to the threat of war—has now itself become a problem. Guided as it is by artificial needs and capitalist values, it has lost sight of real human needs. Human history has arrived at a point where the problem of war has to be faced anew. According to Bergson's dynamical dialectic, a historical tendency keeps pushing further and further, often stopping only at the brink of disaster. This has indeed happened with the industrialization of society. Disaster is imminent because destruction on an industrial scale has also emerged as a real possibility. World War I was a testimony to this, and the pages of *The Two Sources* are saturated with the menace of a future war that could prove itself to be even more destructive.

Bergson stresses that mechanical invention is not unique to industrial modernity. Man has always invented machines—this already happened in Antiquity and is part of human life.[120] But the effects of machinery were limited as long as it was based on "natural" forces like "muscular effort, wind or water power."[121] The tool equipment that was produced provided only a limited continuation of the human body, as in a workman's tool being an extension of his arm. If our organs are natural instruments, states Bergson, the instruments that man creates are artificial organs.

Only when science became involved did the spirit of mechanical invention assume giant proportions: "The machine developed its full efficiency only from the day it became possible to place at its service, by a simple process of releasing, the potential energies stored up for millions of years, borrowed from the sun, deposited in coal, oil, etc."[122] Technological and scientific innovations have distended the human body out of proportion. The invention of machines such as the steam-engine has "imparted to our organism an extension so vast, have endowed it with a power so mighty,

---

118. TS, 306.

119. TS, 307.

120. In *Creative Evolution* Bergson defines intelligence as the ability to construct artificial instruments.

121. TS, 304.

122. TS, 304–305.

so out of proportion to the size and strength of that organism, that surely none of all this was foreseen in this structural plan of our species."[123] This "structural plan" does not of course refer to some pre-existing plan that is being realized in evolution, but to the fact that humans have surpassed the limitations of biological evolution by taking their evolution into their own hands. Modern man now lives in a gigantic body, with a soul that has remained what it was—too small and weak to guide it. Many of the social, political, and international problems of the day, Bergson argues, are "so many definitions" of the gap between body and soul.[124]

Bergson has hereby restated the problem of war in qualitative terms. It has become clear that we cannot continue on the road traveled for centuries. History's pendulum needs to swing in the opposite direction. In order to leave behind the ideal of material progress, "humanity must set about simplifying its existence with as much frenzy as it devoted to complicating it."[125] This does not mean a "return" to the asceticism and simplicity of the Middle Ages. We would then direct our efforts at diminishing the volume of the human body, to bring it into proportion with its weak soul. Bergson does not want to discard the gains of the industrial frenzy. In this respect he is less pessimistic about technological achievements than Spengler and Ortega. Instead, humanity's larger body calls for a larger soul: "What we need are new reserves of potential energy—moral energy this time."[126] This requires a qualitative leap, a turn toward mysticism.

This qualitative leap would have to be directed at the realization of the Enlightenment ideal of humanity. If we want to circumvent the threat of war, internationalism needs to triumph over nationalism and imperialism. One way in which this qualitative leap can be made is, of course, if a privileged individual sets the example for us. This is Bergson's similar but different version of Nietzsche's overman:

> Let a mystic genius appear, he will draw after him a humanity already vastly grown in body, and whose soul he has transfigured. He will yearn to make of it a new species, or rather deliver it from the necessity of being a species; for every species means a collective halt, and complete existence is mobility in individuality.[127]

---

123. TS, 309.
124. TS, 310.
125. TS, 307.
126. TS, 310.
127. TS, 311.

If we wait for a hero to appear, though, progress is highly uncertain and beyond our control. There may be another way by which we can achieve historical progress, and this is by redirecting science. Science has concentrated for three centuries on matter, and for good reason, namely to satisfy basic human needs. As a consequence, humanity has cultivated a metaphysics of materialism. But, as Bergson argued in *Matter and Memory*, spirit cannot be reduced to matter; mental activity is more than cerebral activity. The body is a means of action and therefore limits our perception by putting blinders on us. It has the task of regulating our attention to life, by focusing "straight ahead" in the direction we need to go.

Bergson argues that the time has come to pursue a science of the spirit, with the task of liberating our perception. "Psychical research" has to cultivate "abnormal perceptions," those perceptions that we may obtain when our attention to life is distorted. These abnormal perceptions may provide us with a glimpse of the noumenal, of duration, and thereby of the contingency of our conventional, practical relation to the world. Bergson refers to the reality of telepathic phenomena, which are corroborated by "thousands of statements" but are declared by science to be "null and void." Psychical research may cultivate mystical intuitions that were previously reserved only for privileged individuals, and that bring us in touch with the *élan vital*, the creative essence of life. He admits that psychical research depends on a spiritualist metaphysics that is hypothetical—that a scientist would consider the facts reported by psychical research highly improbable—but he insists that spiritualism is not more hypothetical than the materialist metaphysics that science is based on.

The effects of the mystical intuitions of privileged individuals give us a glimpse of the enormous transformation that psychical research may entail for humanity. A human being is generally accustomed "to accept as existing only what it can see and touch."[128] Even only a slight sense of a "life beyond" that psychical research could give us could turn what has remained for most people something "verbal, abstract, ineffectual" into "a life, acting reality." We would obtain, in other words, an *experience* of life as a whole that reaches beyond the natural confines to which we are condemned as a species. The Enlightenment's ideal of humanity would not remain merely an abstract idea; it would turn into an active reality. This would not be confined to humanity, but would include life as a whole. This experience would have a tremendous attraction—that of the joy of the simplicity of life "diffused throughout the world by an ever-spreading mystic intuition."[129]

---

128. TS, 316.

129. TS, 317.

Until that joy has been realized, we have to be content with smaller measures, with regulations that allow us to circumvent "each successive obstacle that our nature sets up against our civilization."[130] Bergson implicitly refers to the development of international institutions like the League of Nations, instigated after World War I and to which he had contributed as president of the International Committee on Intellectual Cooperation (CIC). An important task of the CIC was to promote a spirit of internationalism by stimulating international cooperation between scholars, as "anyone who is thoroughly familiar with the language and literature of a people cannot be wholly its enemy."[131]

The cryptic last lines of *The Two Sources* are famous. Here Bergson summarizes the historical moment of choice for his contemporaries:

> Men do not sufficiently realize that their future is in their own hands. Theirs is the task of determining first of all whether they want to go on living or not. Theirs the responsibility, then, for deciding if they want merely to live, or intend to make just the extra effort required for fulfilling, even on their refractory planet, the essential function of the universe, which is a machine for the making of gods.[132]

With these lines Bergson concludes not only his last original work, but his entire oeuvre. The universe is moved by a creative tendency, an *élan vital*, which is the essence of life. It is clear that this creative tendency sustains for Bergson an implicit hypothesis of God—a pantheistic God immanent to the universe that has similarities with the God of Spinoza.[133] Because the essence of this immanent God is creation, the crown of divine creation is the creation of creatures which themselves create.[134] This echoes Nietzsche's overman, in the sense that these creatures can be conceived of as gods themselves.

---

130. TS, 317.

131. TS, 286.

132. TS, 317.

133. As Ansell-Pearson and Urpeth put it, "Bergson's spiritualism is unique since it conceives God as life: the divine force is the creative energy at work in the evolution of life." Ansell-Pearson and Urpeth, "Bergson and Nietzsche on Religion," 252–253.

134. "As a matter of fact, the mystics unanimously bear witness that God needs us, just as we need God. Why should he need us unless it be to love us? And it is to this very conclusion that the philosopher who holds to the mystical experience must come. Creation will appear to him as God undertaking to create creators, that He may have, besides Himself, beings worthy of His love." TS, 255.

This is why Bergson sees the "making of gods" as an essential function of the universe. This function can ultimately be fulfilled by humanity. Human beings are the crown of creation, because they have taken their evolution into their own hands—this is, indeed, what constitutes human history. Yet to fulfill the function of the universe and to "make gods," humanity has to make an effort, which requires a qualitative leap. Making this effort requires a historical choice. Bergson criticizes a teleological conception of progress in arguing that humanity finds itself at a moment in history where this historical choice has become indispensable. This is a moment when mankind lies "half crushed beneath the weight of its own progress"—when World War I had offered a glimpse of the destruction to which "progress" may lead.

4. CONCLUSION

If we evaluate Bergson's theory of history, we encounter a number of elements that are clearly prompted by the preoccupations and dominant themes that determined the philosophical agenda around 1930. It is not for nothing that Bergson's theory of history shows certain resemblances to the ideas of Oswald Spengler, José Ortega y Gasset, and other cultural commentators of the day. Bergson's critical attitude toward comfort and modern technology, his plea for a life of simplicity, his notion of heroic individuals who shape human evolution, his embrace of mysticism, and his faith in the development of psychical research, will all at first sight appeal less to intellectuals of our own time.

Yet at the same time we must not forget that Bergson's conception of the closed and open society has had an important influence on twentieth-century political thought. For instance, as I have indicated, Bergson's concepts formed an indirect source of inspiration for liberal political thought and the project of European integration. The Universal Declaration of Human Rights was also in part inspired by Bergson's political ideas.[135] Furthermore, I would like to argue that *The Two Sources of Morality and Religion* still provides us with original insights deserving of study at the beginning of the twenty-first century and that can provide a source of inspiration for questioning dominant perspectives.

Bergson's social and historical theory can be conceived of as an important addendum to the project of Enlightenment. Bergson's relation to the

---

135. Alexandre Lefebvre notes that Bergson had a profound influence on John Humphrey, one of the principal drafters of the Universal Declaration of Human Rights. Lefebvre, *Human Rights as a Way of Life*, xvi.

Enlightenment narrative of progress is ambivalent. On the one hand, he embraces the cosmopolitical ideals of the Enlightenment as the only way of preventing war and destruction. Bergson considers it of crucial importance that humanity transcend itself as a species. Yet on the other hand, Bergson is highly critical of the modern regime of historicity that has shaped this narrative. He points to the dangers of a teleological conception of progress and a rationalistic approach to morality, which are shaped by what Bruno Latour has called the modern Constitution. Progress is a task that we ourselves have to accomplish through creative acts. In this sense, there is a mystic dormant in all of us. Bergson points to the biological aspects of morality and human society and pleads for a recognition of the political meaning of emotions such as love and fear. In this respect, it would be interesting to relate Bergson's contribution to the political ideas of Spinoza, or, more recently, Martha Nussbaum.[136] The political dimension of Bergson's ideas about time, creativity, and human rights is, for instance, also the inspiration of Alexandre Lefebvre's recent book *Human Rights as a Way of Life: On Bergson's Political Philosophy* (2013). A reading of *The Two Sources* allows Lefebvre to argue that the main purpose of human rights is to initiate all human beings into love.

Yet the most interesting feature of Bergson's theory of history in the context of this book is that it places Bergson's entire oeuvre in a whole new light. Many interpreters have considered Bergson's reflections on the problem of war and industrial modernity in the Final Remarks of *The Two Sources* as a somewhat odd appendix to his philosophy of life. Deleuze, for instance, only dedicates a few pages to *The Two Sources* in his influential *Bergsonism*. Many commentators have identified Bergson's philosophy of life as the core of Bergsonism and have argued that this was already fully formed with the publication of *Creative Evolution* in 1907. In this chapter I have argued, however, that *The Two Sources* is of a far greater importance to Bergsonism than is often assumed. We might say that it creates what Bergson himself would call a *retroactive truth* about Bergsonism itself. It highlights a historical dimension within Bergson's philosophy of life that had remained unaccounted for in his previous works, and which I have highlighted throughout this book.

However, it is important to realize that Bergson's account of history does not amount to a substantive or speculative *philosophy of history* per se. Bergson does not provide us with a definitive account of the "laws" according to which the historical process unfolds. As we have seen in chapter 4, Bergsonism is non-systematic. Bergson is always interested in *problems*, rather

---

136. Martha Nussbaum, *Upheavals of Thought: The Intelligence of Emotions* (Cambridge: Cambridge University Press, 2001).

than in a subject matter or discipline.[137] An important characteristic of the Bergsonian intuitive method is that the creation of concepts (in *The Two Sources*, for instance, the concepts of the closed and open society) both begins and ends in a concrete situation.[138] With this method, therefore, Bergsonism attempts, as Frédéric Worms puts it, "to intervene in life, to reform or transform it."[139] In order to evaluate Bergson's theory of history on its merits, it is therefore important to realize that the historical theory that Bergson develops in *The Two Sources* has to be understood in relation to a very specific, historically determined problem, namely that of war. For this reason, also, it is not surprising that Bergson's theory of history breathes the atmosphere of the Interbellum.

Bergson's theory of history, in other words, cannot be sundered from the historically determined problem in relation to which it was formulated. In the context of this book the work is important as a very particular actualization of Bergson's ontology of duration. *The Two Sources* provides us with an example of how we can "historicize the present" by bringing about a transformation of perception with regard to established views in the here and now. This potential to historicize can be of particularly great value now that we are confronted with a crisis of historicity. I concur in this respect with Deleuze, who has argued that an actualization of or "return to" Bergson comprises not only a renewed admiration for an important figure from the history of philosophy but also "a renewal or an extension of his project today, in relation to the transformations of life and society, in parallel with the transformations of science."[140]

---

137. Soulez, "Bergson as Philosopher of War and Theorist of the Political," 109.
138. Lefebvre, *Human Rights as a Way of Life*, 6.
139. Worms, cited in ibid., xvii.
140. Deleuze, *Bergsonism*, 115.

Conclusion

Assessing Presentism

> Wanderer, your footsteps are
> the road, and nothing more;
> Wanderer, there is no road,
> the road is made by walking.
> By walking one makes the road,
> and upon glancing behind
> one sees the path
> that will never be trod again.
> Wanderer, there is no road
> Only wakes upon the sea.[1]
>
> —Antonio Machado, "Proverbios y cantares,"
> *Selected Poems of Antonio Machado*

At the end of this journey, let us very briefly look back at some of the ground that we have covered. The objective of this book has been to alter the prevailing view that Bergsonism is antithetical to historical thought. Its thesis is that, in going "beyond the human state," Bergson's philosophy of life implies a fundamental revision of the conventional, modern significance of "history" that still predominates in contemporary historiography.

The origins of this modern concept of history, as we have seen in chapter 2, can be traced back to the emergence of a modern regime of history in

---

1. Antonio Machado, "Proverbios y cantares" (XXIX), in Antonio Machado and Betty Jean Craige, *Selected Poems of Antonio Machado*, trans. Betty Jean Craige (Baton Rouge: Louisiana State University Press, 1978), 143.

the second half of the eighteenth century. As a result of an acceleration of time, historical time emancipated itself from the rhythms of nature. A notion of history as a general concept or "collective singular" arose, affirming what Bruno Latour designates as the modern Constitution: the separation of reality into two ontologically distinct and purified spheres, that of Nature and Culture, of non-humans and humans. Modern-historical time transformed the asymmetry between Nature and Culture into an asymmetry between past and future. While the past came to stand for the confusion of men and things, the future will no longer confuse them.

Bergsonism implies a critique of this modern concept of history, because it integrates the domains of Nature and Culture (see chapter 6). Bergsonism establishes human history as primarily the history of *living* beings, instead of *rational* beings. Bergson's philosophy of life entails a nonmodern conception of history that situates human history within the broader framework of life as a creative becoming.

A unique feature of this Bergsonian account of history is that the integration of Nature and Culture does not amount to a reductionist sociobiology that explains away "the given" in the here-and-now by means of Darwinian arguments. To the contrary, Bergson's philosophy of life turns historical time into an immanent, positive, and creative force. Bergsonism thereby allows us to introduce a mode of creative time into the philosophy of history and turns human history into a process of creative becoming. Against the background of this Bergsonian historical ontology I have explored two contributions of Bergsonism to historical thought.

The first contribution is an account of the survival of the past, which contrasts, as we saw in chapter 5, with the ontological status of the past as "absence" or nonentity in modern historiography. Historians tend to assume that a "distance" between past and present is a fundamental prerequisite for historical inquiry. Only from a distance can the historian take on his or her role of "impartial bystander."[2] The distance between past and present is brought about by the modern "arrow of time," which sustains the modern discourse of history by assuring that the past is removed from the present. Thus, a relation between past and present is established in which one is the subject or "producer" of history, while the other is what is being represented, the "object" of knowledge.[3]

Thinking history in terms of duration, however, has allowed us to develop an alternative perspective on the ontological status of the past. Bergsonism makes us aware that creative historical change is entangled with a *survival*

---

2. Bevernage and Lorenz, "Breaking up Time," 10.
3. De Certeau, "History: Science and Fiction," 214–215.

of the past. According to Bergson's famous theory of memory, the whole of our past is preserved as virtual, pure memory. Memory-images materialize pure memory in a movement from past to present. The paradox here is that creation and freedom are bound up with a virtual survival of the past. By actualizing the past, living beings are able to withdraw themselves from the mechanistic laws of matter. This Bergsonian perspective offers a compelling alternative to the modern notion of change as "creative destruction," which assumes that innovation necessarily requires the *destruction* of the past.

In contrast to what is often assumed, the Bergsonian time of memory is not fundamentally different from the time of history. Bergsonian pure memory should not be understood as primarily subjective and psychological but as an *ontological* notion. Bergson's theory of memory is part of an ontology of time as duration. This means that the survival of the past does not depend on a notion of the subject or individual psyche, but in the final instance on *duration*.

The second contribution of Bergsonism to historical thought is that a historical interpretation of duration allows us to understand history from within the broader framework of the creative movement of life. The prism of Bergsonism shows us history as a creative becoming.

Important in this respect is that, as became clear in chapter 6, duration has to be conceived of as an organic or virtual *whole*. As virtual whole, duration is a "mode of time" that is immanent to the whole of the universe. We can distinguish two virtual *tendencies* or movements within duration: a "downward" homogeneous tendency toward material repetition and an "ascending" heterogeneous tendency of life and creation. These virtual tendencies are a condition of possibility for organic or historical forms.

Of the two virtual tendencies, the ascending tendency of life and creation is a historical tendency *par excellence*. It places history at the center of Bergson's ontology of duration. The ascending tendency is creative because it incorporates the past in the present. Bergson associates this creative virtual movement with a tendency toward individualization. At the same time, however, Bergson does not let go of his holistic premise. Each individual living organism has to be regarded as a whole. Its organization should be compared with "the whole of the material universe."

There are similarities here with some of the ontological presuppositions regarding the nature of history of nineteenth-century German historicism. Such a comparison seems plausible at first sight, as both place *change* at the center of their worldview. Both assume that the world is in a state of incessant flux and that the (human) world changes with history.[4]

---

4. Beiser, *The German Historicist Tradition*, 2–3.

Like Bergson, the historicists combine a focus on *individuality* with a *holistic* conception of history. Yet in contrast to Bergsonism, the historicists reproduced the modern Constitution by assuming that the social and historical sciences require a fundamentally different approach to that of the natural sciences because of a fundamental difference between the phenomena of nature and those of history.

A Bergsonian objection to the modern Constitution is that human history is being isolated from the history of life as a whole, and that thereby a perspective on duration, or, in other words, on the *creative* aspect of history, is being obscured. Isolating human history from the history of life as a whole means that we "cut out" history from the whole of duration, thereby turning history into a closed system. To regain a sense of the creative nature of history—that is, of both historical continuity and discontinuity—the history of man would have to be understood from within the framework of life as a whole. What I call a Bergsonian "nonmodern historicism" does not seek, as do the historicists, to *legitimate* history as a science, but incites us to *extend* the scope of history as a science "beyond the human state." In this respect, we should conceive of Bergsonism as a movement "beyond historicism," a radicalization of the historicist worldview.

∼

Having established Bergson as an important historical thinker, I would like to briefly point out how Bergsonism contributes to different areas of contemporary philosophy of history.

ONTOLOGY AND HISTORICAL TIME

A Bergsonian historical ontology may add depth to the "ontological turn" in contemporary philosophy of history.[5] The Bergsonian method of intuition, for instance, provides insights into the way in which ontological presuppo-

---

5. Bentley, "Past and 'Presence,'" 349. Another thinker that I have recuperated in this respect is Heidegger (see chapter 2). Heidegger makes us aware that history as a science is grounded in ontology. He draws attention to how historiography presupposes a prescientific existential historicity that has often been neglected by philosophers of history. Despite the differences between Bergson and Heidegger, both thinkers are relevant to contemporary philosophers of history who want to "revisit" historical ontology.

sitions regarding the nature of history shape historiographical practices.[6] In chapter 4, I pointed to the affinities between the method of intuition and what Ian Hacking calls "historical ontology"—a form of "meta-epistemology" that investigates the historically shaped conditions or "conception of the world" within which certain epistemological "objects" have come into existence. Bergson's important works can also be conceived of as forms of meta-epistemology. They are directed not at finding *solutions* to philosophical issues (e.g., the mind-body problem; free will vs. determinism; the nature of evolution) but primarily at the statement of the *problems* themselves. A problem is *badly* stated when we think in terms of "more or less," which is to say, in "differences in degree," where in reality they are "differences in kind." This happens when we think about a qualitative phenomenon like time in quantitative terms—when, in other words, we confuse time with space.[7] Bergson's approach is highly relevant to the modern understanding of history to the extent that it is structured by the timeline.

Several theorists are now implicitly or explicitly questioning the assumption of empty and homogeneous time that structures the modern understanding of history. As we saw in chapter 1, this applies for instance to Eelco Runia, who introduced the notion of "presence" to designate the "unrepresented way the past is present in the here and now." Another testament to the ontological turn in the philosophy of history is Frank Ankersmit's *Sublime Historical Experience* (2005), which investigates how the historian can "enter into a real, authentic, and 'experiential' relationship to the past—that is, into a relationship that is not contaminated by historiographical tradition, disciplinary presuppositions, and linguistic structures as identified by Hayden White in his *Metahistory* of 1973."[8]

A third example is Berber Bevernage's exploration of "transitional justice."[9] Bevernage shows how truth commissions politically deal with the persistence of the past by managing a break with the past through modern-historical discourse. Modern-historical time thus serves as an antidote to memorial time, in which the past continues to haunt the present. My exploration of the case of the London Cenotaph in chapter 1 confirmed this.

These and other reconceptualizations of historical time, and the status of the past, require an alternative ontology of historical time. This may be

---

6. See on the ontological turn in contemporary philosophy of history, chapter 1.
7. Deleuze, *Bergsonism*, 21.
8. Ankersmit, *Sublime Historical Experience*, 4.
9. Bevernage, *History, Memory, and State-Sponsored Violence*.

provided by Bergson's ontology of duration and the nonmodern conception of history that we explored throughout this book.

EPISTEMOLOGY AND METHODOLOGY

Thinking of history in terms of duration also raises epistemological and methodological issues. It forces us to rethink a number of important historical concepts, such as the role of causality in history, the relation between the possible and the real, the historical past as "object" of study, and the problem of representation and historical truth (see chapter 5).

Modern homogeneous time suggests that historical events can be explained by their historical antecedents. We thereby assume that the possibility of things precedes their existence. Bergson, however, argues that there is not less but *more* in the possible than in the real. An unforeseeable and "new" historical reality becomes "retroactively possible." This means that the historical past is not fixed, in the sense of an "object" placed on a timeline that can be studied on its own terms. In duration, the past is constantly being reshaped in the present. Presenting "what actually happened" is impossible, because the historical meaning of an era will only become clear in light of an indeterminate and unforeseeable future.[10] The historical past is not given but actually *changes* within duration.

A Bergsonian historical ontology raises the question of how historians can do justice to historical creation, or, in other words, historical discontinuity. Bergson's critique coincides with the insights of narrativism and representationalism, which have made us aware in the past decades of how historians create meaning through the narrative representation of the past. This raises the question of which narrative tools are available to the historian for capturing historical creation.

I discussed two approaches that can potentially do justice to historical duration and to which a Bergsonian ontology of history may contribute. The first is "the event" as a concept that allows philosophers and historians to account for occurrences that radically interrupt our sense of continuity. By labeling, for instance, the Arab Spring, or the financial crisis of 2008, or 9/11 as "events," theorists emphasize the discontinuous nature of these happenings and prevent them from being dissolved in the continuum of history. Slavoj Žižek, for instance, considers it a great merit of events that they undermine any stable order precisely *by* reconfiguring the past. According

---

10. CM, 13–14.

to Žižek, a true event does not stand by itself but brings about a change in the frame of reference from which we understand and relate to the world: it is a radical change of reality itself.[11]

A second conceptual approach that has an affinity with a Bergsonian ontology of historical creation is the genealogical method as practiced by, for instance, Nietzsche and Foucault. The genealogical method wants to be sensitive to the contingent nature of the historical process. As a "history of the present" it traces the emergence of who and what we have become.[12] According to Foucault, the genealogist can thereby construct a counter-memory toward the present, which shows us the heterogeneous nature of solid historical identities and shatters the myth of the historian as a neutral and objective subject of knowledge, devoid of passions and committed solely to truth.[13] A genealogical approach may potentially do justice to the "heterogeneous continuity" that is historical duration.

HISTORIOGRAPHY

A Bergsonian conception of history that conceives of human history within the broader context of the history of life also sustains recent attempts to develop broader historiographical perspectives.

I mentioned two of these attempts in the introduction, namely *The History Manifesto* and big history. *The History Manifesto* asks for renewed attention to long-term historical narratives in order to provide a counterweight to a "crisis of short term thinking" that has pervaded our whole society and culture. Big history wants to unite human history with natural history, and seeks to integrate different historically oriented disciplines, such as history, biology, geology, and cosmology. It thereby wants to achieve a sense of "global citizenship." Historiographical innovations such as these often lack a consideration of the ontological assumptions regarding the nature of history. A Bergsonian historical ontology can provide this.

Furthermore, a Bergsonian philosophy of life, in its attempt to go "beyond the human state," connects with what has recently become known as the posthuman turn in the humanities. We can think, for instance, of

---

11. Žižek, *Event: A Philosophical Journey Through a Concept*.

12. Gutting, *Foucault*, 35.

13. Genealogy "disturbs what was previously considered immobile; it fragments wat was thought unified; it shows the heterogeneity of what was imagined consistent with itself." Foucault, "Nietzsche, Genealogy, History," 82.

the project by Ewa Domanska on "non-anthropocentric knowledges of the past,"[14] or Manuel DeLanda's influential *A Thousand Years of Nonlinear History*.

Also interesting in this respect is the widely debated concept of the Anthropocene—the notion that "human imprint on the global environment has now become so large and active that it rivals some of the great forces of Nature in its impact on the functioning of the Earth system."[15] The Anthropocene expresses a forceful and even violent "return of the history of the Earth into world history."[16] The "new human condition" that the Anthropocene implies requires, as historians Christophe Bonneuil and Jean-Baptiste Fressoz state, "new environmental humanities to rethink our visions of the world and our ways of inhabiting the Earth together."[17] A Bergsonian historical ontology sustains and may contribute to an awareness of what Boneuil and Fressoz designate as "a double relation of internality" between nature and society.[18]

∼

How can Bergsonism contribute to overcoming the contemporary crisis of the modern regime of historicity?

We have seen that this crisis manifests itself in the form of an omnipresent present. Contemporary presentism may remind us of the famous painting by René Magritte called "Time Transfixed," which depicts a train coming out of a chimney suspended in mid-air. This symbolizes the way in which a progressive notion of time has been stalled, how history seems to have come to a standstill and how we are locked in an eternal present.

We have related presentism through the work of Reinhart Koselleck and especially Hartmut Rosa to an acceleration of time that characterizes modernity and that has "desynchronized" contemporary societies. According to Rosa, it is no longer possible to synchronize the variety of accelerating subsystems in late-modern society. The modern conception of History as a "collective singular," which for two centuries served as an integrating temporal

---

14. Domanska, "Retroactive Ancestral Constitution, New Animism and Alter-Native Modernities."

15. Steffen et al., *The Anthropocene*, 843.

16. Bonneuil and Fressoz, *The Shock of the Anthropocene*, 20.

17. Ibid., xii.

18. Ibid., 36.

authority allowing us to politically manage the acceleration of historical time, has become obsolete. As a consequence, politics has become situational. A common complaint about politics nowadays is that politicians are no longer developing progressive visions about the future of society, but merely react to pressures of the moment (see chapter 2).

Bergsonism can help us to establish a change of perspective with regard to the "omnipresent present," which allows us to restore, as Hartog puts it, some form of communication between past, present, and future. At its core, Bergsonism is a philosophy that endeavors to expand and extend our ordinary perception of reality. In contrast to other metaphysical systems, Bergsonism wants not to rise above our perception of things but to "plunge into it" in order to deepen and widen it.[19] Bergsonism achieves this change of perception by affirming the reality of time. In the conclusion to "The Possible and the Real," Bergson argues that a reflection on duration is a preparation for what he calls the art of living:

> But above all we shall have greater strength, for we shall feel we are participating, creators of ourselves, in the great work of creation which is the origin of all things and which goes on before our eyes. By getting hold of ourselves, our faculty for acting will become intensified.[20]

Bergsonism is therefore not merely a philosophy of contemplation, but is also ultimately aimed, as Alexandre Lefebvre puts it, at transforming "our everyday orientation or way of life."[21]

What Bergsonism can therefore offer us is an alternative perspective on the crisis of the modern regime of historicity. By affirming the *reality* of time—time as a positive and creative force—Bergsonism sheds a new light on the categories of present, past, and future that have become petrified.

With regard to the present, this means that we should no longer take the "given" in the here-and-now as inevitable, a necessity. Bergsonism may remind us of the contingency of the present and forces us to acknowledge that things could always have been different. While the present on a timeline can be reduced to pure presence, a now-point tied in between a nonexistent past and future, the ontology of duration affirms the present as a multiplicity,

---

19. CM, 111.

20. CM, 124.

21. Lefebvre, Introduction to *Henri Bergson*, xvii.

part of a creative process of becoming. "The" present has to be conceived of as a virtualization, a condensation of a multiplicity of interacting and changing temporalities or rhythms of duration.

The Bergsonian conception of time furthermore reminds us that we are embodiments of the evolution of life as a creative temporal process that brings about the new. The persistence of the past is of crucial importance in this respect. To the moderns, the new is brought about through "creative destruction." Only by leaving the past "behind" us are we able to move "forward." Within Bergsonian duration, however, the past is a living resource for creative change. "Change" does not bring about a radical destruction of the past but merely means that we *lose sight of the past*. The past persists as virtuality in the present. The actualization of the past brings about the new and allows us to realize our freedom.

The status of the past in duration is different from the "present past" within a presentistic regime of historicity. The Bergsonian past is not a pure presence. Yet although the past does not coincide with the present, it is also not external to it. As virtuality, the past exists in its actualizations. Now that we are facing a series of global problems that seem to indicate the limitations of "old" processes of modernization based on a model of creative destruction, an alternative, Bergsonian regime of creative change might be of significance. This regime gives critical importance to the past as a vehicle for change. An "enduring" change requires that we find new ways of (re-)connecting with the past within an environment in which this connection is no longer obvious.

Finally, Bergsonism implies a new perspective on the future. Within the modern regime of historicity, the future was envisioned as a utopian destination of History as "collective singular," history as an all-encompassing and singular process. The presentistic future, by contrast, represents the great unknown. Even contemporary protest movements such as Occupy no longer aimed at the realization of a utopian project for the future, but embraced their lack of a "coherent vision for social change."[22] At the most, the presentistic future is being visualized as the disastrous continuation of the present. As a reaction to this uncertainty, the future is being fixated and made predictable. We see this, for instance, in the rise of the figure of the "indebted man," which according to the Italian philosopher Maurizio Lazzarato is characteristic

---

22. The lack of a "coherent vision for social change" has been identified as an important reason for the failure of Occupy. According to Tom Malleson, "it is undeniable that the overall direction of the protests remained vague, the goals remained unclear, and the underlying vision opaque." Tom Malleson, *After Occupy: Economic Democracy for the 21st Century* (Oxford: Oxford University Press, 2014), xvii.

of contemporary society.²³ The debtor makes it impossible for us to imagine a future as "different" from the present. Debt thus functions as a "technique of social safety" that has deprived many people not only of political power and wealth, but also "of the future, that is, of time, time as decision-making, choice, and possibility."²⁴

Thinking of the future in terms of duration entails that the future is more than merely the realization of *possibilities* contained in the present. Instead, as Elizabeth Grosz puts it, the future is the result of "the unpredictable, uncertain, diverging, often impromptu processes of actualization."²⁵ A Bergsonian perspective on the reality of time as a positive and creative force makes us aware that the future may be an *invention*.

In this book, I have further argued that the "end of history" which we are currently experiencing is merely the end of a very specific, modern conception of history that came into being at the end of the eighteenth century. I have wanted to show that a Bergsonian perspective on time and history can achieve an alternative form of historicity. This is not a strictly modern form of historicity, based on a conception of history as collective singular and grounded in the modern Constitution traditionally bound up with the nation-state.

By taking the *reality of time* as its point of departure, Bergsonism turns history from a modern collective singular into a nonmodern "*multiplicitous singular.*" As a virtual whole, duration is actualized in the form of a multiplicity of countless interacting "rhythms of duration." This historical ontology can potentially account for the condition of globalized and desynchronized late-modern acceleration societies by providing the "integrating temporal authority" that is currently lacking.

By integrating the domains of Nature and Culture, Bergsonism lays the foundations for a nonmodern regime of historicity. While, according to the German historicists, human action obtained a historical meaning within the context of the nation-state, a Bergsonian concept of history as multiplicitous singular situates human history in a global, or even cosmological, perspective. This sustains recent attempts by historians to reverse the retreat of history

---

23. "Everyone is a 'debtor,' accountable to and guilty before Capital. Capital has become the Great Creditor, the Universal Creditor." Maurizio Lazzarato, *The Making of the Indebted Man: An Essay on the Neoliberal Condition*, trans. Joshua David Jordan (Los Angeles, CA: Semiotext(e), 2012), 7. Thanks to Thijs Lijster for this reference. Bergsonism may also be relevant to a critique of post-Fordism. For a comparison between Marx and Bergson, see Gregory Dale Adamson's *Philosophy in the Age of Science and Capital*.

24. Lazzarato, *The Making of the Indebted Man*, 8.

25. Grosz, *The Nick of Time*, 242.

from the public realm by developing wider historiographical perspectives. More important, however, is the consequence of Bergsonism's nonmodern perspective for our understanding of *res gestae*. The integration of Nature and Culture sheds light on a vital and creative dimension of history that remained unaccounted for within the modern regime of historicity.

With the retreat of history from public life, the three contributions of Bergsonism to historical thought that I have identified—(1) a reconceptualization of the past and (2) a perspective on historical creation, which provide the basis for (3) a nonmodern historical ontology—can reinvigorate the significance of history as a vital source of orientation in our society and culture.

BIBLIOGRAPHY

Adamson, Gregory Dale. *Philosophy in the Age of Science and Capital.* London: Continuum, 2002.
Agamben, Giorgio. *Infancy and History: On the Destruction of Experience.* Translated by Liz Heron. London: Verso, 2007.
Anderson, Benedict. *Imagined Communities.* London: Verso, 1985.
Ankersmit, Frank R. *Denken over geschiedenis: Een overzicht van moderne geschiedfilosofische opvattingen* [Thinking about History: An Overview of Modern Perspectives on the Philosophy of History]. 2nd ed. Groningen: Wolters-Noordhoff, 1986.
———. *Historical Representation.* Stanford, CA: Stanford University Press, 2001.
———. "Historicism: An Attempt at Synthesis." *History and Theory* 34 (1995): 143–161.
———. *De navel van de geschiedenis: Over interpretatie, representatie en historische realiteit* [The Navel of History: On Interpretation, Representation, and Historical Reality]. Groningen: Historische Uitgeverij, 1990.
———. *Sublime Historical Experience.* Stanford, CA: Stanford University Press, 2005.
———. "The Transfiguration of Distance into Function." *History and Theory* 50 (2011): 136–149.
Ansell-Pearson, Keith. *Philosophy and the Adventure of the Virtual: Bergson and the Time of Life.* London: Routledge, 2002.
Ansell-Pearson, Keith, and Jim Urpeth. "Bergson and Nietzsche on Religion: Critique, Immanence, and Affirmation." In *Bergson, Politics, and Religion*, edited by Alexandre Lefebvre and Melanie White, 246–264. Durham, NC: Duke University Press, 2012.
Ansell-Pearson, Keith, John Mullarkey, and Melissa McMahon, eds. *Henri Bergson: Key Writings.* New York: Continuum, 2002.
Antliff, Mark. *Inventing Bergson: Cultural Politics and the Parisian Avant-Garde.* Princeton, NJ: Princeton University Press, 1993.
Augustine. *The Confessions of St. Augustine.* Translated by E.B. Pusey. 1921. Reprint, Auckland: The Floating Press, 2008.
Badiou, Alain. *Deleuze: The Clamor of Being.* Translated by Louise Burchill. Minneapolis: University of Minnesota Press, 2000.

Barnard, William G. *Living Consciousness: The Metaphysical Vision of Henri Bergson.* Albany: State University of New York Press, 2011.

Barnes, Julian. *The Sense of an Ending.* London: Cape, 2011.

Beiser, Frederick C. *The German Historicist Tradition.* Oxford: Oxford University Press, 2011.

———. *Hegel.* New York: Routledge, 2005.

Benjamin, Walter. "Experience and Poverty." In *Selected Writings,* vol. 2, *1927–1934,* translated by Rodney Livingstone and others, edited by Howard Eiland, Michael W. Jennings, and Gary Smith, 731–736. Cambridge, MA: Harvard University Press, 1999.

———. "On Some Motifs in Baudelaire." In *Charles Baudelaire: A Lyric Poet in the Era of High Modernism,* 107–154. Translated by Harry Zohn. London: Verso, 1997.

———. "Theses on the Philosophy of History." In *Illuminations,* 253–264. Translated by Harry Zohn. Edited by Hannah Arendt. New York: Schocken Books, 1968.

Bentley, Michael. "Past and 'Presence': Revisiting Historical Ontology." *History and Theory* 45 (October 2006): 349–361.

Bergson, Henri. *Creative Evolution.* Translated by Arthur Mitchell. 1911. Reprint, Mineola, NY: Dover Publications, 1998. (Abbreviated herein as CE.)

———. *The Creative Mind: An Introduction to Metaphysics.* 1946. Translated by Mabelle L. Andison. Reprint, Mineola, NY: Dover Publications, 2007. (Abbreviated herein as CM.)

———. "De la simulation inconsciente dans l'état d'hypnotisme." *Revue Philosophique* 22 (1886): 525–531.

———. *Matter and Memory.* Translated by Nancy Margaret Paul and W. Scott Palmer. 1912. Reprint, Mineola, NY: Dover Publications, 2004. (Abbreviated herein as MM.)

———. *Mélanges.* Edited by André Robinet. Paris: Presses Universitaires de France, 1972. (Abbreviated herein as ML.)

———. *Mind-Energy: Lectures and Essays.* Translated by H. Wildon Carr. London: Henry Holt and Company, 1920. (Abbreviated herein as ME.)

———. *Oeuvres.* Edited by André Robinet. Paris: Presses Universitaires de France, 1959. (Abbreviated herein as OE.)

———. *Time and Free Will: An Essay on the Immediate Data of Consciousness.* Translated by F.L. Pogson. 1913. Reprint, Mineola, NY: Dover Publications, 2001. (Abbreviated herein as TFW.)

———. *The Two Sources of Morality and Religion.* Translated by R. Ashley Audra and Cloudesley Brereton. 1935. Reprint, Notre Dame, IN: University of Notre Dame Press, 2006. (Abbreviated herein as TS.)

Berman, Marshall. *All That Is Solid Melts into Air: The Experience of Modernity.* New York: Penguin Books, 1982.

Bevernage, Berber. *History, Memory, and State-Sponsored Violence: Time and Justice.* New York: Routledge, 2012.

———. "Writing the Past Out of the Present: History and the Politics of Time in Transitional Justice." *History Workshop Journal* 69 (Spring 2010): 111–131.

Blencowe, Claire. "Destroying Duration: The Critical Situation of Bergsonism in Benjamin's Analysis of Modern Experience." *Theory, Culture & Society* 25 (2008): 139–158.
Bloch, Marc. *The Historian's Craft*. 1954. Translated by Peter Putnam. Manchester: Manchester University Press, 1992.
Blom, Philipp. *Fracture: Life and Culture in the West, 1918–1938*. London: Atlantic Books, 2015.
———. *The Vertigo Years: Europe, 1900–1914*. New York: Basic Books, 2008.
Bonneuil, Christophe, and Jean-Baptiste Fressoz. *The Shock of the Anthropocene: The Earth, History and Us*. Translated by David Fernbach. London: Verso, 2017.
Boomkens, René. *Erfenissen van de Verlichting: Basisboek cultuurfilosofie* [Inheritances of the Enlightenment: Basic Book of Cultural Philosophy]. Amsterdam: Boom, 2011.
Bor, Jan. *Bergson en de onmiddellijke ervaring* [Bergson and Immediate Experience]. Meppel: Boom, 1990.
Borg, Alan. *War Memorials: From Antiquity to the Present*. London: Cooper, 1991.
Bos, Jacques. "Agency and Experience: Changing Views of the Subject in Gender History." *Jaarboek voor Vrouwengeschiedenis* 45 (2005): 25–48.
———. "Nineteenth-Century Historicism and Its Predecessors: Historical Experience, Historical Ontology and Historical Method." In *The Making of the Humanities*, edited by Rens Bod, Jaap Maat, and Thijs Weststeijn, vol. 2, *From Early Modern to Modern Disciplines*, 131–147. Amsterdam: Amsterdam University Press, 2012.
———. "Renaissance Historiography: Framing a New Mode of Historical Experience." In *The Making of the Humanities*, edited by Rens Bod, Jaap Maat, and Thijs Weststeijn, vol. 1, *The Humanities in Early Modern Europe*, 351–365. Amsterdam: Amsterdam University Press, 2010.
Brunner, Otto, Werner Conze, and Reinhart Koselleck. *Geschichtliche Grundbegriffe: Historisches Lexikon zur politisch-sozialen Sprache in Deutschland*. 8 vols. Stuttgart: Klett-Cotta, 1972–1997.
Burckhardt, Jakob. *The Civilization of the Renaissance in Italy*. Translated by S.G.C. Middlemore. London: Penguin Books, 2004.
Canales, Jimena. *The Physicist and the Philosopher: Einstein, Bergson, and the Debate that Changed our Understanding of Time*. Princeton, NJ: Princeton University Press, 2015.
Cannadine, David. "War and Death, Grieving and Mourning in Modern Britain." In *Mirrors of Mortality: Studies in the Social History of Death*, edited by J. Wiely, 187–242. London: Europa Publications, 1981.
Čapek, Milič. *Bergson and Modern Physics: A Re-interpretation and Re-evaluation*. Dordrecht: Reidel, 1971.
Carr, David. "Reinhart Koselleck: 'Futures Past: On the Semantics of Historical Time.'" *History and Theory* 26 (1987): 197–204.
———. *Time, Narrative, and History*. Indiana: Indiana University Press, 1986.
Carr, Herbert Wildon. *Henri Bergson: The Philosophy of Change*. London: Jack, 1911.

Caygill, Howard. "Heidegger and the Destruction of Tradition." In *Walter Benjamin's Philosophy: Destruction and Experience*, edited by Andrew Benjamin and Peter Osborne, 1–31. London: Routledge, 1994.

Certeau, Michel de. "History: Science and Fiction." In *Heterologies: Discourse on the Other*, translated by Brian Massumi, 199–224. Manchester: Manchester University Press, 1986.

Christian, David. *Maps of Time: An Introduction to Big History*. Berkeley: University of California Press, 2005.

———. "The Return of Big History." *History and Theory* 49 (December 2010): 6–27.

Cohen, Richard A. "Philo, Spinoza, Bergson: The Rise of an Ecological Age." In *The New Bergson*, edited by John Mullarkey, 18–31. Manchester: Manchester University Press, 1999.

Collingwood, R.G. *The Idea of History*. 1946. Reprint, Oxford: Oxford University Press, 1973.

Conrad, Peter. *Modern Times, Modern Places*. New York: Knopf, 1999.

DeLanda, Manuel. *A Thousand Years of Nonlinear History*. New York: Swerve Editions, 1997.

Deleuze, Gilles. *Bergsonism*. Translated by Hugh Tomlinson and Barbara Habberjam. New York: Zone Books, 1991.

———. "Bergson's Conception of Difference." In *The New Bergson*, edited by John Mullarkey, translated by Melissa McMahon, 42–65. Manchester: Manchester University Press, 1999.

Domanska, Ewa. "The Material Presence of the Past." *History and Theory* 45 (October 2006): 337–349.

———. "Retroactive Ancestral Constitution, New Animism and Alter-Native Modernities." *Storia della storiografia* 65 (2014): 61–75.

Driessche, Joost van. "Muishond: Techno-wetenschappelijke, literaire en ethische bewegingen van taal" [MouseDog: Techno-Scientific, Literary, and Ethical Movements of Language]. PhD diss., University of Groningen, 2016.

Edelstein, Dan. *The Enlightenment: A Genealogy*. Chicago: University of Chicago Press, 2010.

Edkins, Jenny. *Trauma and the Memory of Politics*. Cambridge: Cambridge University Press, 2003.

Ellenberger, Henri F. *The Discovery of the Unconscious: The History and Evolution of Dynamic Psychiatry*. New York: Basic Books, 1970.

Encyclopaedia Britannica. "Henri Bergson: French Philosopher." Accessed October 15, 2014. http://www.britannica.com/biography/Henri-Bergson.

Ermarth, Elizabeth Deeds. *Sequel to History: Postmodernism and the Crisis of Representational Time*. Princeton, NJ: Princeton University Press, 1992.

Foucault, Michel. "Nietzsche, Genealogy, History." Translated by Donald F. Bouchard and Sherry Simon. In *The Foucault Reader*, edited by Paul Rabinow, 76–100. New York: Pantheon Books, 1984.

———. *The Order of Things: Archeology of the Human Sciences*. 1970. Reprint, London: Routledge, 2008.

———. "What is Enlightenment?" In *Essential Works of Foucault 1: Ethics, Subjectivity and Truth*, edited by Paul Rabinow, translated by Catherine Porter, 303–319. New York: The New Press, 1997.

François, Arnaud, and Roxanne Lapidus. "Life and Will in Nietzsche and Bergson." *SubStance* 36 (2007): 100–114.

Fritzsche, Peter. *Stranded in the Present: Modern Time and the Melancholy of History*. Cambridge, MA: Harvard University Press, 2004.

Frye, Northrop. "'The Decline of the West' by Oswald Spengler." *Daedalus* 103 (Winter 1974): 1–13.

Fukuyama, Francis. "The End of History?" *The National Interest* (Summer 1989): 1–18.

Fussell, Paul. *The Great War and Modern Memory*. New York: Oxford University Press, 1975.

Gilbert-Walsh, James. "Revisiting the Concept of Time: Archaic Perplexity in Bergson and Heidegger." *Human Studies* 33 (2010): 173–190.

Gillies, Mary Ann. *Henri Bergson and British Modernism*. Montreal: McGill-Queen's University Press, 1996.

Glasser, Richard. *Time in French Life and Thought*. Manchester: Manchester University Press, 1972.

Gleick, James. *Faster: The Acceleration of Just about Everything*. New York: Pantheon Books, 1999.

Gliddon, Gerald, and Timothy John Skelton. *Lutyens and the Great War*. London: Frances Lincoln, 2008.

Gray, John. *Straw Dogs: Thoughts on Humans and Other Animals*. London: Granta Books, 2002.

Greenberg, Allan. "Lutyens's Cenotaph." *The Journal of the Society of Architectural Historians* 48 (March 1989): 5–23.

Gregory, Adrian. *The Last Great War: British Society and the First World War*. Cambridge: Cambridge University Press, 2008.

Grogin, Robert C. *The Bergsonian Controversy in France 1900–1914*. Calgary: University of Calgary Press, 1988.

Grosz, Elizabeth. *The Nick of Time: Politics, Evolution and the Untimely*. Sydney: Allen and Unwin, 2004.

———. *Time Travels: Feminism, Nature, Power*. Durham, NC: Duke University Press, 2005.

Guerlac, Suzanne. "Bergson, the Void, and the Politics of Life." In *Bergson, Politics, and Religion*. edited by Alexandre Lefebvre and Melanie White, 40–60. Durham, NC: Duke University Press, 2012.

———. *Thinking in Time: An Introduction to Henri Bergson*. Ithaca, NY: Cornell University Press, 2006.

Guldi, Jo, and David Armitage. *The History Manifesto*. Cambridge: Cambridge University Press, 2014.

Gutting, Gary. *Foucault: A Very Short Introduction*. Oxford: Oxford University Press, 2005.

Habermas, Jürgen. "De nieuwe onoverzichtelijkheid: de crisis van de welvaartsstaat en de uitputting van utopische krachten" [The New Indistinctiveness: The Crisis of the Welfare State and the Exhaustion of Utopian Forces]. In *De nieuwe*

onoverzichtelijkheid en andere opstellen, translated by Geert Munnichs and René von Schomberg, 31–55. Meppel: Boom, 1989.
Hacking, Ian. *Historical Ontology*. Cambridge, MA: Harvard University Press, 2002.
Hammer, Espen. *Philosophy and Temporality from Kant to Critical Theory*. Cambridge: Cambridge University Press, 2011.
Hanson, Neil. *Unknown Soldiers: The Story of the Missing of the First World War*. London: Doubleday, 2005.
Harbers, Hans. "Van mensen en dingen: Bespreking van: Bruno Latour, Wij zijn nooit modern geweest" [Of Humans and Things: A Review of: Bruno Latour, We Have Never Been Modern]. *Krisis* 58 (1995): 6–15.
Hartley, L.P. *The Go-Between*. London: Hamish Hamilton, 1953.
Hartog, François. *Regimes of Historicity: Presentism and Experiences of Time*. Translated by Saskia Brown. New York: Columbia University Press, 2015.
———. "Time and Heritage." *Museum International* 227 (2005): 7–18.
———. "Time, History and the Writing of History: The *Order* of Time." *KVHAA Konferenser* 37 (1996): 95–113.
Harvey, David. *The Condition of Postmodernity: An Inquiry into the Origins of Cultural Change*. Cambridge, MA: Blackwell, 1989.
Hegel, Georg Wilhelm Friedrich. *The Philosophy of History*. Translated by J. Sibree. 1857. Reprint, Kitchener, ON: Batoche Books, 2001.
———. *The Philosophy of Nature*. 1842. Reprint, Whitefish, MT: Kessinger, 2004.
———. *Sämtliche Werke VI: Grundlinien der Philosophie des Rechts* [Collected Works VI: Elements of the Philosophy of Right]. 1821. Reprint, Hamburg: Felix Meiner, 2009.
———. *Science of Logic*. 1816. Reprint, Whitefish, MT: Kessinger, 2001.
Heidegger, Martin. *Being and Time*. Translated by John Macquarrie and Edward Robinson. 1962. Reprint, Oxford: Blackwell, 2001.
Hermsen, Joke. *Stil de tijd: Een pleidooi voor een langzame toekomst* [Silence the Time: A Plea for a Slow Future]. Amsterdam: De Arbeiderspers, 2009.
Hoffmann, Stefan-Ludwig. "Koselleck, Arendt, and the Anthropology of Historical Experience." *History and Theory* 49 (2010): 212–237.
Hollander, Jaap den, Herman Paul, and Rik Peters. "Introduction: the Metaphor of Historical Distance." *History and Theory* 50 (2011): 1–10.
Hölscher, Lucian. *Semantik der Leere: Grenzfragen der Geschichtswissenschaft* [A Semantics of the Empty: The Demarcation of the Historical Sciences]. Göttingen: Wallstein, 2009.
Horkheimer, Max. "On Bergson's metaphysics of time." *Radical Philosophy* 131 (2005): 9–19.
Hoy, David Couzens. "History, Historicity, and Historiography in Being and Time." In *Heidegger and Modern Philosophy: Critical Essays*, edited by Michael Murray, 329–353. New Haven, CT: Yale University Press, 1978.
———. *The Time of Our Lives: A Critical History of Temporality*. Cambridge, MA: MIT Press, 2009.

Huijer, Marli. *Ritme: Op zoek naar een terugkerende tijd* [Rhythm: In Search of a Repeating Time]. Zoetermeer: Uitgeverij Klement, 2011.
Huizinga, Johan. *The Waning of the Middle Ages: A Study of the Life, Thought, and Art in France and the Netherlands in the Fourteenth and Fifteenth Centuries*. Translated by F. Hopman. London: Arnold, 1924.
Humboldt, Wilhelm von. "On the Historian's Task." *History and Theory* 6 (1967): 57–71.
Hussey, Christopher. *The Life of Sir Edwin Lutyens*. London: Antique Collectors Book Club, 1984.
Hyppolite, Jean. "Various Aspects of Memory in Bergson." Translated by Athena V. Colman. In Leonard Lawlor, *The Challenge of Bergsonism. Phenomenology, Ontology, Ethics*, 112–127. New York: Continuum, 2004.
Iggers, Georg G. *The German Conception of History: The National Tradition of Historical Thought from Herder to the Present*. Middletown, CT: Wesleyan University Press, 1968.
———. *Historiography in the Twentieth Century: From Scientific Objectivity to the Postmodern Challenge*. Middletown, CT: Wesleyan University Press, 1997.
———. "Historiography in the Twentieth Century." *History and Theory* 44 (October 2015): 469–476.
Ingles, K.S. "War Memorials: Ten Questions for Historians." *Guerres mondiales et conflits contemporains* 167 (July 1992): 5–21.
Jakobson, Roman, and Morris Halle. *Fundamentals of Language*. The Hague: Mouton, 1956.
Jameson, Fredric. *Postmodernism, or, the Cultural Logic of Late Capitalism*. New York and London: Verso, 1991.
Janik, Allen, and Stephen Toulmin. *Wittgenstein's Vienna*. New York: Simon and Schuster, 1973.
Jankélévitch, Vladimir. *Henri Bergson*. Translated by Nils F. Schott. Durham, NC: Duke University Press, 2015.
Jarvie, Ian. "Popper's Ideal Types: Open and Closed, Abstract and Concrete Societies." In *Popper's Open Society After Fifty Years: The Continuing Relevance of Karl Popper*, edited by Ian Jarvie and Sandra Pralong, 72–83. London: Routledge, 1999.
Jarvie, Ian, and Sandra Pralong. "Introduction." In *Popper's Open Society After Fifty Years: The Continuing Relevance of Karl Popper*, edited by Ian Jarvie and Sandra Pralong, 2–15. London: Routledge, 1999.
Jay, Martin. *Downcast Eyes: The Denigration of Vision in Twentieth-Century French Thought*. Berkeley: University of California Press, 1993.
Jenkins, Keith. "Inventing the New from the Old—from White's 'Tropics' to Vico's 'Topics' (Referee's Report)." *Rethinking History* 14 (2010): 243–248.
Jordheim, Helge. "Against Periodization: Koselleck's Theory of Multiple Temporalities." *History and Theory* 51 (2012): 151–172.
Kahneman, Daniel. *Thinking, Fast and Slow*. New York: Farrar, Straus and Giroux, 2011.
Kant, Immanuel. *An Answer to the Question: What is Enlightenment?* Translated by H.B. Nisbet. 1991. Reprint, London: Penguin Books, 2009.

———. *Critique of Practical Reason*. Translated by Werner S. Pluhar. Indianapolis, IN: Hackett, 2002.

———. *The Critique of Pure Reason*. Translated by J.M.D. Meiklejohn. Reno, NV: Everyman Paperbacks, 1991.

———. *Prolegomena to Any Future Metaphysics*. Translated by Paul Carus. Boulder: NetLibrary, 1997.

Kennedy, Ellen. "Bergson's Philosophy and French Political Doctrines: Sorel, Maurras, Péguy and de Gaulle." *Government and Opposition* 15 (January 1980): 75–91.

Kern, Stephen. *The Culture of Time and Space, 1880–1918*. Cambridge, MA: Harvard University Press, 1983.

Kerslake, Christian. "Becoming against History: Deleuze, Toynbee and Vitalist Historiography." *Parrhesia* 4 (2008): 17–48.

Khandker, Wahida. "The Idea of Will and Organic Evolution in Bergson's Philosophy of Life." *Continental Philosophy Review* 46 (2013): 57–74.

Kolakowski, Leszek. *Bergson*. Translated by H. van den Haute. Kampen: Klement, 2003.

Kosellek, Reinhart. *Critique and Crisis: Enlightenment and the Pathogenesis of Modern Society*. Cambridge, MA: MIT Press, 1988.

———. *Futures Past: On the Semantics of Historical Time*. Translated by Keith Tribe. New York: Columbia University Press, 2004.

———. *The Practice of Conceptual History: Timing History, Spacing Concepts*. Stanford, CA: Stanford University Press, 2002.

Kövecses, Zoltán. *Metaphor: A Practical Introduction*. Oxford: Oxford University Press, 2002.

Krol, R.A. *Het geweten van Duitsland: Friedrich Meinecke als pleitbezorger van het Duitse historisme* [Germany's Conscience: Friedrich Meinecke as Advocate of German Historicism]. PhD diss., University of Groningen, 2013.

Kwinter, Sanford. *Architectures of Time: Toward a Theory of the Event in Modernist Culture*. Cambridge, MA: MIT Press, 2001.

Lakoff, George, and Mark Johnson. *Metaphors We Live By*. Chicago: University of Chicago Press, 1980.

Landes, D.S. *Revolution in Time: Clocks and the Making of the Modern World*. Cambridge, MA: Belknap Press, 1983.

Latour, Bruno. "Some Experiments in Art and Politics." *E-flux Journal* 23 (March 2011): 1–7.

———. *We Have Never Been Modern*. Translated by Catherine Porter. Cambridge, MA: Harvard University Press, 1993.

Lazzarato, Maurizio. *The Making of the Indebted Man: An Essay on the Neoliberal Condition*. Translated by Joshua David Jordan. Los Angeles, CA: Semiotext(e), 2012.

Lefebvre, Alexandre. *Human Rights as a Way of Life: On Bergson's Political Philosophy*. Stanford, CA: Stanford University Press, 2013.

———. Introduction to *Henri Bergson*, by Vladimir Jankélévitch, xi–xxviii. Durham, NC: Duke University Press, 2015.

Lefebvre, Alexandre, and Melanie White. "Introduction: Bergson, Politics, and Religion." In *Bergson, Politics, and Religion*, edited by Alexandre Lefebvre and Melanie White, 1–24. Durham, NC: Duke University Press, 2012.

Le Goff, Jacques. *History and Memory*. Translated by Steven Rendall and Elizabeth Claman. New York: Columbia University Press, 1992.
Lehan, Richard. "Bergson and the discourse of the Moderns." In *The Crisis in Modernism: Bergson and the Vitalist Controversy*, edited by Frederick Burwick and Paul Douglass, 277–305. Cambridge: Cambridge University Press, 1992.
Lijster, Thijs. *De grote vlucht inwaarts: Essays over cultuur in een onoverzichtelijke wereld* [The Great Flight Inward: Essays on Culture in a Chaotic World]. Amsterdam and Antwerp: De Bezige Bij, 2016.
Lindsay, A.D. *The Philosophy of Bergson*. London: Dent, 1911.
Lloyd, D.W. *Battlefield Tourism: Pilgrimage and the Commemoration of the Great War in Britain, Australia, and Canada, 1919–1939*. New York: Berg, 1998.
Lorenz, Chris. "Blurred Lines: Memory, History and the Experience of Time." *International Journal for History, Culture and Modernity* 2 (2014): 43–62.
Lorenz, Chris, and Berber Bevernage. "Breaking up Time—Negotiating the Borders between Present, Past and Future." In *Breaking up Time: Negotiating the Borders between Present, Past and Future*, edited by Chris Lorenz and Berber Bevernage, 7–38. Göttingen: Vandenhoeck & Ruprecht, 2013.
Lübbe, Hermann. "The Contraction of the Present." In *High-Speed Society, Social Acceleration, Power, and Modernity*, 159–178. University Park, PA: Penn State University Press, 2009.
Lukács, Georg. *History and Class Consciousness: Studies in Marxist Dialectics*. Translated by Rodney Livingstone. Cambridge, MA: MIT Press, 1971.
Lundy, Craig. "Bergson, History, and Ontology." Paper presented at the conference The Future of the Theory and Philosophy of History, Ghent, Belgium, July 10–13, 2013.
Lyotard, Jean-François. *The Postmodern Condition: A Report on Knowledge*. Translated by Geoff Bennington and Brian Massumi. Manchester: Manchester University Press, 1984.
Machado, Antonio, and Betty Jean Craige. *Selected Poems of Antonio Machado*. Translated by Betty Jean Craige. Baton Rouge: Louisiana State University Press, 1978.
Machiavelli, Niccolò. "Discourses on the First Decade of Titus Livius." In *The Chief Works and Others*, vol. 1, translated by Allan Gilbert, 175–532. Durham, NC: Duke University Press, 1989.
Malleson, Tom. *After Occupy: Economic Democracy for the Twenty-First Century*. Oxford: Oxford University Press, 2014.
Mandelbaum, Maurice. *History, Man, and Reason: A Study in Nineteenth-Century Thought*. Baltimore, MD: The Johns Hopkins Press, 1971.
Matthews, Eric. "Bergson's Concept of a Person." In *The New Bergson*, edited by John Mullarkey, 118–134. Manchester: Manchester University Press, 1999.
McGettigan, Andrew. "As Flowers Turn Towards the Sun: Walter Benjamin's Bergsonian Image of the Past." *Radical Philosophy* 158 (2009): 25–35.
McNamara, Patrick. *Mind and Variability: Mental Darwinism, Memory, and Self*. Westport, CT: Praeger, 1999.
Megill, Allan. "Was There a Crisis of Historicism?" *History and Theory* 36 (1997): 416–429.

Merleau-Ponty, Maurice. "Bergson in the Making." In *Signs*, translated by Richard C. McCleary, 182–191. Evanston, IL: Northwestern University Press, 1964.

Metzinger, Thomas. *The Ego Tunnel: The Science of the Mind and the Myth of the Self.* New York: Basic Books, 2010.

Michalski, Sergiusz. *Public Monuments. Art in Political Bondage 1870–1997.* London: Reaktion Books, 1998.

Montebello, Pierre, and Roxanne Lapidus. "Matter and Light in Bergson's 'Creative Evolution.'" *SubStance* 36 (2007): 91–99.

Moore, F.C.T. *Bergson: Thinking Backwards.* Cambridge: Cambridge University Press, 1996.

Mulhall, Stephen. *Routledge Philosophy Guidebook to Heidegger and Being and Time.* 2nd ed. London: Routledge, 2005.

Mullarkey, John. *Bergson and Philosophy.* Notre Dame, IN: University of Notre Dame Press, 2000.

———. "Forget the Virtual: Bergson, Actualism, and the Refraction of Reality." *Continental Philosophy Review* 37 (2004): 469–493.

———. "Introduction: La Philosophie nouvelle, or Change in Philosophy," in *The New Bergson*, edited by John Mullarkey, 1–17. Manchester: Manchester University Press, 1999.

Mumford, Lewis. *Technics and Civilization.* 7th ed. London: Routledge and Kegan Paul, 1955.

Munslow, Alun. "Editorial." *Rethinking History* (2010): 161–163.

Nietzsche, Friedrich. *On the Use and Abuse of History for Life.* Translated by Ian Johnston. Arlington: Richer Resources Publications, 2010.

———. *Thus Spoke Zarathustra.* Edited by Adrian Del Caro and Robert Pippin. Translated by Adrian Del Caro. Cambridge: Cambridge University Press, 2006.

Norman, Larry. *The Shock of the Ancient: Literature and History in Early Modern France.* Chicago: The University of Chicago Press, 2011.

NOS. "Volgende generaties slechter af" [Coming generations worse off]. Accessed January 2, 2016. http://nos.nl/artikel/236012-volgende-generaties-slechter-af.html.

Nussbaum, Martha. *Upheavals of Thought: The Intelligence of Emotions.* Cambridge: Cambridge University Press, 2001.

Olsen, Niklas. *History in the Plural: An Introduction to the Work of Reinhart Koselleck.* New York: Berghahn Books, 2012.

The Open Society Foundations. Accessed July 19, 2014. http://www.opensocietyfoundations.org.

Ortega y Gasset, José. *The Revolt of the Masses.* Anonymous translation. 1932. Reprint, New York: W.W. Norton, 1993.

Osborne, Peter. "Marx and the Philosophy of Time." *Radical Philosophy* 147 (2008): 15–22.

———. *The Politics of Time: Modernity and Avant-Garde.* London: Verso, 1995.

Percy, Clayre, and Jane Ridley, eds. *The Letters of Edwin Lutyens to His Wife Emily.* London: Collins, 1985.

Peters, Peter. *De haast van Albertine: Reizen in de technologische cultuur: naar een theorie van passages* [Albertine in a Hurry: Travel in Technological Culture: Towards a Theory of Passages]. Amsterdam: Uitgeverij De Balie, 2003.

Phillips, Mark Salber. *On Historical Distance*. New Haven: Yale University Press, 2013.
Plato. *Plato: Complete Works*. Edited by John M. Cooper. Indianapolis, IN: Hackett Publishing Company, 1997.
Popper, Karl. *The Open Society and Its Enemies: New One-Volume Edition*. 1945. Reprint, Princeton and Oxford: Princeton University Press, 2013.
Prigogine, Ilya, and Isabelle Stengers. *Order Out of Chaos: Man's New Dialogue with Nature*. Toronto: Bantam Books, 1984.
Quirk, Thomas V. *Bergson and American Culture: The Worlds of Willa Cather and Wallace Stevens*. Chapel Hill: The University of North Carolina Press, 1990.
Ramírez, Sandra Lucía. *Conocimiento y formas de vida: Elementos para la construcción de espacios públicos en cuestiones científico-tecnológicas* [Knowledge and Forms of Life: Elements for the Construction of Public Spaces in Scientific-Technological Questions]. Mérida: Universidad Nacional Autónoma de México, 2011.
Richter, Melvin, and Michaela W. Richter. "Introduction: Translation of Reinhart Koselleck's 'Krise,' in Geschichtliche Grundbegriffe." *Journal of the History of Ideas* 67 (2006): 343–356.
Ricoeur, Paul. *Memory, History, Forgetting*. Translated by Kathleen Blamey and David Pellauer. Chicago: University of Chicago Press, 2006.
Ridley, Jane. *The Architect and His Wife: A Life of Edwin Lutyens*. London: Chatto and Windus, 2002.
Roberts, Adam. *Fredric Jameson*. London: Routledge, 1991.
Rosa, Hartmut. *Social Acceleration: A New Theory of Modernity*. Translated by Jonathan Trejo-Mathys. New York: Columbia University Press, 2013.
———. "Social Acceleration: Ethical and Political Consequences of a Desynchronized High-Speed Society." In *High-Speed Society, Social Acceleration, Power, and Modernity*, 77–112. Edited by Hartmut Rosa and William E. Scheuerman. University Park, PA: Penn State University Press, 2009.
Runia, Eelco. *Moved by the Past: Discontinuity and Historical Mutation*. New York: Columbia University Press, 2014.
———. "Namen Noemen [Naming Names]." *Tijdschrift voor Geschiedenis* 119 (2006): 242–248.
———. "De Pissende Pulcinella" [The Pissing Pulcinella]. *De Gids* 168 (2005): 397–416.
———. *De Pathologie van de Veldslag: Geschiedenis en geschiedschrijving in Tolstoj's Oorlog en Vrede* [The Pathology of Battle: History and Historiography in Tolstoj's War and Peace]. Amsterdam: Meulenhoff Boekerij, 1995.
———. "Presence." *History and Theory* 45 (February 2006): 1–29.
Rushkoff, Douglas. *Present Shock: When Everything Happens Now*. New York: Penguin Group, 2013.
Russell, Bertrand. *A History of Western Philosophy, and Its Connection with Political and Social Circumstances from the Earliest Times to the Present Day*. New York: Simon and Schuster, 1945.
Safranski, Rüdiger. *Martin Heidegger: Between Good and Evil*. 2nd ed. Translated by Ewald Osers. Cambridge, MA: Harvard University Press, 1998.
———. *Nietzsche: A Philosophical Biography*. Translated by Shelley Frisch. London: Granta Books, 2002.

Scharff, Robert. "Heidegger's 'Appropriation' of Dilthey before Being and Time." *Journal of the History of Philosophy* 35 (1997): 105–128.
Schure, Leon ter. "Presence: De tegenwoordigheid van het verleden in het heden" [Presence: The presence of the past in the here and now]. *Tijdschrift voor Geschiedenis* 116 (2006): 230–241.
Singer, Peter. *Hegel: A Very Short Introduction.* 1983. Reprint, Oxford: Oxford University Press, 2001.
———. *Marx: A Very Short Introduction.* 1980. Reprint, Oxford: Oxford University Press, 1996.
Society for Psychical Research. Accessed September 30, 2018. http://www.spr.ac.uk.
Soulez, Philippe. "Bergson as Philosopher of War and Theorist of the Political." In *Bergson, Politics, and Religion*, edited by Alexandre Lefebvre and Melanie White, 99–125. Durham, NC: Duke University Press, 2012.
———. *Bergson politique.* Paris: Presses Universitaires de France, 1989.
Sowerwine, Charles. *France since 1870: Culture, Politics and Society.* New York: Palgrave, 2001.
Spengler, Oswald. *The Decline of the West, Part 1: Form and Actuality.* Translated by Charles Francis Atkinson. New York: Knopf, 1926.
Spiegel, Gabrielle. "Memory and History: Liturgical Time and Historical Time." *History and Theory* 41 (2002): 149–163.
Steffen, Will, Jacques Grinevald, Paul Crutzen, and John McNeill. "The Anthropocene: conceptual and historical perspectives." *Philosophical Transactions of the Royal Society* 369 (2011): 842–867.
Swaab, Dick. *We Are Our Brains: A Neurobiography of the Brain, from the Womb to Alzheimer's.* Translated by Jane Hedley-Prôle. New York: Spiegel and Grau, 2014.
Tanner, Michael. *Nietzsche.* Oxford: Oxford University Press, 1996.
De Telegraaf. "Consumentenvuurwerk is cultureel erfgoed" [Consumer Fireworks are Cultural Heritage]. Accessed October 19, 2016. http://www.telegraaf.nl/binnenland/24812086/__Vuurwerk_is_cultureel_erfgoed__.html.
Thompson, E.P. "Time, Work-Discipline, and Industrial Capitalism." *Past and Present* 38 (1967): 56–97.
Toffler, Alvin. *Future Shock.* New York: Bantam Books, 1971.
Tuin, Iris van der. "'A Different Starting Point, a Different Metaphysics': Reading Bergson and Barad Diffractively." *Hypatia* 26 (Winter 2011): 22–42.
Tukhanen, Mikko. "Ontology and Involution." *Diacritics* 35 (2005): 20–45.
White, Hayden. *Metahistory: The Historical Imagination in Nineteenth-Century Europe.* Baltimore, MD: Johns Hopkins University Press, 1973.
———. *Tropics of Discourse: Essays in Cultural Criticism.* Baltimore, MD: Johns Hopkins University Press, 1978.
Wilcox, Donald. *The Measure of Times Past: Pre-Newtonian Chronologies and the Rhetoric of Relative Time.* Chicago: University of Chicago Press, 1987.
Wilson, Timothy. *Strangers to Ourselves: Discovering the Adaptive Unconscious.* Cambridge, MA: The Belknap Press of Harvard University Press, 2002.

Winter, Jay. *Remembering War: The Great War Between Memory and History in the Twentieth Century.* New Haven: Yale University Press, 2006.
———. *Sites of Memory, Sites of Mourning: The Great War in European Cultural History.* Cambridge: Cambridge University Press, 1995.
Worms, Frédéric. "The Closed and the Open in The Two Sources of Morality and Religion: A Distinction That Changes Everything." In *Bergson, Politics, and Religion*, edited by Alexandre Lefebvre and Melanie White, 25–39. Durham, NC: Duke University Press, 2012.
Zammito, John. "Koselleck's Philosophy of Historical Time(s) and the Practice of History." *History and Theory* 43 (2004): 124–135.
Žižek, Slavoj. *Event: A Philosophical Journey through a Concept.* London: Penguin Books, 2014.
———. *First as Tragedy, Then as Farce.* London: Verso, 2008.
———. *Living in the End Times.* London: Verso, 2010.

INDEX

9/11, 55, 141, 216

Absolutism: Absolutist State, 41, 180
acceleration: cycle, 48–50; of history, 39–45, 48, 50, 121, 218; in the pace of life, xxvi, 49; social, 48–50; of social change, 48–49; societies, 49, 54, 221; technological, 48–49, 54; of (historical) time, xv, 23, 25, 47, 54, 56, 61n6, 121, 145–146, 212, 218–219
Achilles, 98, 123, 171
Action Française, 70
action(s): and the adaptive unconscious, 93; associationists on, 91; Bergson on, 83, 97; the body as center of, 96n90, 131, 205; creative, 96n90, 146, 200; determinism and, 93; free, 92–93, 101–102, 134, 168; German historicism on, 155, 221; "of a hand through iron filings," 106; Hegel on, 163–164; and historical ontology, 115n181; and the historical past, 141, 146; and historiography, 135; and the intellect, 166–167; Kahneman on, 91n75; categorical imperative and, 185; Koselleck on, 36; and memory, 131–134; moral, 193; Nietzsche on, 33; and organic instruments, 109; in the prelude to World War I, 60; and social acceleration, 49; Sorel on revolutionary, 70; superficial and fundamental self and, 91
the actual, 108, 151n9, 157
actualization: of Bergson, 151n9, 209; duration as, 157; future as, 221; of memory-images, 96n90, 130–134; of the past, 130, 138, 158, 186, 220; phase of memory, 133–134; and the virtual, 108n161, 157. *See also* selectionism
adaptive unconscious, 93
affirmative method, xxvii
agency, 155, 146
Alexanderschlacht (Altdorfer), 40
Alexander the Great, 40, 164
alienation: Bergson on, 66, 149; of *Dasein* from authentic existence, 33; of Spirit, Hegel on the, 162
Altdorfer, Albrecht, 40–41
Ankersmit, Frank: on historical distance, 124–125; on historical experience, 215; on historical representation, 2–4; on historicism, 152–153, 155n22; on memory, 136
Ansell-Pearson, Keith, 82–83, 103n126, 105n137, 108n161, 151n8, 157, 195n80
the Anthropocene, 119n5, 218
anti-intellectualism, Bergson and, xx, 78
Antiquity, 41, 179, 203
antinomies, 80

antiquarianism: Bergson and, 135, 146; Nietzsche on, 5n10, 33
apocalypse, xvi
Arab Spring, 141, 216
archeology, Foucault on, 36
Aristotle, 64n22; on memory, 127–128, 132
Armitage, David, xvii, 119n5
ascetic frenzy, 202. *See also* industrial frenzy; law of two-fold frenzy
asceticism, 204
associationist psychology, 85, 91
atomic bomb, 176
atomism, 64, 65n25, 152, 155
Augustine, xxi, 64n22
authenticity: Benjamin on, in Bergson, 113n174; Heidegger on, 28–35; of historical experience, 215; memory studies and, 136
Ayotzinapa, 6

Bachelard, Gaston, 149–150
Badiou, Alain, 151n9
becoming 83n35; vs. being, 61; Bergson on, 70, 112, 123; Deleuze and Badiou on, 151n9; duration as, xxvi, 131, 151n9, 219–220; fluid concepts and, 116; Hegel on, 169; history as, 43, 119, 212–213; language and, 88; life as, 104, 195n80, 212; Nietzsche on, 196; the self and, 91; the universe as, 76n6, 113
Being and Time (Heidegger), 24–35, 37–38
Beiser, Frederick: defining historicism, 153–154, 158; on Hegel's holism, 164; on historicisms' nominalist holism, 156, 171
Belle Époque, xix, 67, 73, 176
Benda, Julien, xx
Benjamin, Walter, 5, 57; critique of Bergson, 113; on historicism, 125–126, 161; on World War I, 60–61
Bentley, Michael, 5, 20

Bergson, Henri: biography of, 65; debate with Einstein, xx, 72; influence of, 69–72; during the Interbellum, 196, 197, 198; and nineteenth-century physics, 99; popularity of, xix–xxi, 67–68, 72; as president of the CIC, 175–176; style of writing, 75; during World War I, 175, 176, 189–190. *See also* Bergsonism
Bergsonism: Bachelard on, 150n7; and overcoming the crisis of the modern regime of historicity, 218–222; as cultural phenomenon, 59, 66–74 passim; and Hegel's philosophy of history, 161–172; as nonmodern historicism, xxvii, 79n18, 108n162, 148, 151, 156–161, 172; as non-systematic, 76, 113, 208; as philosophy of the virtual, 87n54, 95, 151; as philosophical revolution, xix–xxi; revival of, 73. *See also* Bergson, Henri; history: Bergson and
Berlin Wall, xiv, xv, 46
Berman, Marshall, 47, 138
Bevernage, Berber, xxv, 5n14, 19n75, 20, 123, 125, 215
the body: Bergson on, 95, 96n90, 100n110, 129, 164n57; as center of action, 96n90, 131, 205; disappeared, 5, 7n18; foreign, 15; -mind problem, 115, 215; of the nation, 71; and the problem of war, 203–204
Bonneuil, Christophe, 119n5, 218
Bor, Jan, 94n84, 112, 114n178
Borges, Jorge Luis, 117
Braudel, Fernand, 45, 57
Burckhardt, Jacob, 3, 4, 128

Canales, Jimena, xx
Čapek, Milič, 94, 95, 99n105
capitalism, xiv, xvi, 61; Benjamin on, 113n174; Bergson and, 138, 203, 221n23; and homogeneous time,

63, 67–72, 148; late, 52; and social acceleration, 48, 50n100
Carpenter, William, 93n81
Carr, David, 25, 33, 34n35, 38, 128–129
categorical imperative, 185–186
causality: and the acceleration cycle, 49; associationism and, 85, 91; and Bergson's memory-cone, 133; in Hegel's philosophy of history, 164; in history, 119, 138, 147, 216
Cenotaph, the London, xxv, 1–3, 60; history of, 6–12; and the presence of the past, 12–21, 122–123, 215
Certeau, Michel de, xxii, 17, 18
Chaplin, Charlie, 146, 149
Chladenius, Johann Martin, 154n18
Christian, David, xviii, 119n5
chronology, historical, 121–122, 124–125, 138–139
Cicero, Marcus Tullius, 40
civilization(s): Hegel on, 169–170; modern, and historical culture, 51; and progress, 177, 182, 183n30, 206; the war instinct and, 177, 190; Western, 197–198
clock–time, xxi, 62–64, 148–149; Heidegger on, 32
closed society: Bergson on: xxvii, 176, 184, 187–191 passim, 194, 198; Popper on, xxvii, 176, 181–183. *See also* open society; morality
Cold War, 180
Collège de France, 65, 67–68
Collingwood, R.G., 136–137
comfort, 202–203, 207
commemoration. *See* World War I: practices of commemoration; Cenotaph, the London
Conceptual History, 36–38, 46–47. *See also* Koselleck, Reinhart
consciousness: as attention to life, 129; Bergson on, 71, 83–84, 85–89; the brain and, 131; Cubism and, 69; and the egotunnel, 83; evolution of, 109–112; and freedom, 90–93; Heidegger on, 27, 34n35; historical, xxv, 24, 33, 50–51, 118, 121, 144, 152, 179; Husserl on, 26; Koselleck on time-, 47n89; life as, 69, 102–104, 158, 166; matter as, 100–101; the past and, 126, 130; memory and, 134; stream-of-, novel, 63; "the Whole" and, 160; of "World-Historical Individuals," 164.
continuity: Bergson on, 83; duration as, 108n157, 148–151, 217; and the event, 141–142, 216; between experiences and expectations, 40; Foucault on, 143–144; and historicism, 155; and history, 36, 48, 51, 60, 147–148, 161, 168, 214; of life, 102; matter as, 99, 100; time as, 152
creative destruction, 47, 50, 138, 213, 220
Creative Evolution (Bergson): causality in, 164; duration in, xxii, xxvi, 94–95, 108n157, 152; on human society, 184; Bergson's concept of identity in, 155; impact of, 65, 68; intelligence in, 203n120; James on, xix–xx; Bergson's philosophy of life in, 102–108, 157; and modernity, 70; Nietzsche in, 195; objective of, 112; Popper on, 182n26; in relation to *The Two Sources*, 176, 208
Critique of Practical Reason (Kant), 185, 193
Critique of Pure Reason (Kant), 64n22, 77, 78, 79–82
Cubism, xix, 69

Darwin, Charles, 104, 196
Darwinism, 116, 212. *See also* mental Darwinism
Dasein, 26–27, 34n35; authentic and inauthentic, 27–28, 30–33; Koselleck on, 37n47, 38

debt, 220–221
decadence, 197, 198
Decline of the West, The (Spengler), 197
déjà vu, 129
DeLanda, Manuel, 119n5, 218
Delboeuf, Joseph, 86
Deleuze, Gilles, xxi, 72, 73, 95, 209; on dialectics, 170, 201; on history, 199; on intuition, 114; on memory, 129, 132; and *The Two Sources*, 208; on the virtual, 87n54, 151; on the whole, 119, 172.
democracy, 36n42; Bergson and, 71, 144–145; liberal, xiv, 70, 197; Popper and, 181
Descartes, René, 76, 95
desynchronization, 54, 146, 218, 221
determinism: Bergson and, 66, 68, 93, 104, 110, 115, 215; psychological, 85; technological, 61n6
Dewey, John, xix
dialectic(s), 53; Bergson's dynamical, 200–203; and duration, 169–171
Diamond Dust Shoes (Warhol), 52
dichotomy, xx; the law of, 199–201; of Nature and Culture, 42n68, 124. See also modern Constitution
difference: Badiou and Deleuze on, 151n9; between closed and open society, 187, 191–193, 198–199; in degree vs. in kind, 86, 115, 177, 215; dialectics and, 170–171; qualitative, 86, 115, 118
differentiation: "functional," 54; history as, 142; and the law of dichotomy, 201; and the whole, 157–158
Dilthey, Wilhelm, 25, 26, 154n18; Heidegger on, 29–30
discontinuity: duration and, 108n157, 147–152, 142, 214; of *epistèmes*, 39; and the event, 141, 216; in evolution, 108; historical, 5, 142, 144, 147–148, 168; historicism and, 51, 148, 161, 214; matter and, 98–99, 100; postmodernism and, 52; and World War I, 13n49, 61
dissociation: evolution as, 107–109, 199; and genealogy, 144; of the past, 44, 51
Domanska, Ewa, 5–6, 17; on the posthuman turn, 119n5, 218
Du Cubisme (Gleizes and Metzinger), 69
duration, xxii, xxvi: and the art of living, 219; Benjamin's critique of, 113n174; Collingwood on, 136–137; comparison with music, 90; Cubism and, 69; development of, 76; dialectics and, 169–171; the event and, 138–142; fluid concepts and, 116; freedom and, 91–93; the future and, 221; genealogy and, 142–146; Hegel and, 166–171; Hermsen on, 148–151; as heterogeneous continuity, 147–148; historical, 120–124, 160; and historical epistemology, 136–146; and historicism, 155, 171–172; and history, 117–120, 147, 160, 216, 217; Horkheimer's critique of, 112–113; Huijer on, 149–151; intuition of, 77, 78n12, 93, 94, 106, 109, 112, 114–116; language and, xxi, 39n56, 88–89; of matter, 94–102; and the mechanistic worldview, 65; memory and, 131, 133–134, 137; metaphysics of, 84, 95–102; and the modern Constitution, xviii, 214; and the modern regime of historicity, xxiv, 126; ontology of, xxvi, 76, 97n90, 131, 137, 147, 148, 157–159, 172, 193, 198, 201, 209, 213, 216, 219; the past and, 220; as philosophy of life, 69, 71, 94–95, 102–108; psychical research and, 205; psychological, xxii, xxvi, 76, 86–90 passim, 94–96, 100, 102–103, 108n157; pure, 85, 90; rhythms of, 76, 97n90, 100–101, 157, 172, 220, 221; thinking in, 93,

106, 112–116, 130, 161, 212–213;
as vague concept, 75; as virtual
whole, 148, 151–152, 156–161, 172,
193–194, 213–214, 221. *See also under*
discontinuity
Duration and Simultaneity (Bergson), 94n84
Durkheim, Émile, 65, 177n6

Edelstein, Dan, 44n76, 165, 178–179
Edkins, Jenny, 15, 18
the egotunnel, 83
Einstein, Albert, xx, 64, 72
élan vital, 71; Bergson's philosophy
of life and the, 69, 102–108, 199;
evolution and, 109, 110; God and,
206; and Nietzsche's "will to power,"
196; privileged individuals and, 194,
205; as vague concept, 75, 116; and
the law of dichotomy, 201
electrons, 99n106
emotion(s), 8; the adaptive unconscious
and, 93; Bergson on, 86, 87, 193–
194, 208; and the Cenotaph, 13; and
intuition, 84; Kahneman on, 91n75;
in postmodernism, 52
empiricism: Bergson's philosophy as,
xxvi, 77, 84, 103, 115n184; Kant on,
82; Toynbee on, 81n27
the Enlightenment: Bergson and, 116,
204–205, 207–208; concepts of time
and space in, 64; Hegel and, 161,
166, 170; historicism and, 153–155;
narrative of, 44, 176–182, 202;
progress and, 44, 50, 52; project of,
50; *The Two Sources* as critique of,
182–183, 186–188
épistème(s), 36n39, 45
epistemology: Bergson and historical,
120, 136–146, 161; Bergson's
evolutionary, 81–82, 109–112;
Foucault on, 36n39; Heidegger and,
25, 35; and history, xxv, 3, 4, 19,
20–21, 24, 25, 56, 216–217; meta-,
115, 215

Ermarth, Elizabeth, 122
European Union, 183
event, the (philosophical concept), 120,
138–142, 216–217
evolution: Bergson on, xxii–xxvii
passim, 69, 82–83, 102–116, 215,
220; of the eye, 104–106; of free
actions, 92; and history, 110, 118,
124, 159–160, 166, 177, 179, 195,
198–201; and holistic individualism,
157–158; and human society, 184,
185; of mankind, Fukuyama on the,
xiv; and memory, 102, 133–135,
160; Popper on Bergson's creative,
182n26; role of privileged individuals,
194–195, 198, 207; and the problem
of war, 202–205; Sorel on, 70.
existentialism, xx, 53
extensity, 96–97, 99–101

fascism, xiv, 71
Fechner, Gustav, 86
finalism, xxii, 104–106
forgetting: Bergson on, 131; Heidegger
on, 32, 33; Ricoeur on, 126–128
Foucault, Michel, 72; on Enlightenment,
178; and genealogy, 142–144, 217; on
history, 35–36, 37n42, 45
freedom, 69; and the Absolutist State,
180; Bergson on, 66, 85, 90–93, 97,
168; Deleuze on, 199; and evolution,
102, 110, 148; Fukuyama on, xiv;
Hegel on, 162–166, 169–170, 184–
185; Hyppolite on, in Bergson, 95;
Kant on, 180; and memory, 96n90,
101; negative, 163; in the open
society, 181; the past as resource for,
110, 126, 135, 213, 220; rhythm as,
149
Fressoz, Jean-Baptiste, 119n5, 218
Freud, Sigmund, 53, 89
Fukuyama, Francis, xiv
future: collective, 53, 56; Heidegger on
the, 28–33 passim; invention of the,

future *(continued)*
  xiv, xxiv, 135, 221; modern, xv, 43; presentistic, 220; public, xvii; "shock," xv; "slow," 148; unforeseeable, 140, 145, 216; utopian, xiv, 180; view from the, xv, 46, 56
futurists, Italian, 64

Gadamer, Hans-Georg, 38n52
genealogy, xxvi, 120, 142–144, 217
George, Lloyd, 9
Gleick, James, xiv
Gleizes, Albert, 69
God, 183; death of, 195–196, Bergson on, 206–207
Greenwich Mean Time, 62
Gregory, Adrian, 8n22, 12
Grosz, Elizabeth, xxiv, 104, 138, 142, 195, 196, 221; on the affirmative method, xxvii
Guldi, Jo, xvii, 119n5

Hacking, Ian, 114, 115n181, 215
Hamilton, William, 93n81
Hartog, François, xxv, 4n9; on the challenge of presentism, 51–52, 55–56, 146, 219. *See also* the modern regime of historicity; presentistic regime of historicity
Harvey, David, 47–48, 50, 72. *See also* time–space compression
Hegel, G.W.F., xxvii, 3, 128, 141, 148, 153n16; comparison with Bergson, 166–171, 172, 184–185, 195; on dialectics, 169–170; historical distance and, 124; philosophy of history of, 161–172, 182n26; Popper on, 181–182
Heidegger, Martin, xxv, 24; on "fundamental ontology," 26–28, 29; on historicity, 28–32, 34; on historiography, 32–33; Koselleck and, 37–38; and the theory of history, 25–26, 35, 57, 114, 214n5

Herder, Johann Gottfried von, 3, 153n16, 154n18, 156
heritage, xvi, 55; Heidegger on, 30–32
hermeneutics, 33, 53
Hermsen, Joke, 148–152
heterogeneity: as aspect of duration, 100n109, 147, 148–151; and genealogy, 143, 217; as tendency of life, 157, 213; of time, 63–64
historical distance, xiv, xxii, xxvi, 17, 19, 41, 55, 121, 140, 212; as metaphor, 124–126; and transitional justice, 123
historicism, xxvi, 3–5, 60, 195; Benjamin on, 125–126, 161; Bergsonism as nonmodern, xxvii, 79n18, 108n162, 148, 151, 156–161, 172; comparison with Bergson, 156–161, 171–172, 213–214, 221; crisis of, 38; German, 50–51, 79, 152–156, 179n13; Heidegger and, 29, 38; and the modern regime of historicity, 21; Nietzsche and, 33; Popper on, 181
historicity: crisis of, 24–25, 46, 47, 51–52, 57, 209; Foucault on, 36; fragmentation of, 145–146; historicism and, 160; and historiography, 24, 26; Koselleck on, 37, 38n52; of a memory, 127; modern, 20, 46; "of the universe," 138; weakening of, in postmodernism, 53. *See also* Heidegger: on historicity; regime of historicity
historiography, xxv, 4–5, 119, 211; implications of Bergsonism for, 135, 217–218; Collingwood on Bergson and, 137n73; Foucault on, 144; and memory studies, 136; modern, 5–6, 17, 19–21, 44, 120–121, 125, 212; postmodern, 128n41; Toynbee's Bergsonian, 81n27; Wilhelm von Humboldt on, 140n81. *See also under* Heidegger; historicity

history: acceleration of, 39–45, 48, 50, 121, 218; as becoming, 43, 119, 212–213; Bergson and, xxii–xxiii, xxv–xxvii, 74, 77, 81n27, 115n181, 117–120, 123–124, 126n31, 135, 137, 146, 147–148, 172–173, 176–177, 182n26, 184–202 passim, 208–222 passim; big, xviii, 119n5, 217; causality in, 119, 138, 147, 216; of the London Cenotaph, xxv, 6–12; as a general concept, 43, 212; continuity and, 36, 48, 51, 60, 147–148, 161, 168, 214; cultural significance of, xvii, 24, 46–47, 51, 153; Deleuze on, 199; as differentiation, 142; as a discipline, xvi, xxii, 23–24, 30, 33–35, 45, 118, 124; duration and, 117–124, 147, 160, 216, 217; end of, xiv, 165, 221; epistemology of, xxv, 3, 4, 19, 20–21, 24, 25, 56, 216–217; and evolution, 110, 118, 124, 159–160, 166, 177, 179, 195, 198–201; Foucault on, 35–36, 37n42, 45; Hegel's philosophy of, 161–172, 182n26; Heidegger on, 25–35, 57, 114, 214n5; historicism and, xxvi, 50–51, 147, 153–159, 172, 181, 214, 216, 217; Koselleck on, 25, 36–45, 47, 48, 121, 166, 183, 218–219; laws of, 181, 198–202; memory and, 125, 136–137; modern concept of, 24, 45, 54, 56–57, 59, 118–124, 166, 183, 211–212, 218, 221–222; and modernity, 19n75, 24, 36, 42, 47–48, 56, 61n6, 62, 70; and the modern regime of historicity, xviii, xxv, 21, 56, 222; as multiplicitous singular, 221; pendulum of history, 196, 200–202, 204; of philosophy, xx, 32, 35, 66, 77, 78, 209; standstill of, xv–xvii, 146, 218; temporality and, 122, 136; truth in, 136, 138, 140, 216; universal, xviii, 119n5, 165; virtual, 152n9. *See also* chronology, historical; Conceptual History; consciousness: historical; discontinuity: historical; the event; genealogy; historical distance; ontology: historical; past: historical; presentism; progress: historical; representation: historical; trauma: historical

History Manifesto, The (Guldi and Armitage), xxvii–xxviii, 119n5, 217
historia magistra vitae, 40, 43, 121
historia rerum gestarum, 19, 136, 142
Historie, 43
Historik, 37
Hitler, Adolf, 32, 198
Hobbes, Thomas, 183n30
holism: Bergson's, 83n35, 98, 148, 151–152, 156–161, 172, 193–194, 213–214, 221; of Hegel's philosophy of history, xxvii, 164; and historicism, 155–156, 171–172, 214
holistic individualism, 158
Holocaust-Mahnmal, 7
horizon of expectation, 38–42, 48, 55, 62. *See also* space of experience; Koselleck, Reinhart
Horkheimer, Max, 112–113, 114n176
Hoy, David Couzens, 34
Huijer, Marli, 149–152, 156
Huizinga, Johan, 4, 125
Humboldt, Wilhelm von, 140, 154n18
Hume, David, 85n48, 179n13
Humphrey, John, 207n135
Husserl, Edmund, 26–27
hypnosis, 69n36, 93
Hyppolite, Jean, 95

idealism, xiv; Bergson on, 96n90, 100; Hegel's absolute, 162, 169
identity: Bergson on, 89, 155; Deleuze and, 151n9; modern life and, 48; situational form of, 54; of the unknown soldier, 7
image(s): matter as, 96n90; memory-, 127, 130–134, 213; postmodernism as "new culture of the," 52, 53

Imperial War Graves Commission, 8, 15
imperialism, 204
impressionists, 64
In Search of Lost Time (Proust), 63
individuality: Bergson on, 80, 157–158, 172, 192, 195, 204, 213; as ontological principle of historicism, 148, 155–156, 171, 214. *See also* holistic individualism
industrial frenzy, 202–204. *See also* ascetic frenzy; law of two-fold frenzy
inhibition(s): intuition as removal of, 84; and memory, 84, 131, 134–135
instinct, 144; in evolution, 109–112, 186n44, 188; intelligence and, 199; compared with intuition, 111–112, 114; Russell on, in Bergson, 78; war, 177, 184, 190
instructionism, 127, 134–135
the intellect: Bergson on, 78, 81–82, 139, 167–168, 170; Deleuze on, 199n104; evolution of, 109–112; Kant and, 66. *See also* anti-intellectualism, Bergson and
intentionality, 27
Interbellum, xxvii, 2, 72, 176, 177, 196, 209
International Committee on Intellectual Cooperation (CIC), 175, 206
Introduction to Metaphysics (Bergson), 78, 94n84
intuition(s), xxi, 69, 70; Bergson on, xxvi, 75, 77–84, 96n90, 205; of duration, 77, 78n12, 93, 94, 106, 109, 112, 114–116; and evolution, 109–112; compared with Hegel's dialectics, 169–171; Kant and, 64n22, 66, 80; of matter, 97–100; as philosophical method, 77–79, 85n45, 90, 103, 113–116, 144n101, 214–215; Popper on, 182n26. *See also under* instinct; mysticism; perception

Jakobson, Roman, 13n50

James, William, 65n25, 134
Jameson, Fredric, 52–53
Jenkins, Keith, 19, 125n26
Jetztzeit, 126n31
Joyce, James, 64

Kafka, Franz, 63
Kahneman, Daniel, 91–92
Kant, Immanuel, xix, 77, 112, 181; and Bergson, 65–66, 77–84; on Enlightenment, 178–179; and Bergson on morality, 185, 193; on time and space, 64, 66, 80. *See also* categorical imperative; *Critique of Practical Reason*; *Critique of Pure Reason*
Kolakowski, Leszek, 72, 73, 76, 77
Koselleck, Reinhart, xxv, 25, 166, 181; on the acceleration of history, 39–45, 121, 218–219; and the crisis of the modern regime of historicity, 46–47, 48; on the Enlightenment narrative, 180; and the modern Constitution, 183; on the *Sattelzeit*, 37, 41–42, 45, 47, 121; theory of historical times, 36–45 passim. *See also* Conceptual History

Latour, Bruno, xviii, xxiii, 5, 42, 56, 118, 159, 183, 208, 212. *See also* modern Constitution
law of two-fold frenzy, 200–201. *See also* industrial frenzy; ascetic frenzy
Laycock, Thomas, 93n81
Lazzarato, Maurizio, 220–221
Lefebvre, Alexandre, 193, 207n135, 208, 219
Lindsay, A.D., 81
linguistic turn, 2, 20
Locke, John, 85n48, 183n30
love: Bergson on, 186, 187, 190, 202; as event, 141; language and, 89; the open society and, 191–194
Lukács, Georg, 63

Lutyens, Edwin, 2, 6, 7–11, 15, 16, 18. *See also* Cenotaph, the London
luxury, 190, 202–203
Lyotard, Jean-Francois, 52

Machiavelli, Niccolò, 40, 121n10
Magritte, René, 218
das Man, 28, 34
Mandelbaum, Maurice, 153n16, 154
Maritain, Jacques, 176n4
Marx, Karl, 3, 47, 50n100; 70n43, 128, 138, 154n16, 181, 221n23
Marxism, 52, 63, 70, 71
mass: culture, 28; destruction, 176; man, 197–198; production, 63
mathematics: Bergson on, 81, 86; Dilthey on the human sciences and, 29; and duration, xxi, 98, 160; Kant on the possibility of, 80–81; Newtonian physics and, 64, 79
matter: Bergson on, 76, 85, 87, 91n72, 95–102; "double genesis" of intellect and, 82, 110–112, 167; duration and, 94–102; in evolution, 106–112, 199; mentioned, 162, 213; science and, 205; tendency of, toward repetition, 107–108, 159. *See also under* image(s), intuition(s), memory
Matter and Memory (Bergson), 83n39, 94–102 passim, 205; Benjamin on, 113n174, 126n31
Maurras, Charles, 70
McNamara, Patrick, 132–135
mechanism(s): Bergson on, 69, 79, 85, 90–91, 159, 213; in culture, 68–69; and evolution, xxii, 103–106; historical change and, 123–124, 138, 147; historicism and, 155; in Kant, 80–83; mentioned, 99n105; motor, 131; Spengler on, 197; and time, 81, 91n72, 124, 152; as worldview, 65, 80, 85, 91, 116
Meinecke, Friedrich, 152, 154n17
memorial(s). *See* monument(s)

memory, 11; Benjamin on Bergson's theory of, 113n174, 126n31; Bergson's theory of, xxvi, 120, 129–134, 137, 213; counter-, toward the present, 143–144, 217; evolution and, 101–102, 133–135, 160; history and, 125, 136–137; history as pendulum endowed with, 196, 200–202, 204; Huijer on, 150; -images, 127, 131–134, 213; intuition and, 84; of matter, 101; and mental Darwinism, 134–135; relation to perception, 96n90; Ricoeur on, 127–128; studies, 19, 125, 136; time of, 20, 63, 125, 137, 213, 215; and the virtual, 128n40, 130–132, 213
mental Darwinism, 134
Merleau-Ponty, Maurice, xxii–xxiii, 117, 118
metaphor(s): Bergson and, 75, 89, 160; historical representation as, 4; mentioned, xxiii, 39, 42, 79, 83, 107, 124n23, 127, 131, 134n63, 140, 165, 183; and metonymy, 13–14; in monuments, 2, 6, 7, 16–17; of time, xxi, 17, 64n22
metaphysics, xx, 77; Bergson on, xxvi, 78–79, 83–84, 89, 184, 205; Bergsonism as process, 151n9; of duration, 84, 95–102; Heidegger on, 26–28, 35; relation of historicism to, 154, 156; Horkheimer on Bergson's, 112–113, 114n176; Kant on, 80; of time, 4, 17, 112, 150, 152
metonymy: and the Cenotaph, 2, 15–17; and monuments, 7; Runia on, 14–15, 16–17. *See also under* metaphor
Metzinger, Jean, 69
Metzinger, Thomas, 83
Michelet, Jules, 3, 128
Middle Ages, 4, 62, 122, 202, 204
Mill, John Stuart, 85n48, 94n81
Minerva, owl of, 124, 141

modern Constitution, xviii–xix, xxiii–xxiv, 42–43, 56, 118, 159, 165–166, 183–184, 208, 212, 214, 221. *See also* Latour, Bruno

modernity, xxv, 23, 46; Bergson's relation to, 172–173; Enlightenment's project of, 188; historicism and, 51; history and, 19n75, 24, 36, 42, 47–48, 56, 61n6, 62, 70; industrial, 90, 113n174, 177, 202, 203, 208; late, 54, 145–146; Latour on, 183; paradox of, 188, 191; politics in, 43, 44n75; and social acceleration, 48–50, 218. *See also* nonmodern; postmodernism

Modern Times (1936), 149

modernism, xix, 53, 71, 116n186; "Bergsonian," 138

the modern regime of historicity, 46; Bergson and, 116, 126, 144, 145, 172, 208, 218–221; crisis of, xv, xxi, 45–46, 56–57, 59, 73, 116, 145, 218–219; Enlightenment and, 179; Heidegger and, 31n26; Hegel and, 148, 172; history and, xviii, xxv, 21, 56, 222. *See also* Hartog, François; presentistic regime of historicity

monism, Bergsonism as, 94, 95, 108n161, 118

Montesquieu, Charles de, 179n13

monument(s), xvi, xxv, 2–18 passim, 55; World War I, 2, 7–8.

morality, 115n181: in the Absolutist State, 180; Bergson on, 176, 177, 208; in closed society, 182–183, 191–194; mentioned, 77; open, 192–195; social function of, 185–187, 190, 191

morphology, 197

Möser, Justus, 154n18

Mullarkey, J., xxi, 72, 76n6, 84, 107–108, 105n140, 113, 132, 151n9, 157

multiplicity, 97, 150, 151n9; continuous or virtual, 87–95 passim; discrete, 87, 93; of historical times, 45; the present as, 219–220

mysticism: Bergson and, 207–208; intuition and, 77, 182n26; and open morality, 192, 194–195, 204–205, 206n134

myth–making faculty, 188

Napoleon, 164, 165

narrativism, 3–5, 20, 53, 56, 128–129, 216

nationalism, 70, 71; the Cenotaph and, 16; Enlightenment and, 204; and the European Union, 183; historians and, 136, 153; monuments and, 7

the Netherlands, xv, xvi, 55, 149

Newton, Isaac, 64, 79–80, 81, 121–122, 123

Nietzsche, Friedrich, 5n10, 104n134, 128; and Bergson, 195–196, 204, 206, 217; and genealogy, 143; Heidegger on, 33

nominalism, 156, 171

nonmodern: Bergson's philosophy as, xviii–xxvii passim, 124n21, 148, 156, 165–169, 184, 212; historicism, Bergsonism as, xxvii, 79n18, 108n162, 148, 151, 156–161, 172. *See also* modern Constitution

Norman, Larry, 179n13

now-time: see *Jetztzeit*

noumenal, 80, 82, 205

Nussbaum, Martha, 208

obligation: moral, 185–187, 191, 193n71; social, 192

Occupy, 220

Ockham, William of, 156

ontology: Bergson's historical, 142, 148, 161, 212–222 passim; Bergson's nonmodern, xviii, xxiv, 165–169, 184; of duration, xxvi, 76, 97n90, 131, 137, 147, 148, 157–159, 172, 193, 198, 201, 209, 213, 216, 219; the event and Bergsonian, 141; Heidegger's fundamental, 26, 28,

29; historical, xxvi, 20, 24, 56, 114, 115n181; and historicism, 195; of history, Heidegger's, 38; modern, 177; Toynbee and Bergson's, xxiin48
open society: Bergson on, xxvii, 176, 187, 188, 191–196, 199, 207; Popper on, xxvii, 176, 177, 182–183. *See also* closed society; morality
Open Society Foundations, 181
Ortega y Gasset, José, 197–198, 204, 207
Osborne, Peter, 118, 120
oscillation, 200–202
overman, 195–196, 198, 204, 206. *See also* Nietzsche, Friedrich

pantheism, 206
past: absent, xvii, xxvi, 3, 4, 5, 17, 19, 20, 25, 51, 53, 56, 119, 127, 212; actualization of the, 130, 138, 158, 186, 220; collective, 136; destruction of the, 126, 213, 220; dissociated, 44, 51; existence of the, 126–130, 135; as "foreign country," 51, 121; "futures," 38; haunting, 123; historical, xxvi, 3, 17–20, 25, 51, 53, 119, 120, 128, 138, 139, 141, 142, 216; as non-absent, 6, 18; as nonentity, xxv, 2, 119, 212; as object of study, 18, 51, 121, 138, 216; objectification of the, xxii; persistence of the, 20, 102, 160, 215, 220; premodern, 43; "present," xxv, 2, 3, 6, 20, 39, 220; pure, 96n90, 129, 130, 132, 141, 220; social, 33, 34n35; survival of the, xxvi, 90, 117, 119, 120, 124–126, 128n40, 130n48, 137, 150, 155, 212–213; uncanny, 6; virtual, 135, 140, 141n85, 220
Peace Day Parade, 2, 9, 11, 15
Péguy, Charles, 57, 67
pendulum of history, 196, 200–202, 204
perception: Bergson on, 87, 89, 93n81, 96n90, 100, 145, 209, 219; Husserl's transcendental phenomenology and, 26; hypnosis and, 69n36; intuition and, xxvi, 84, 171; of matter, 82; memory and, 127–134 passim; psychical research and, 205; pure, 96n90
phenomenology, xx; Bergsonism and, 77, 128n40; Heidegger's hermeneutical, 27; Husserl's transcendental, 26–27, 64n22
physics, xx, 64, 65n25, 79–81, 99, 120
Plato, 127, 134n63
politics, xxvi, 71, 135, 181; absolutist, 41, 180; Bergson and, 65, 70n41, 118, 175, 176, 193; of commemoration, 9, 13, 14, 16; in modernity, 43, 44n75; situational, 54, 219; of time, 5n14, 20n76, 125
Popper, Karl, xxvii, 176, 181–182, 187
post–Fordism, 221n23
posthuman turn, 119, 218
postmodernism, 4, 52–54, 128
predestination, 141n85
presence, xxv, 2, 13–21 passim, 125, 189, 215, 219, 220; of absence, memory as, 127–128, 132; metaphysics of, 26
present: contraction of the, 48–49; eternal, xvi, 85, 92, 218; extended, 53, 55; fragmented, 32, 60; genealogy as "history of the," 143; living, 155; omnipresent, xxiv, 24, 46, 51, 55, 56, 218, 219
presentism, xvi, xviii, xxiv, xxv; xxvii, 24, 46, 51–56, 145–146, 218–220
presentistic regime of historicity, 52, 56, 145, 220. *See also* Hartog, François; modern regime of historicity
Prigogine, Ilya, 79n19
privileged individuals, 192, 194, 195, 198, 204–205, 207
progress, xvi, xxiv, 4, 5, 41–55 passim, 67, 102, 116; Benjamin's critique of, 126; Bergson on, 86, 91, 93, 102, 176–177, 191–192, 199, 201–207

progress *(continued)*
  passim, 208; Hegel on, 162, 163, 184; historical, xxvii, 4; 46, 54, 118, 176–177, 196–197, 201–207 passim; narrative of the Enlightenment and, 44, 50, 52, 178–184, 187, 208
proliferation phase, 133
Proust, Marcel, 63, 65
psychoanalysis, 18, 61
psychology, xx, 77, 79, 81, 85, 90, 91, 93, 94, 120. *See also* duration: psychological
psychophysics, 77

railway system, 60, 62
Ranke, Leopold von, 3, 51, 128, 153, 154n18
rationalism, 67, 71, 78, 82, 182n26, 186, 208
recognition, 128n40
recollection, 131–132
refraction, 87, 101
relativity, theory of, 61, 64, 72
religion, 41, 44, 47, 188; Bergson on, 77, 176, 177, 182n26, 193; dynamic, 194; Nietzsche on, 195; static, 189–190
representation: Bergson on, 96n90, 116, 123, 193n71, 218–220; consciousness and, 83n37, 87; historical, 2–5, 18–20, 43, 53, 128, 136, 138, 142, 152n9, 216; memory and, 127, 131–134; mentioned, 61; in monuments, 2, 7, 17, 18; political, xxiii, 159, 42, 183; scientific, xxiii, 42, 159, 183
representationalism, 3, 20, 216
res gestae, 19, 53, 136, 142, 222
revolution, 37n42, 70; of Bergsonism, xix, xxi; Copernican, 41, 47, 69, 80; digital, 24; French, 4n9, 51, 122, 139, 165, 170, 180; historicism as intellectual, 152, 154n17; scientific, 66, 79, 179

rhythm(s): of duration, 76, 97n90, 100–101, 157, 172, 220, 221; Huijer on, 149; mentioned, 134; of nature, 41, 71, 121, 166, 183, 212
Rhythmism, 69
Rickert, Heinrich, 154n18
Ricoeur, Paul, 31, 126–130 passim
Rimbaud, Arthur, 50
Romanticism, 50, 70, 117n3, 140
Rosa, Hartmut, xvi, xxv, 43–44, 48–50, 54, 146, 218. *See also* acceleration
Rousseau, Jean-Jacques, 140, 183n30
Runia, Eelco, xxv, 2, 14–19 passim, 165, 215
Rushkoff, Douglas, xv
Russell, Bertrand, xx, 75, 78, 85n48, 112, 114n177

Sattelzeit: *See* Koselleck
Schlegel, Friedrich, 40–41
Schopenhauer, Arthur, 78n12, 196n86
Schumpeter, Joseph, 138
science(s), xx, 4, 50, 54, 152n9, 179; Bergson on, 65n25, 69, 78–79, 90, 9399n105, 102, 112, 120, 134, 160–161, 166 167, 176, 203, 205, 209, 214; Dilthey on, 29; earth, xviii; Heidegger on, 28–29, 34; historical, xxiv, 3, 21, 28–29, 34, 35, 121, 129n43; historicism on history as a, 153–159 passim, 172, 181, 214; Kant and modern, 66, 79–81; of life, 102–104; mentioned, 67, 188; political, 52; semiotic, 13n50; social, 37. *See also* representation: scientific; revolution: scientific
scientific management, 63
selectionism, 133–135
self, superficial vs. fundamental, 87–92 passim
semiotics, 53
Simmel, Georg, 154n17
simplicity, xxi, 105, 204, 205, 207

slippery–slope phenomenon, 50n100
socialization, 88–89
Society for Psychical Research, 69
space, 47, 122: Bergson on, xx, 66, 90–101 passim, 104, 107, 113n173, 116, 160; and culture, xix, xxvi, 59, 61, 63–64, 69, 73; historical time and, 123–124, 160; Kant on, 64, 66, 80; Newton on, 121; in postmodernism, 53; time as, 4, 65–66, 85, 87, 90, 93, 101, 115, 120, 123, 145, 157, 215; of "the uncanny," 6. *See also* time-space compression
space of experience, 38, 40, 48, 62. *See also* horizon of expectation; Koselleck, Reinhart
Socrates, xix, 127, 170, 192
Sorel, Georges, 67, 70
Soros, George, 181
Spencer, Herbert, 65n25, 154n16
Spengler, Oswald, 81n27, 197–198, 204, 207
Spiegel, Gabrielle, 125
Spinoza, Baruch, 206, 208
spirit(s), 13n48, 156, 202, 203; Bergson on, 96n90, 205–206; Hegel on, 162–166, 170, 172, 195; philosophical, 44n76, 178–179; war-, 194
spiritualism, 78, 205, 206n133
steam-engine, 62, 203
Stein, Gertrude, 60
Stengers, Isabelle, 79n19
structuralism, xx
symbolism, xix, 12n42, 69
Syndicalist movement, 70

Taylorism, 61, 63
technology, xiv, xv, xix, 41, 47, 59, 60, 67, 178, 188; Bergson on, 107, 203–204, 207; Spengler on, 197–198. *See also under* acceleration; determinism
The Open Society and its Enemies (Popper), 176, 181

teleology: Bergson on, 172, 207–208; evolution and, 105; and Hegel's concept of history, 161–162, 164; and history, 144, 152n9
telepathy, 96n90, 205
temporality: Bergson on, 70, 76, 81, 118; "functional differentiation" and, 54; Heidegger on, 24–34 passim; and history, 122, 136; Kant and, 64n22; Koselleck on, 37–45 passim; linear, 14; mentioned, 61, 79; modern, 4, 145; postmodernity and, 53; Taylorism and, 63
time: absolute, 64, 71, 119, 121n13, 122; arrow of, xviii, xxiv, 5, 43, 118, 134, 212; Bergson's philosophy of, xix, 59, 120; creative, xix, xxii, xxiv, 69, 102–104, 116, 119, 123–124, 148, 184, 196, 201, 212, 219–221; crisis of, xxv, 21, 46, 50, 55, 57; experience of, xvi, xxii, 47, 52, 61, 76, 77, 85, 90, 116, 148; Heidegger on, 26, 28, 32; historical, xxii, 19, 20, 25, 37–45 passim, 47, 54–56, 63, 122, 123, 126n31, 136–137, 145, 166, 212, 214–215, 219; homogeneous, xxi, xxii, 62–71 passim, 80, 85, 87, 90, 101, 107, 116, 119–126 passim, 39, 150–151, 156, 213, 215, 216; of life, xxiii, 166; -line, xxii, 5, 17, 80, 121, 122, 124, 138, 139, 142, 215, 216, 219; linear, xvii, xix, 4, 5n10, 14, 17, 32, 54, 64; of memory, 20, 63, 125, 137, 213, 215; philosophical, xx and postmodernism, 52–54; premodern experience of, 40; progressive notion of, xv, xix; reality of, 123, 219, 221; relative, 71; social, 148–149; spare, xiv, 49; subjective, xx, 63–64, 77; universal, 64, 121–122, 148. *See also* acceleration: of (historical) time; capitalism: and homogeneous time; clock–time; duration; heterogeneity:

time *(continued)*
  of time; *Jetztzeit*; Kant, Immanuel: on time and space; Koselleck, Reinhart: theory of historical times; mechanism(s): and time; metaphysics: of time; politics: of time; space: time as; temporality; time-space compression
Time and Free Will (Bergson), 65, 66, 76, 78, 84–86, 93–96
time-space compression, 48, 60
Tocqueville, Alexis de, 128
Toffler, Alvin, xv
Two Sources of Morality and Religion, The (Bergson), xxvii, 65, 103, 118, 120, 124, 147, 175–177, 182–184, 188, 196, 198, 199, 203, 206–209
Tomb of the Unknown (Soldier), 7, 12, 14
totalitarianism, 181
Toynbee, Arnold, xxiin48, 81n27
trace theory, 127
transitional justice, xxv, 20, 123, 215
trauma, 115n181, 121n10; historical, 123, 125; and World War I, 12–13
Troeltsch, Ernst, 38
truth: Bergson on, 81, 113, 114n176, 116, 167n73; commissions, 20, 215; Foucault on, 143–144, 217; Heidegger on, 33–35, 169; in history, 136, 138, 140, 216; retroactive, Bergson on, 140–141, 208

UNESCO, xvi
the universe, 47, 64, 79, 138; Bergson on, 96n90, 98–99, 105, 113, 153, 158, 159, 167, 207; duration as immanent to, xxii, 76, 94, 102, 152, 156–157, 206, 213

Verdinglichung, 101
Vico, Giambattista, 3, 19n74, 25
virtual: in the Cenotaph, 18; history, 152n9; memory and the, 128n40, 130–132, 213; multiplicity, 87–95 passim; past as, 135, 140, 141n85, 220; tendencies, 108–109, 159, 168, 172, 177, 193–194, 198; whole, duration as, 148, 151–152, 156–157, 172, 193–194, 213, 221. *See also* Bergsonism: as philosophy of the virtual; duration: as virtual whole; Deleuze, Gilles: on the virtual
vitalism, Bergson and, 71, 103, 105
Voltaire, 179n13

war(s): Bergson on the problem of, xxvii, 120, 176–177, 182–209 passim; class, 70; Cold, 180; and commemoration, xxv, 2, 6–9, 13n48, 14–15, 18; Franco-Prussian, 189; and haunting pasts, 123; religious, 41, 47. *See also* World War I; World War II; instinct: war
Warhol, Andy, 52
wax metaphor, 127, 131, 134n63
Weber, Max, 50n100, 154n18
White, Hayden, 2–4, 52, 128, 215
White, Melanie, 193
Whitehall, 1, 9, 11, 15
Wilcox, Donald, xxiin49, 121, 122
Wilson, Woodrow, 175
Windelband, Wilhelm, 154n18
World War I, xix, xx, xxv, xxvi, 2, 6, 15, 60–61, 196; Benjamin on, 60–61; Bergson and, 65, 69, 71, 72, 175, 176, 196; and the crisis of the modern regime of historicity, 57, 73; mentioned, 38, 63, 67, 139; practices of commemoration, 2, 6–9, 12–13; and *The Two Sources*, 176, 182, 184, 189–190, 203, 206, 207; as trauma, 12–13
World War II, 182, 183
worldview: Bergsonian, xx, 171, 213, 214; historicist, xxvi, 4, 51, 60, 152–154, 171, 213, 214; mechanistic, 65, 80, 85, 91, 116

Worms, Frédéric, 182, 209

Zarathustra, 195

Zeno of Elea, paradoxes of, 98
Žižek, Slavoj, xvi; on the event, 141, 216–217

www.ingramcontent.com/pod-product-compliance
Lightning Source LLC
Chambersburg PA
CBHW030531230426
43665CB00010B/846